STUDIES IN TRANSACTIONAL EVALUATION

EDITED BY

ROBERT M. RIPPEY

UNIVERSITY OF ILLINOIS
AT CHICAGO CIRCLE

McCutchan Publishing Corporation
2526 GROVE STREET
BERKELEY CALIFORNIA 94705

©1973 by McCutchan Publishing Corporation
The contributions by Hubert S. Coffey and William P. Golden Jr.,
and Francis G. Caro are reprinted by permission of their publishers,
The National Society for the Study of Education, and The American
Educational Research Association, respectively.
Printed in the United States of America

Library of Congress Catalog Card Number: 72-83477
ISBN: 0-8211-1713-0

To the person who said,
"This theory sounds great,
but how do you really do it?"

CONTENTS

III   *TRANSACTIONAL EVALUATION*
IN THEORY
The Philosophy

CONTRIBUTORS

FRANCIS G. CARO is Associate Professor of Social Research at the Florence Heller School for Advanced Studies in Social Welfare, at Brandeis University. He received his Ph.D. from the University of Minnesota in 1962, with a major in Sociology and a minor in Psychology.

VICTOR G. CICIRELLI is Professor of Human Development at Purdue University. Previously, he was a U.S. Office of Education Post Doctoral Fellow in Educational Research at the Center for Cognitive Learning, University of Wisconsin. He holds a Ph.D. in Educational Psychology from the University of Michigan, and a Ph.D. in Developmental Psychology from Michigan State University. His current research includes a study, supported by the U.S. Office of Education, of the influence of sibling structure and interaction on young children's categorization style, and the design of an experimental study to assess day care centers, for the Office of Economic Opportunity.

WAYNE DOYLE was a teacher in Missouri and Illinois public schools for eleven years and a junior high school administrator for five years. After graduating from Washington University with a Ph.D. in

Educational Administration, he served as Director of Research and Evaluation for an ESEA Title III Project in St. Louis county, studying a new organizational structure for the innovation and diffusion of elementary school practices. Since the summer of 1969, he has been the Director of Research and Evaluation of the Ford Training and Placement Program at the University of Chicago.

MAURICE J. EASH is Professor of Education and Director of the Office of Evaluation Research at the University of Illinois at Chicago Circle. He has been active as an evaluator of social and educational programs, both state and national, and has written articles and papers on the problems of program design and evaluation in field settings.

WILLIAM P. GOLDEN, JR., is currently Professor of Public Health, at the University of Hawaii's School of Public Health. Previously, from 1952 through 1970, he was Professor of Education and Psychology at San Francisco State College. Concerned with research, service, and teaching in Community Health Education and the application of behavioral science to planning for change in the delivery and maintenance of health care, his major professional interest is the application of T-group and laboratory methodology to problems of personal growth and organizational development. Professor Golden's most recent publication, an article entitled, "On Being a T-Group Trainer," is included in *Modern Theory and Method in Group Training,* edited by W. Dyer.

DENNIS D. GOOLER is Assistant Professor of Education at Syracuse University. He received his Ph.D. from the University of Illinois at Urbana-Champaign in 1971. His primary interests include curriculum development, evaluation, and educational priorities.

GORDON HOKE is currently an Associate Professor of Education at the University of Illinois at Urbana-Champaign, serving as an evaluation specialist and program developer for the Center for Instructional Research and Curriculum Evaluation (CIRCE). He received his Ph.D. in Education and Sociology from Michigan State University in 1965. Today, he is deeply involved in school, community, and regional development.

ERNEST R. HOUSE is at the Center for Instructional Research and Curriculum Evaluation, University of Illinois at Urbana-Champaign. He has recently completed a large-scale, four-year evaluation study and is editing a book on educational evaluation for administrators. His interests include educational change, evaluation, and administration.

EDWARD F. KELLY is Associate Director for Research and Evaluation at the Center for Instructional Development, Syracuse University. He received his Ed.D. from the University of Illinois at Urbana-Champaign in 1971. His primary interest is curriculum evaluation.

W. RAY RHINE is Associate Professor in the Department of Behavioral Studies and Research in the School of Education at the University of Missouri-St. Louis. From 1968 to 1971 he was a Senior Research Psychologist in the Urban and Social Systems Division of the Stanford Research Institute, where he worked on the Follow Through longitudinal evaluation.

ROBERT M. RIPPEY, after fifteen years as a high school teacher and curriculum coordinator, received his Ph.D. from the University of Chicago in 1964. Following that, he joined the faculty of the University of Chicago Department of Education where he was also Director of the Center for the Cooperative Study of Instruction, and Dean of Students of the Division of Social Sciences.

Now at the University of Illinois at Chicago Circle, Professor Rippey teaches courses in evaluation and change. He is also involved in the evaluation of numerous educational innovations through the Office of Evaluation Research at the university. He has written more than sixty papers on evaluation, instructional theory, and educational change.

DOUGLAS SJOGREN is presently Director of the Human Factors Research Laboratory and Professor of Education at Colorado State University. He received his Ed.D. in Education, Psychology, and Measurements at the University of Nebraska in 1961. He has had seven years experience in public school teaching and counseling, and has been evaluating educational programs for the past six years.

HARRIET TALMAGE, Associate Professor of Education, is Head of the Division of Curriculum and Instruction, and a Staff Associate of the Office of Evaluation Research, of the College of Education, University of Illinois at Chicago Circle. She received her Ph.D. from Northwestern University.

JOHN M. THRONE is Associate Director of the Center for Mental Retardation and Human Development, Director of the Lawrence unit of its clinical training component, and Professor of Education and Psychology, at the University of Kansas. His previous positions have included those of Chairman of the Department of Special Education at Indiana University, Associate Director of the Joseph P. Kennedy Jr. Foundation, Research Associate in the Department of Psychiatry at the University of Chicago, and clinical psychologist in institutions for the mentally retarded in Minnesota and Tennessee. He received a Ph.D. degree in psychology from George F. Peabody College in 1960.

HERBERT J. WALBERG, now at the College of Education, the University of Illinois, Chicago, was formerly at the Educational Testing Service, Harvard University, and the University of Wisconsin. He received his Ph.D. from the University of Chicago in 1964. Since then he has served as consultant, to a wide variety of private and public institutions and agencies, in program and curriculum design and evaluation research. He is author of more than eighty books, monographs, and research papers on creativity, developmental and social psychology, the social environments of learning, and other topics. He is on the editorial board of the *American Educational Research Journal* and is currently editing *Rethinking Urban Education.*

INTRODUCTION

The actual meaning of transactional evaluation is emerging. It is not fully developed. The authors represented here are not all of a like mind on the definition. However, they do agree that in the field there is an important "something else" in need of exploration.

Transactional evaluation is concerned with the system undergoing change rather than with the outcomes of the system's activity. Any social system undergoing change is embedded in forces. Without an analysis of these forces, a study of change in a school will be missing an important part of the picture. In addition, an understanding of systemic forces and role relationships will be valuable in overcoming resistance to change.

Transactional evaluation might perhaps mistakenly be thought of as a catchall term for those activities performed by the evaluator that are outside the line of duty of checking out the accomplishment of alleged objective. Such is not the case, for many of the concerns of transactional evaluation are often not attended to at all in the formal evaluation of social change programs and educational innovations. The basic model of transactional evaluation, outlined in chapter two, includes a range of ideas extending back at least as far as George Herbert Mead and his idea of the intimate relationship between one's self and one's milieu. Also subsumed under this model are Lewin's ideas on the inaccessibility of the central regions of the personality, and the Getzels' model outlining the parallelism between the personal and the organizational aspects of institutional functioning. The role of evaluation in monitoring institutional behavior was pointed out several decades ago by J. A. C. Brown. One cannot, of course, pay tribute to all the progenitors of an idea because of the multiple relations that develop among ideas—especially in areas as exploratory as this. Likewise, two rather contradictory traditions, those of the community organization schools of Saul Alinsky and those of the organizational movement, have contributed extensively to an understanding of the vicissitudes of change. And, as Throne points out in his contribution, there may even be a few genes inherited from behaviorism.

The book has been organized into three sections, the first covering the process of transactional evaluation, the second covering the perspective of the evaluator, the third covering the theory of transactional evaluation.

THE PROCESS

In chapter two, a transactional evaluation model is described and its applicability to changing conditions in schools defined. In chapter three, illustrations are given of the use of transactional evaluation in three disruptive, malfunctioning situations. In chapter four, Talmage discusses the case study as an important tool for the planning of a formal evaluation, especially when a wide variety of social forces must be taken into consideration. In chapter five, Hoke recounts his experiences as an evaluator working with the Effingham, Illinois, public schools, and the difficulty he had getting his work accepted and understood. In chapter six, Eash describes a fairly successful field evaluation study and puts forward an evaluation design model that is adaptable to a changing program of innovation. His model distinguishes between the evaluation needed at the early stages of any innovation and the evaluation needed once a program is developed and operating under favorable conditions. In chapter seven,

Rippey recounts his experiences as the evaluator of a project characterized by intense polarization and conflict among parents, teachers and students.

THE PERSPECTIVE

The introduction of an evaluator into a previously unevaluated situation is, in itself, a large change and may threaten roles as much as the change being evaluated. How can the evaluator respond to this fact? Can the evaluator use transactional evaluation to expedite his own task? Walberg, in chapter eight, reports on an evaluation that developed from an initially apparently simple assessment of outcomes. He concludes that the educational consultant must be competent, sensitive and persuasive—all traits of a good transactional evaluator. Companion pieces, chapters nine and ten describe the unexpected consequences of Operations Head Start and Follow Through respectively. In chapter eleven, Gooler and Kelly discuss, in dialogue, their evaluation of a project that remains nameless to protect the innocent. In chapter twelve, Doyle, thrust into a melee of conflicting interests—school, community, university and teacher training college—describes his own difficulties in gaining acceptance as an evaluator.

THE PHILOSOPHY

In chapter thirteen, Coffey and Golden describe their own model, based extensively on ego psychology, for explaining the sources of conflict associated with change. This model may be used to describe a number of the specific changes mentioned in earlier chapters. In both chapters fourteen and fifteen, the conflict between truth and success is analyzed. In chapter fourteen, House describes the conflict that develops between the evaluator in his search for truth and the practitioner in his search for success. In chapter fifteen, Sjogren analyzes the evaluator's own schism: the conflict within the evaluator as he seeks the truth through his ability to be detached and objective, and as he seeks success through his ability to become involved and point out defects and dysfunction. Throne, in chapter sixteen, eliminates one half of the problem in suggesting, as a behaviorist, that the evaluator *must* become involved in the process of change, that detached objectivity is not only unwise, but also impossible. In chapter seventeen, Eash, regarding transactional evaluation as the bridge between change propelled by research and practice prompted by tradition, describes the application of Simmel's coaction model to change in the classroom. In chapter eighteen, Caro presents a comprehensive review of current research on the evaluation of programs for social change.

I TRANSACTIONAL EVALUATION IN ACTION

The Process

1

WHAT IS TRANSACTIONAL EVALUATION?

ROBERT M. RIPPEY

Transactional evaluation is a developing aspect of educational accountability. It looks at the effects of changed programs—in schools and other institutions—on the incumbents of the roles in the system undergoing change, i.e. on the changers themselves. It does not focus exclusively on the outcomes of the changed programs as they affect a target population. For example: if a school system were planning to introduce a performance contracting system, transactional evaluation would look, not at improving reading scores of students, but at changed role relationships and latent apprehensions among those responsible for the educational services—teachers, administrators, and perhaps parents. A comparison with traditional summative and formative evaluations shows that the target of evaluation is different: the subject of the evaluation is the system, not the client of the services rendered by the system. The variables relate to the social, psychological, and communications aspects of the system, rather than to the manifest objectives. The information is continuously fed back into the system. The evaluator himself is more a part of the operating system. The conventional considerations of reliability, validity and objectivity are less important than those of timeliness, relevance, and the observable effects of generating evaluation information. Primarily evaluation is intended to transform the conflict energy of change into productive activity; to clarify the roles of those persons involved in the program changes, not to produce new knowledge or ascribe causality.

Change often threatens the roles of incumbents in an organization. Changing programs require new skills and behaviors. Persons holding positions feel that a considerable investment on their part may be threatened by planned change: conflict, procrastination, and subversion can often be expected. In schools, reaction to change ranges from small talk in the teachers' lounge to active subversion in the community or faculty. Although resistance can be expected as a universal consequence of change, there are several responses open to the educator. One common, though deficient, response follows a sequential strategy:

1. A single plan is developed carefully. The likelihood of its success is documented. Change is restricted to non-contentious steps.
2. Legitimation is obtained from external agencies. Published reports of successes are circulated.
3. Further backing is obtained from a local teachers' committee, which recommends universal adoption.
4. Arguments defending the plan against all possible criticism are prepared.
5. The plan is introduced to the entire system.
6. Publicity value is obtained from the program, but the consideration of whether the program is being carried out is not questioned too carefully. Teachers are free to modify the program to suit their comfort and to reduce phone calls from parents.
7. Either the program is proved to be a success, or it is not evaluated at all.

Such a picture of inconsequential changes, highly publicized, carelessly implemented, and unevaluated is not entirely foreign to education.

Transactional evaluation suggests a different strategy. The first step is similar: a problem is carefully studied and the likelihood of success documented. Several optional solutions might be entertained from the very start. The second step, legitimation from external agencies, though useful, is perhaps not so important. The third step is quite different: the change is recommended only to those who are really enthusiastic about it, so that the program starts on a small scale with its most enthusiastic, energetic supporters. Conflict begins when praise or reward for a successful new program constitutes a threat to those not originally involved. It is at this point that transactional evaluation becomes a useful tool in the change process.

Transactional evaluation has two main phases. In the first phase one uncovers sources of conflict; in the second, one uses proponents and opponents to develop and implement an evaluation plan. One might determine the sources of conflict and apprehension by using a transactional instrument, such as the questionnaire below (used in a bilingual, inner-city, teacher training program), with items developed by all who are involved in the change.

EVALUATION QUESTIONNAIRE

(A = strong agreement; a = agreement; d = disagreement; D = strong disagreement)

	A	a	d	D
1. We need more courses directed toward the understanding of the inner-city child.	10	7	2	0
2. My experience with the staff and Principal of school leave something to be desired. There are too many inconsistencies about rules, and about what is accepted as proper procedure for discussing problems.	2	6	8	2
3. I enjoy classes though I find the ten weeks too short a time to understand each subject fully.	7	5	4	1
4. Lack of experience in bilingual education, and the unconcern of a teammate, hinder the development of an integrated program at our school.	2	7	4	1
5. The program, being dominated by the administration, suffers and, because it is not controlled by the communities in which we teach, does not receive their support.	9	2	4	2
6. We need more time to share teaching ideas and experiences with fellow interns. We could learn a great deal from one another, but have no time for such exchanges.	11	7	0	1

	A	a	d	D
7. So far my experience has been extremely fruitful.	5	5	6	2
8. Our experiences in the community have been helpful and rewarding.	7	7	4	0
9. Experiences with the administration have been exciting but not always rewarding.	4	7	1	3

Such an instrument may contain items from a single group, or items submitted by several groups, such as parents, students, and teachers.

The second phase of transactional evaluation follows: proponents and opponents of the program, or of any particular aspect, develop and implement an evaluation plan, with technical assistance from professional evaluators. The presence of both protagonists and antagonists in project monitoring teams has several salubrious effects. Monitoring can include not only outcomes expected by proponents, but also unexpected outcomes suggested by opponents. Nonbelievers apprehensive about their roles can be reassured by direct action of the project, in-service training, where necessary, and clarification of policy. Obviously not all role apprehensions can be solved in this way, but many can be. The initial opponents can be given a legitimate, constructive, albeit skeptical, role in the program, a role that can lead to their incorporation and conversion. An opponent may have a legitimate objection. The new plan may really need modification. Opponents may provide just the skills or ideas necessary to keep a project off the rocks or out of the slough of despond.

It is perhaps when a program of change is first criticized that one can tell whether or not transactional evaluation is being used. If the response to criticism is an answer, an explanation, or a defense, regardless of whether the defense is based on data, opinion, or the scriptures, transactional evaluation is not spoken here. If the response to criticism is another question, an exploration of substance and apprehension, the appointment of doubting Thomas to a monitoring committee, we can assume that transactional evaluation is on the agenda. When a program of change looks beyond the immediate outcomes of its manifest goals, and begins to examine it roles and the apprehensions of all parties to the system (including the client), when a program attempts continuously to monitor its total effects and respond to clarifying information, it is participating in transactional evaluation.

Transactional evaluation may be a necessary part of effective change. As House states in his evaluation of the Illinois Demonstration Centers:

> If Havelock is correct, research and development models of change assume a passive user population which is shaped by the dissemination process itself. The facts belie this assumption. Of far greater importance are the variables controlling the would-be adopter's everyday world in his home district. The individual is caught in a powerful social web that determines his behavior more than do his individual impressions gleaned at a demonstration visit. The variables that influence whether he will adopt [an innovation] are those that shape this home environment. The findings in this study are consistent with the "social interaction" change model which sees change as a result of the social relations network within the adopting unit.[1]

Unfortunately, examples of transactional evaluation are not readily available. The methodology has not been perfected. Applications are few and far between. The data collected may not be clean enough to appear in more formal journals. Persons engaged in transactional evaluation, perhaps not realizing the importance of what they are doing, may not be motivated to publish. Some of the following chapters will describe the effects of attempts to move into the area of transactional evaluation. It is fairly untraveled ground, subject to criticism from the research purist on the right and the threatened ideologist on the left. It is a road not often taken, yet if we have educational promises to keep, we should perhaps travel it at least a few miles before we sleep.

FOOTNOTE

1. Ernest House, Thomas Kerins, and Joe M. Steele, *The Demonstration Center—An Appraisal of the Illinois Experience* (Urbana, Ill.: Center for Instructional Research and Curriculum Evaluation, University of Illinois, 1970), p. 35.

2

THE NATURE OF
TRANSACTIONAL
EVALUATION

ROBERT M. RIPPEY

Evaluation is demanded by the United States Office of Education as a prerequisite for funding, yet rejected as an honest livelihood by most professionals. As Rossi (1969) describes it,

> evaluation research is more of a service industry rather than either a professional activity or a primary production industry, and as such suffers from low prestige, a sense of alienation, and feelings of impotence.

Perhaps nowhere is evaluation more severely attacked than in the programs aimed at elevating the quality of life for various disadvantaged people. Examples of the heat placed on evaluators are numerous. David Fox's tribulations (documented in the *Urban Review* of May 1968) after he reported the More Effective Schools Program, and Donald Erickson's last stand with the Navajos and the anthropologists (see the *School Review* of November 1970) should be ample warning of the rocky path awaiting the well-intentioned evaluator.

Most evaluations to date have been useless. Formative evaluations usually come too late—often after a program has lost, or retained, its funding. Summative evaluations, despite their intent, have been inconclusive. In analyzing the evaluations of seventeen national and local compensatory programs, McDill, McDill, and Sprehe (1969) concluded that: "[evaluation research] fails to meet even minimum standards for program design, data collection, and data analysis." In reviewing the research on curriculum, Baker (1969) concurs and adds that:

> Too often, the preoccupation with satisfying requirements of design and statistical models violates the instructional treatment and reduces the utility of the research to zero. Conversely, the lack of specificity of treatment has often made the application of elegant procedures a waste of time and money at best and a smokescreen at worst.

At the moment, there seems to be no evidence that evaluation, although the law of the land, contributes anything to educational practice other than headaches for the researcher, threats for the innovators, and depressing articles for journals devoted to evaluation.

This state of affairs has led McDill, McDill and Sprehe to suggest that an investigation should be conducted to contrast the outcomes of programs rigorously evaluated, and with unusually high budgets for evaluation, with the outcomes of programs completely free from the strictures of evaluation. They believe that evaluation is part of innovation. This belief raises an important question: what are the consequences of the evaluation of educational change under varying conditions, and under varying evaluation models? In field projects, the models of evaluation that have been encountering difficulty conform more or less to the formative and summative models first elaborated by Scriven (1967). In summative evaluation, as Scriven defines it, terminal judgments are made about a curriculum or instruction program, or the effectiveness of two kinds of programs are compared. In formative evaluation information about specific content, units, instructional materials, and classroom procedures are derived in an attempt to guide the improvement of a single program while it is underway. The evaluator may find it difficult to limit himself to the two models. However, there is another evaluation model, honored more in the breach than in the observance, which I refer to as transactional evaluation.

TRANSACTIONAL EVALUATION AND
EDUCATIONAL THEORY

Transactional evaluation differs from formative evaluation in two major aspects. First, it involves not only the protagonists and the designers of an innovation, but also a representative sample of persons likely to be affected adversely or disturbed by the consequences of the change. Second, transactional evaluation, as well as attempting to improve the program, will also attempt to analyze the dysfunction of the changing organization. This dysfunction is largely due to the threats that change imposes on stable roles.

Katz and Kahn (1966), in rejecting the theoretical organizational models of Weber, Gulick, and Taylor, have developed an open systems theory, which supplements previous theories in attempting to deal with transactions between organizations and their environments. Organizations designed to provide a fixed output under constant conditions can be less complex than those that are constantly faced with changing demands and changing resources. The second type of organization is more descriptive of today's school than the first. Schools aimed primarily at transmitting the traditions of the past might function quite well under Katz and Kahn's model of stable organizations. A medieval monastery, the school Madame de Maintenon developed for the orphans of the French court, or a school for keypunch operators would do quite well without the adaptive or boundary subsystems that Katz and Kahn associate with more mature, elaborate organizations. At the heart of successful adaptive systems, Katz and Kahn place institutional research and development functions:

> Too often changes in the social arrangements of organizations are lagging and fragmentary adjustments to technical changes already made. We automate the equipment first and repair the social dislocations afterwards. The same rational considerations, however, that operate within the framework of technology can be utilized to determine social objectives and thus make the technical system [the] means rather than the master of social organization . . . More serious organizational experimentation, more trial and evaluation sequences, and more data on the effects of organizational alternatives are needed.
>
> As an end state, the perfect ability of human society must perhaps remain an article of faith; never-

theless, some of the conditions necessary to give the
perfectability notion reality as a social process are
known. They include an increased understanding of
human organizations and a concomitant willingness
to test that understanding by trial experiment and the
scrutiny of research.

Katz and Kahn's open systems theory emphasizes the importance of
the adaptive and maintenance subsystems within an organization.
These subsystems, looking respectively outward and inward, provide
the information and intelligence necessary for institutional survival in
the face of changing demands and resources. It is this continuous
scanning outwardly and inwardly, this continuous attention to information about the institutional role that distinguishes formative from
transactional evaluation. Both can be carried on simultaneously. It is
possible to have formative without transactional evaluation, but
transactional evaluation is best grounded in a good plan for formative
evaluation.

Promising research findings are often not implemented in the
schools (Sullivan, Grant and Grant 1955; Bixler and Foulke 1963;
Rippey 1966). Cost, time, and effort are the usual reasons given for
not adopting promising educational changes. However, the primary
source of resistance to change is, apparently, not economic or technical, but is due to the effect that change has on the roles of school
personnel.

This is by no means a new idea. Crucial to the Katz and Kahn
argument (1966), it first appeared in the 1957 yearbook of the
National Society for the Study of Education. Coffey and Golden
argued that the chief source of resistance to change is the threat to
roles, and that this resistance can be alleviated by well-planned
strategies. The article is reprinted as chapter thirteen of this book.

The Transactional Evaluation Model

In my own study of change, I have reduced and modified their
rationale somewhat. In a planned strategy it seems important to:
establish   disequilibrium;   to   increase   differentiation;   to   begin
change on a small scale under the best possible conditions; to
improve the climate and the organizational mechanism for change;
and, finally, to implement all new programs as temporary experiments with an evaluation scheme which requires both the protagonists
and the antagonists of the change to set up the criteria for assessing
and measuring the planned and unplanned outcomes.

To employ such a strategy, change agents must be skilled themselves or have the assistance of persons skilled in interpersonal relations, which includes an understanding of the roles that people assume in groups and what inhibits open discussion. People are inhibited by norms for appropriate behavior, fears of personal rejection, and stereotyped perceptions of others. Since educational institutions have built-in mechanisms for maintaining stability, significant change affecting the central rather than the peripheral behavior of students, parents, teachers, or administrators is bound to be accompanied by hostility, frustration, and conflict. These mechanisms are predominantly the roles, expectations, and sanctions operating formally and informally in the institution. Change, introduced in response to external needs and pressures, will have the following results:

1. It will have unexpected consequences as well as those intended.
2. It will affect the entire organization, not just the part included in the formal plan.
3. It will cause a certain amount of dislocation because of the competition for resources (including the students' time) and the shift of roles and expectations, which may place an individual in a situation incongruent with his needs.

The key to the transactional model's effectiveness is the continuous evaluation, by both the protagonists and the antagonists, of both the expected and unexpected consequences of change. This evaluation will modify and improve the program. If the program functions effectively, concerns and anxieties are alleviated, and, if the evaluation is properly managed, persons initially opposed to a change may become quite cooperative.

Transactional evaluation makes a number of contributions to a good program of formative evaluation. Formative evaluation design is improved by the inclusion of a wider range of opinions and values. Organizational efficiency improves because of the attention to potential role threats. The evaluator's concern for human values as well as program outcomes gives him a better relationship with those involved in the change, leads to greater honesty of interchange, and provides more valid data. The evaluation, involving a wide range of personnel, will create a supply of organizational and evaluative skills that will be available after the original program has been completed.

Practical Concerns in an Innovative Situation

A program of change is not straightforward. Not all sources of anxiety about a change are standing in the wings ready to come on stage. The change agent must find the individuals who are potential sources of resistance and encourage their involvement. Not all opponents of a project will express themselves in terms that can easily be measured by standard, readily available instruments, so unobtrusive measures, direct observation and ratings by volunteer trained observers may be necessary. Not all school systems may be able to budget for sufficient personnel for a proper evaluation. However, students and parents can help. Students can be trained within the school curriculum for a wide range of behavioral research, including statistics, research design, questionnaire construction and analysis, interviewing, test scoring, keypunching, and computer operation and programming. Parents with adequate research skills could be recruited as volunteers.

Because transactional evaluation requires both top administrative support, and skilled operating personnel, it has yet to be employed on a large scale. The successful application of these techniques on a small scale will be reported in several of the following chapters.

REFERENCES

Baker, R. L. "Curriculum Evaluation." *Review of Education Research* (June, 1969): 339-358.

Bixler, R., and Foulke, E. *Comprehension of Rapid Speech by the Blind.* Cooperative Research Report 1370. Louisville, Kentucky: University of Louisville, 1963.

Katz, D., and Kahn, R. *The Social Psychology of Organizations.* New York: John Wiley and Sons, 1966.

McDill, E., McDill, M., and Sprehe, J. *Strategies for Success in Compensatory Education.* Baltimore: Johns Hopkins Press, 1969.

Rippey, R. "A Contrast Between the Teacher and Materials." *School Review* (Autumn 1966): 283-291.

Rossi, P. "Evaluating Educational Programs." *Urban Review* 3, no. 4 (February 1969): 17.

School Review 69, no. 1 (November 1970).

Scriven, M. "The Methodology of Evaluation." In *Perspectives of Curriculum Evaluation,* edited by R. W. Tyler, R. M. Gagne, and M. Scriven, pp. 39-83 Chicago: Rand McNally, 1967.

Sullivan, C., Grant, M., and Grant, J. "The Development of Interpersonal Maturity." *Reports on Our Projects 174-177 and 174-023.* Mimeographed. San Francisco: San Francisco Family Relations Center, 1955.

Urban Review 2, no. 6 (May 1968).

3

UNCOVERING APPREHENSIONS WITH TRANSACTIONAL EVALUATION INSTRUMENTS

ROBERT M. RIPPEY

Although transactional evaluation is based on a study of the internal conflict concommitant to change it is sometimes difficult to determine just what crucial issues need to be evaluated. The following chapter will illustrate an instrument that is useful in uncovering the conflicts that need to be dealt with as a part of a transactional evaluation.

One solution proposed for resolving interinstitutional conflict is the use of the confrontation group. By face-to-face confrontation, groups may understand what causes division in an institution. But confrontations are often impracticable because of the inherent threat of confronting someone you must work or live with for long periods of time. At times, with face-to-face confrontations, groups may grapple momentarily with an issue and then allow it to recede into a warm bath of verbal agreement or target shifting.

Face-to-face discussion has a number of disadvantages. Groups may be controlled by dominant individuals who do not always have the expertise to match their influence. Because anonymity is impossible social acceptability may govern behavior. Much discussion time may be devoted to biased or irrelevant points of view. Individual judgments may be altered by pressure from the group. Because of these disadvantages, a special type of instrument was developed for transactional evaluation. In this type of instrument, the items are taken verbatim from the subjects. Although the meaning of some items may not be clear, and the technical issue of validity is not pursued, the instruments are of value in providing springboards to discussion and planning of additional steps in evaluation. The reader may notice some similarity to the Delphi method (Helmer 1966), which however, is used to obtain consensus on goals or future trends. In transactional evaluation, consensus may be noted, but the resolution of initial differences is not considered particularly important. Instead of spending time in approaching agreement, transactional evaluation identifies divergence and then proceeds to monitor the situation while considering several divergent views.

A key aspect of transactional evaluation is the development of instruments to discover issues important to individuals and to see, subsequently, whether there is any consensus of opinion on the issues from which to develop a platform for action. A range of responses indicates further discussion, fact finding and a careful evaluation of the expected consequences of action that is based on various, conflicting options. A few isolated dissenters may be persuaded to return to the fold because they are so few, or because of the group's persuasive action. What do the instruments look like? Are they particularly different from commercial climate inventories? I believe they are.

The instruments that will be discussed in this chapter were developed under similar conditions in a variety of school situations. In each case, a problem had created a need for group action; in each case a simulation of the problem preceded the collection of data about goals, needs, or concerns. The statements of the participants were then read and selected with the following criteria in mind: the wording was to be kept as near to the original as possible; statements that seemed to duplicate others were to be rejected; and, wherever possible, at least one statement was to be selected from each participant. At times I would add a provocative question or two when it seemed that a key point brought up in the simulation was missed in the contributed statements. Occasionally, I would add a statement to reflect the concerns that tended to inhibit change, but were seldom expressed. Often such contributions were unnecessary, and some-times the statements submitted exceeded my wildest projections of the nature of the group's anxieties.

The items themselves constitute an interesting collection of causes of organizational malfunction and divergent goals. Once responses were compiled, they were distributed to the participants to examine. Then came the questions: "What does all this mean?" "Where do we go from here?" "How shall we proceed?"

To illustrate transactional evaluation in action, I will discuss the programs used in three educational institutions—an integrated, urban school, a college-level training program in human relations, and a suburban high school. The questionnaires used in each of these evaluations are reproduced in the Appendixes to this chapter, begin-ning on p. 26. The names that appear in all of the accounts are, of course, fictional.

THE SCHOOL LEARNING CENTER

Irwin School is a stable, integrated school in Chicago. Equal numbers of students come from affluent and impoverished areas. The school has a long history of parental participation and, as a result of parental leadership in the PTA, a learning center was planned and funded. The center was to stimulate gifted students and to provide special help and motivation for less successful students. Consisting of two large adjoining classrooms and office space, the Center is staffed by a director, two instructors, a secretary, and a part-time research assistant and evaluator.

Background

The history of the Learning Center illustrates the transactional evaluation model's appropriateness in helping a developmental inno-vative program to become a systematic functioning reality. A history of the Center would probably identify at least three crises that were overcome. The first was the common crisis of goals and roles. What were the staff supposed to be doing? During the life of the center there was a movement away from independent study to individual research, then to remediation, and then to amusement. No single concept dominated and, luckily, the Center was able to offer students a variety of instruction methods which did not duplicate or compete excessively with classroom activities. At times, however, the staff developed a territoriality: each person set off his own area in the rooms and restricted himself to a particular, limited set of responsibilities. At other times, almost everyone responded to a particular child's needs, in a flurry of excessive cooperation.

The second crisis was that of acceptance. Staffed by persons from outside the school, the Center was initially a burr under the saddle to a number of teachers. It took up classroom space and students were missing classwork. The Center's work on the computer interfered with the lessons of one of the math teachers. This type of conflict was resolved through the concern of the Learning Center staff for the apprehensions of the classroom teachers. Instruments were administered to keep track of the climate and valid expressions of concern received direct action.

The third crisis was that of broadening its constituency. To be effective, the Center had to reach many students and its impact needed to be felt in the classroom. Movement toward this goal generated an internal crisis as much as an external one. Initially there were some Learning Center staff members who were opposed to opening the Center to all students.

Early in the Center's history, its students had been sent there because they were remedial students, because they had misbehaved, or because they were researchers independent to a fault. But most students did not ever step inside the front door. After some anguish, vigorous discussion, and an analysis of the staff's responses to a questionnaire on their attitudes toward the Center, it was decided to schedule all classes into the Learning Center once a week. Time was still reserved for groups with special interests and for individual work. This new program, initiated experimentally and evaluated after a month, turned out to be most successful. Teachers, given a better understanding of the center, were enthusiastic and insisted on continuing the new arrangement; some ideas and materials went back to the classrooms with them.

Operations

Writing in *American Education* (1969) Wille gave a detailed description of the operation of the Center. The Learning Center definitely met the children's needs, but its life span might easily have been shortened, had its staff not been committed to a sound strategy of change involving transactional evaluation.

The Learning Center was begun, not at the suggestion of the teachers, but of the PTA, and not with a staff from within the school, but with a staff recruited from the outside. The surprising acceptance and impact of the Learning Center was due to a number of factors. The children found the center extremely attractive. It provided the time, the space, the flexibility, and the people necessary to make a concerted attack on problems that had previously kept particular students back. The role of evaluation in change was carefully and deliberately planned, and to those involved in the Center, it seemed to have played an important role in transforming the inevitable resistance into support. It was the continuous evaluation that undoubtedly kept the Center afloat during its critical first six months of operation.

Even before it was opened, the staff was aware of a degree of apprehensiveness about the Center. In particular teachers and parents wondered whether the children would learn as much in the Center as they would in the classroom. On this account a number of records were kept, to determine the time spent in the Center, and work accomplished while students were in the Center. Instruments to sample student anxiety, sense of power, alienation, and school climate were administered. The most useful instruments turned out to be those developed by the classroom teachers and the students.

The first of the transactional instruments was developed by the Learning Center staff to evaluate their own attitudes. It is well known whenever five or more gather together, in no matter whose name, that disagreement is inevitable. Facing destruction from internal pressures, the Learning Center staff agreed to submit anonymous statements of their concerns and apprehensions to the evaluation. Most questions were self-evident. Should children be scheduled into the Center by classes, or individually? Was the Center to provide remediation, stimulation, or independent study? Should the director of the Center spend his time directing and managing or should he spend time working with the children? From the statements were constructed eighty items intended to elicit a range of responses: strong agreement, agreement, disagreement, and strong disagreement. The instrument included statements such as: "The director gets in everyone's hair," "Entire classes need to be scheduled into the Center on a regular basis," and "If the Center doesn't get more students involved, it is dead." A graph of the responses showed that on some issues the staff agreed, on others they did not and the knowledge then became a basis for discussion in the staff planning meetings. Among other things, the director was able to find out why he was getting in the hair of one of the staff members. An experiment to schedule entire classes into the Learning Center was initially a source of severe disagreement among staff members. It turned out to be very successful in involving students and teachers, and has been kept as part of the program.

The Learning Center staff felt that their experience had been profitable and asked that a similar instrument be prepared with the teachers. This was done at a faculty meeting. Naisbitt (1970) has made a detailed analysis of the instrument, which is given in Appendix I on p. 26. The results may be summarized fairly briefly:

Summary of Results

1. The teachers' general attitude toward the Learning Center and its staff was positive. The staff was seen to be helpful and the Center an asset to the school.

2. There was substantial agreement on all twenty-five of the items listed as objectives, goals, and purposes of the Learning Center; items that were in fact the actual objectives of the Center.

3. There was substantial agreement that the faculty should be included in the planning, consultation, and development of the Learning Center, and that better follow-up practices were needed. Instruction about materials and equipment was desired.

4. There was substantial agreement that the Learning Center needed more materials for individual classrooms, language arts, black studies, gifted students, slow learners, EMH (educable mentally handicapped) students, primary students, and teacher research. It also needed more typewriters and an inventory of available materials.

5. There was general, but not complete, agreement that more work with slow learners was needed. Sufficient help seemed to be given to high achievers.

6. While the teachers liked the Learning Center's equipment they could not agree on the benefits of extending its philosophy into their classrooms.

7. Although there was substantial disagreement with the statement that the Learning Center did not serve academic needs, it was agreed that the Center had not raised test scores. There was also general disagreement with the contention that the Center had actually frustrated the instructional program in many cases. While the teachers disagreed that they felt threatened by the "competition" of the Learning Center, one-third agreed that, because theirs was a special project, Learning Center teachers received too much attention while the classroom teachers were taken for granted.

The Learning Center staff found that many of the criticisms and suggestions were exactly the same as their own. It was necessary to confer with the classroom teachers about some of the specific suggestions and, in the opinion of the Learning Center staff, the feedback from the teachers proved very helpful. The findings of this questionnaire became the basis for constructive dialogue and action and, because of the success of the first two questionnaires, a third one was prepared to evaluate the students' attitudes.

A Student-Written Questionnaire

Seventh and eighth grade students were asked to submit, anonymously and in writing, as many statements or questions as they wished about any aspect of the school. Nearly two hundred students participated and from the hundreds of items, the research assistant selected 158 to be compiled into a questionnaire. This questionnaire was given to the students verbally and they were asked to mark an answer sheet indicating their agreement or disagreement with each item. Usually they had less than forty minutes to complete the questionnaire. The students were very responsive and often answered out loud, sometimes with cries of "Right on!" One eighth grade boy pointedly crumpled up his answer sheet at the beginning and announced that he wouldn't take the questionnaire. I assured him that he didn't need to, but added, "There's an item in here that says 'I hate school' which you won't get a chance to agree with." Instantly he pulled out a second answer sheet, which he had hidden in the desk, and agreed to take the questionnaire. The students were asked not to put their names on the paper, but to indicate their grade and sex.

Naisbitt's report on this questionnaire appears as part B of Appendix I, on p. 45. Of it he remarked: "The responses were startling and reveal a depth of feeling, anger, thoughtfulness, sensitivity. The raw version may anger and upset the teachers. But if we don't face what our students really feel, we will never be able to formulate and educational program which will serve them."

WOODSVILLE WORKSHOP

The next instrument is perhaps the one most memorable to me. I had agreed to spend some time one summer with a workshop established to train human relations personnel for a large city system. I was to work with the participants on the development of skills in evaluating human relations programs. The week before I was to meet the group, a number of events occurred which caused the workshop director to telephone me on the weekend and, remarking, "I don't think they are going to listen to a word you say," he proceeded to explain the mess into which the workshop had fallen.

The situation would not have been quite so bad, were it not that all the participants were supposed to know something about human relations, and the situation in which they had gotten themselves was a threat to their professional skill. As one of the staff put it: "They have created a monster." The human relations of the group on that Monday morning could not have been worse had they been planned by Ghengis Khan, Marie Antoinette, and the Marquis de Sade in committee.

The Problem

The problem centered about the plans for a workshop which the trainees had drawn up on the weekend just past. The workshop was to be conducted in Woodsville, a nearby black high school. It would be an excellent training experience and would allow the participants to put their new skills to a practical test. Furthermore, each of the participants was to be paid handsomely for his time. A committee decided that only black members of the workshop should go. The psychological effect of this decision on a racially mixed group assembled to learn how to help alleviate tensions of all sorts, was devastating. The basic argument was summed up in the statements: "Whites shouldn't go where they're not wanted" and "How do you know I'm not wanted just because I'm white?" But there were many other undercurrents that had not been uncovered.

I had done a lot of thinking about what I might say to a group in such turmoil. My initial remarks went something like this: "I've heard that you are really angry with one another. I've heard that no one would be interested in evaluation today—that no one would want to listen to what I had to say. You have had enough consultants already, and you are in the middle of a problem that you're going to have to be able to solve if you are going to feel that any of you has any skills at all in human relations." There were a few moments of silence. Then I said, "I'm not going to give the usual introduction. I'm not going to do a simulation of a conflicted situation because we have the real thing right here. Let's get on with the task and do what I was only going to talk about." Then I asked them to give me anonymous statements about their concerns, anxieties, and possible remedies.

The Solution

Luckily, good secretaries were able to put together a copy of the instrument within an hour. The participants' responses were tabulated during lunch time and are shown on the instrument that has been reproduced as Appendix II to this chapter, on p. 58. During lunch there was also time to think about what to do with the responses. Unfortunately, thought does not always lead to solutions —at least over lunch, and I decided to put the question to the group. After giving them about twenty minutes to look at the results, I simply asked, "How should we proceed? What should we do with the information we now have?"

Early agreement was reached that the attitude expressed as *I wonder if we cannot deal with those concerns that continue to divide us,* was of crucial importance. It was clear that the group felt that something should be done, and they claimed, rather loudly, that they knew the identity of the one person who strongly disagreed; some said that she had helped to precipitate the present crisis. None of the suggestions about the specific means of dealing with the information seemed to gather much support, until somebody said: "This really is something we have to all be together on. We can't do it in small groups. That will just lead to a continuation of the division. Let's stay together till we work this out, but start by just going around the room and letting everyone say whatever he feels he needs to say. No one will respond, or get to talk out of turn. We won't do anything until everyone has had a chance to speak."

There were sighs of relief when the suggestion was made. What emerged was that many people had been hurt—not so much because they had been left out of the workshop, but because their feelings and motivations had not been understood by those who wanted to defend the decision. It wasn't just the money, or the feeling of being rejected for not being black which bothered many of the participants. Each one expressed a unique feeling of his own and when we finished going around the circle we realized that there were at least as many feelings about the workshop as there were people. When I asked: "Where should we proceed from here?" they told me: "Now that we know this, [we] think we all know what we need to do." The next day, it was easy to sense a relaxation in the group. We began working on the tasks. A week later, the workshop ended in a party; I was there, and I don't think there has ever been such a party, before or since. However, this was not the only outcome of the workshop, although in more reflective moments, I sometimes think that such a party would be justification enough. A number of the workshop participants are effectively functioning in the area of human relations, and making significant contributions to the system that employs them.

HIGH SCHOOL EVALUATION

The third instrument was developed to evaluate a program which had been running for about fifteen years in an established suburban high school. The curriculum, originally exciting, new, and responsive, had become comfortable, accepted and, perhaps, what Thelen would refer to as Vulgarized (Thelen, 1964). The superintendent and some faculty members had planned a fairly large change. Numerous consultants had been employed to prick the conscience of the entrenched, and a steering committee of faculty members had reported on the necessity of change. A new building program and bond issue had been supported and now the faculty was called to action—a call that was not enthusiastically answered. Internecine strife was raging and the concerns of the provoked are reflected in the instrument that appears as Appendix III on p. 61.

One word of caution: transactional evaluation of a faculty of 120 is not to be undertaken lightly. Luckily the school was able to place eight secretaries at my disposal for the day and they were barely enough for the task. One hundred faculty members will generate at least three hundred questions. Many questions are sure to be duplicated, but a hundred items cannot be made into an instrument in less than an hour. The items must be screened, some reworded, and then placed on ditto masters for copies to be run off, collated, and stapled. The most time-consuming activity is the data tabulation. Ditto masters should be preserved so that tabulated data may then be placed on the original masters. If more than one hundred faculty members are involved, some other duplication process may be preferred as ditto masters tend to lose their courage after the first one hundred copies.

Responses to the questionnaire, discussed in small faculty groups and used by the faculty steering committee, resulted in modifications of the development plan. One need clearly evinced by the responses was for increased in-service training. A three-year program to accomplish this has been planned. One immediate benefit was that the faculty were able to discuss their differences freely. Although the program is just beginning, it will be interesting to see if the flow of information already begun can be maintained and if the improved communications will lead to a more direct handling of crucial internal issues.

A PRACTICAL CONSIDERATION

Any transactional evaluation, but especially one involving a large number of people in various roles, needs adequate secretarial help and carefully preplanned forms, such as the one illustrated on p. 25. This particular form was used to ascertain the responses of various groups:

P/C = parents or the community
Stu = students
Sch = school teachers and administrators
Univ = university personnel.

Statements obtained from subjects may be typed into the blank spaces of the form and then whoever is completing the questionnaire indicates his response by checking the appropriate box: A = strong agreement; a = agreement; d = disagreement; D = strong disagreement.

SUMMARY

Recent developments in organizational theory suggest that evaluation of change is a concern of both the protagonists and the antagonists of any new program. If those concerned are involved in periodic monitoring, the new programs may be saved from deteriorating into aggression or apathy. Monitoring may also strengthen both the substance and the acceptance of the evaluation. Extension of involvement, far from being anathema, may be a necessary part of evaluation.

> Evaluation has not yet been accorded its proper place as playing a major role in policy formation and change . . . In sum, the problem presented by evaluation research lies not in research methodology but in the politics of research (Rossi 1969).

FIGURE 1

Transactional Evaluation Instrument

A - strong agreement; a - agreement; d - disagreement; D - strong disagreement

Role: _____

Statements	*Roles	Responses			
		A	a	d	D
#1	P/C				
	Stu				
	Sch				
	Univ				
#2	P/C				
	Stu				
	Sch				
	Univ				
#3	P/C				
	Stu				
	Sch				
	Univ				

*Roles: P/C = Parents and/or Community; Stu = Students; Sch = School Teachers and Administrators; Univ = University Personnel.

APPENDIX I

Transactional Evaluation of a Learning Center Established at a Chicago School

A. Questionnaire Prepared to Ascertain Teachers' Attitudes Toward the Learning Center

Classroom teachers submitted between three and five anonymous statements describing their feelings about the Learning Center, its goals, procedures, needs for improvement, and so forth. All the statements were incorporated in a questionnaire, of eighty-one items, which was answered, also anonymously, by the classroom teachers and several auxiliary staff members. Responses were limited to their agreeing or disagreeing with the items:

A = strong agreement
a = agreement
d = disagreement
D = strong disagreement.

The statements in the questionnaire were then reorganized into seven categories of attitude, among the teachers who were not on its staff, toward the Learning Center:

1. General attitudes toward the Learning Center and its staff
2. Attitudes toward the goals, purposes, objectives, and activities of the Learning Center
3. Attitudes toward the procedures of the Learning Center
4. Opinions on the materials, equipment and space of the Center
5. Opinions on the special educational needs that ought to be filled by the Center
6. Attitudes toward the extension of the Learning Center philosophy to the classrooms
7. Miscellaneous criticisms of the Learning Center.

The Responses

In the bar graphs of the responses, certain patterns were observable—patterns which indicated the degree of feeling among the teachers for the Center. The graphs used as illustrations are taken from the questionnaire.

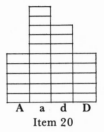

1. Normal Distribution
This pattern follows a bell-shaped curve; the choice of responses follows a continuum.

A   a   d   D
Item 20

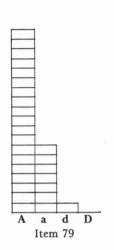

A   a   d   D
Item 79

2. Substantial Agreement
Most responses agree with the statement.

3. Substantial Disagreement
Most responses disagree with the statement.

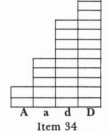

A   a   d   D
Item 34

NOTE: It may be observed that, in the two patterns above, the teachers agree with one another in either agreeing or disagreeing with the statement.

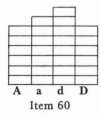

A   a   d   D
Item 60

4. Dispersion
Responses are almost evenly divided among the four alternatives.

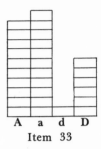

5. Polarization
Most responses agree with the statement, but a significant minority strongly disagrees.

A   a   d   D
Item 33

The Questionnaire

(Numbers in parentheses refer to the items in the original instrument (Naisbitt 1970); the responses are indicated by bar graphs.)

1. *General Attitudes Toward the Learning Center and its Staff*

Response   **Statement**   **Response**

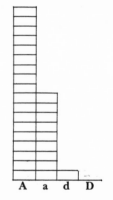

The Learning Center is an asset to the school's total learning environment (4).

A   a   d   D

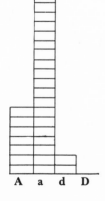

The Learning Center's staff members are sensitive to the needs and desires of students and teachers. They are human professionals (5).

A   a   d   D

Response	Statement	Response

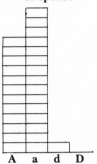

The Learning Center staff is flexible in their planning and execution of plans (6).

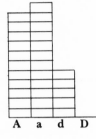

I think the Center has "done fine" so far! (15).

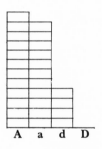

The Learning Center, its equipment, and its staff are always helpful (26).

The Learning Center has been very helpful in sharing its materials with teachers (36).

The Learning Center is very beneficial to the teachers as well as the students (44).

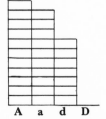

Response   Statement   Response

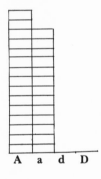

The Learning Center and its staff are
very flexible (70).

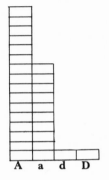

I am glad to be included in coming to
the Learning Center (51).

The Learning Center is a great addition
(71).

I hope the Learning Center continues
after the Federal funding runs out
(79).

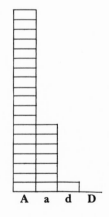

2. *Goals, purposes, objectives, activities of the Learning Center*

Response   **Statement**   **Response**

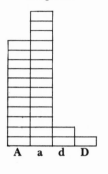

The Learning Center promotes creativity (1).

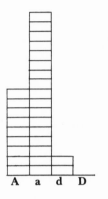

It provides independent study for students (2).

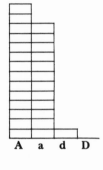

The Learning Center provides a free learning experience (3).

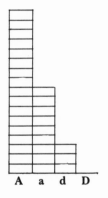

Children enjoy learning in the Learning Center. This, to me, makes it great! (16).

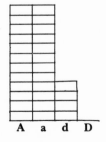

The Learning Center is a place where very bright children gain added interest and challenge (23).

Response   **Statement**   **Response**

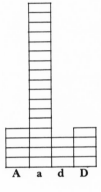

The Learning Center helps motivate the slower child (24).

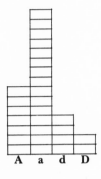

The Learning Center assists pupils' problems on their grade level (27).

The Learning Center provides material so that pupils can work from one level (such as math) to another (29).

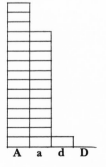

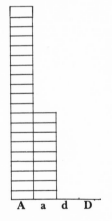

The Learning Center should continue to function to develop more dynamic approaches to the process of learning (37).

The Learning Center should develop an extensive approach toward the ideal goal of understanding between all children and ethnic groups (38).

Response	Statement	Response

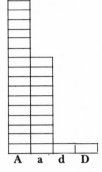

The Learning Center is a place where children can relax in a natural way and learn what they want, in a relaxed and friendly fashion (40).

The Learning Center is helpful in obtaining supplementary materials which are not provided by regular school funds (56).

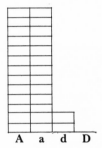

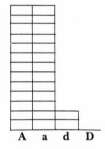

The Learning Center period helps children realize that learning can be fun especially when they can choose learning areas in terms of their interests (57).

The availability of "black studies" materials for use in the Learning Center and for classroom loan is very helpful (58).

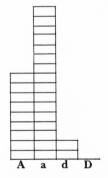

Response	Statement	Response

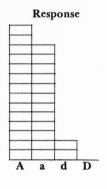

A   a   d   D

In principle, the Learning Center stimulates the curiosity of students and enriches their knowledge, benefitting average and superior students (31).

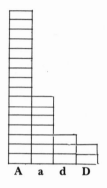

A   a   d   D

The Learning Center provides children [with] an opportunity to explore educational materials in a manner which is free, but not irresponsible (45).

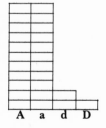

A   a   d   D

The Learning Center helps children develop self-confidence (46).

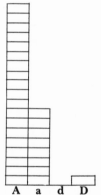

A   a   d   D

Children have an opportunity to use equipment not available in their own rooms (47).

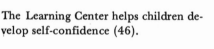

A   a   d   D

The Learning Center helps primary children work with manipulative materials which are sadly missing from our own primary classrooms (48).

Response   **Statement**   **Response**

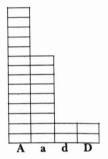

Students seem involved in what they are doing when they are in the Learning Center (52).

Students have commended the Learning Center for the knowledge they have gained there (53).

The Learning Center period for my class gives me a chance to mingle among my pupils, help them with academic problems, or play games with them (61).

I like the fact that it is possible to schedule a time for individual pupils to do special work (62).

I like the flexibility which cannot be accomplished in a classroom with immovable desks (63).

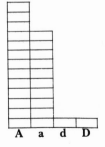

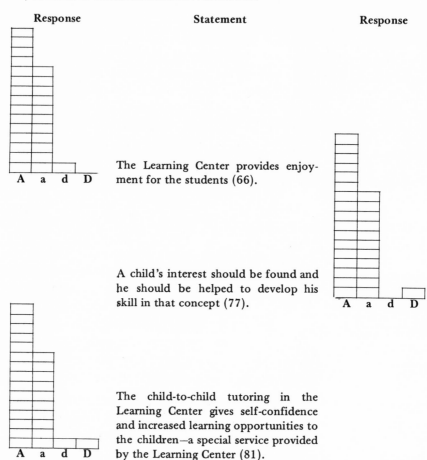

Response   **Statement**   **Response**

The Learning Center provides enjoyment for the students (66).

A child's interest should be found and he should be helped to develop his skill in that concept (77).

The child-to-child tutoring in the Learning Center gives self-confidence and increased learning opportunities to the children—a special service provided by the Learning Center (81).

3. *Procedures of the Learning Center*

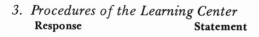

Response   **Statement**   **Response**

The Learning Center is not organized (8).

Response   **Statement**   **Response**

The Learning Center has inadequate follow-up procedures (9).

The Learning Center should be used during social center time to serve students not accommodated during school hours (14).

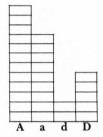

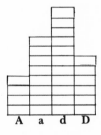

The Learning Center does not actively include the faculty in planning and development. Only a chosen few are invited to participate (19).

The Learning Center correlates work done there by conferences with room teachers (28).

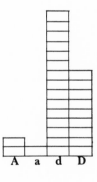

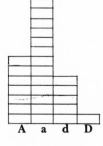

The Learning Center seems to be well-equipped generally, but requirements for referrals sometimes conflict with what the school administration says (30).

Response   Statement   Response

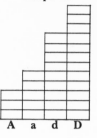

The Learning Center is not organized
with their materials (34).

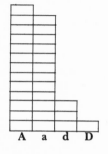

There should be greater consultation
between teachers and Learning Center
staff in order to work on the specific
problems of the child (35).

The Learning Center should make its
facilities, media, materials and staff
readily available to the community,
children and faculty (39).

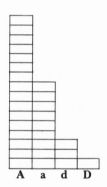

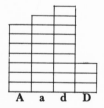

The teachers are not familiar with the
Learning Center when they come in,
which hinders the classes (42).

There should be more instruction on
how to operate equipment in the
Learning Center (59).

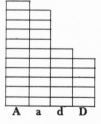

Response	Statement	Response

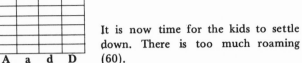

It is now time for the kids to settle down. There is too much roaming (60).

Many students play in the Learning Center rather than learn particular skills (64).

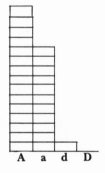

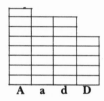

The Learning Center has an inadequate system for keeping track of what students in the Learning Center are doing (69).

The Learning Center should provide exacting instruction in the care of equipment to the younger children (72).

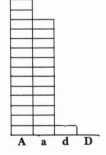

Each area of materials should be shown to all, so that the children know what is available (73).

Response   Statement   Response

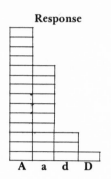

More adult *regular* assistants would be of great value to the younger children (74).

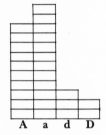

When two or three teachers have their classes in the Center at the same time, there should be some type of guideline as to voice range and movement—that is, if tutoring is to take place at the same time (75).

All staff should become involved with children who come to the Center. Many children walk out because they are either ignored or told to go to the "other room" or told "hands off." This is not encouraging to a student (76).

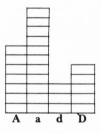

4. Materials, equipment, and space of the Learning Center

Response   Statement   Response

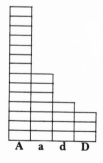

The Learning Center needs more material that can be used by individual teachers in their particular classrooms (7).

Response	Statement	Response

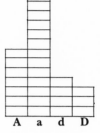

The Learning Center needs more individual resources for study of the English language (11).

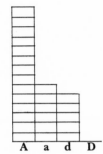

The Learning Center needs another typewriter or two (12).

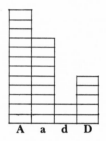

It could use more physical space so it wouldn't be so crowded (13).

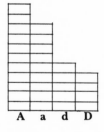

There are insufficient materials for gifted pupils and for teacher research. I would suggest including faculty growth also (17).

The Learning Center staff should develop a complete inventory of materials to be distributed to teachers so that they may know what is available to them (22).

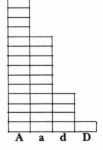

Response **Statement** **Response**

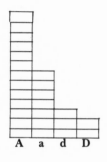

The Learning Center needs more materials on a primary level (43).

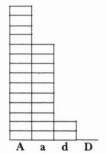

The Center for "black studies" is desperately needed by our upper grade students and should be expanded (54).

EMH students need more materials in all subjects designed for slower learners (55).

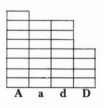

The Learning Center should have rugs for better acoustics (80).

5. Special Education needs to be filled by the Learning Center

Response **Statement** **Response**

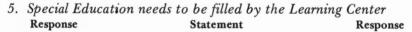

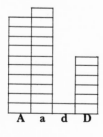

The Learning Center might possibly involve itself more specifically in remedial work with slow learners (33).

Response	Statement	Response

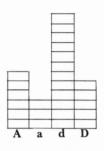

The Learning Center is geared to provide individualized instruction for the slow learner (65).

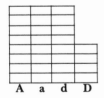

The Learning Center doesn't give enough individual help to the slow learner (67).

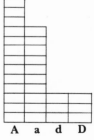

The Learning Center doesn't give enough help to high achievers (68).

6. Extension of Learning Center philosophy into the classroom

Response	Statement	Response

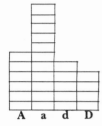

Classrooms should be patterned after a Learning Center idea (41).

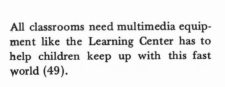

All classrooms need multimedia equipment like the Learning Center has to help children keep up with this fast world (49).

Response	Statement	Response

Every child should be able to explore and to do his own thing in the classroom (50).

7. Miscellaneous criticism of the Learning Center

Response	Statement	Response

The Learning Center does not serve academic needs (10).

The Learning Center has not improved the academic standing (in terms of standardized test scores) (18).

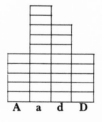

The Learning Center occupies a "dessert" position. The children need a "main course" first (20).

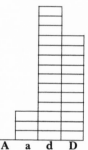

Response	Statement	Response

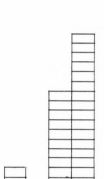

The instructional program is actually frustrated many cases by activities and operational methods used by the Learning Center (21).

The Learning Center *unfortunately* is a place where some teachers send problems so that they can gain goof-off time! (25).

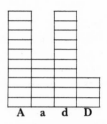

Teachers are reluctant to use resources of the Learning Center because they feel threatened by the competition (32).

Learning Center teachers get too much "credit" and attention because it is a special project, while the hard work of the classroom teacher is taken for granted (78).

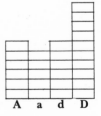

B. Questionnaire Prepared to Ascertain the Attitudes of the Students Toward the School and the Learning Center

The questionnaire was developed as follows: students contributed questions or statements about the school which were incorporated into a questionnaire designed to reflect more accurately the concerns of the students. They had no more than five or ten minutes for this task.

Following are some of the original statements provided by eighth grade students and subsequently included in the evaluation instrument:

Can you improve the lunch?
Teachers like James and Smith accusing pupils of things they don't do.
I like the girl's washroom in the basement but the other's need fixing to.
This is my first year hear and I think [this] school is the neatest school I've been to.

teachers don't give you a fare chance and other teachers always believe teachers. We should have a chance to wear what we want and another thing teachers don't give us good reasons for not wearing them what? *pants* teachers should not threaten us.
teachers are always accusing us and they do lie sometimes too.

One day Thomson accuse me of talking about someone. I was upset because I hadn't said that person's name. He likes to hurt students. He wants them to treat him like some sort of king. I refuse to do so.

We should be allowed to wear neat, clean, appropriate pants to school. All the other schools have this code. Why can't [this one. This] is the best school I've went to. I plan to stay here a little while longer regardless of the dress code.

We should have our own menu for lunch.
longer lunch period
More descussion for the whole school.

I hate one teacher on this floor who just don't like our homeroom and he know who he is.
I like eating in the lunchroom but some food are just old and you can tell that it is old.
the teacher are allways threatening use abot Springfield telling use we will not go, but we can't be good all the time.

The food they give you in the lunchroom is a bunch of *Krap*.
We should have more gym periods instead of free periods.
Some teachers should teach us something insted of giving us free periods all the time.
We should do something with the free periods like the suggestions above.

The food is not hot.
Stop Robbins from critizising other teachers.
Allen is a good principle.

The food is bad.
We need a good long hour for lunch.

I wish I was allowed to go to the Learning Center more.
I also wish we had more freedom here to where what you would like and to do more of what you want to do.

This is the *worst* food I ever ate.
Some teachers at this school aint' no good.
We need a school baseball (team).
We need an hour four lunch.
We need teachers who TEACH!
We need books.

Allen I think is to much. He tries to put to much disapline on the 7 and 8th grades Students.
I think [the school] stinks. It is a pain in the tail. And every teacher in it (except Block, Sherwin, and Green.)

I think the Learning Center is Great but I thought it was set up for the blacks to help them with things which were neglected from there education *but* in the computer programming I only saw very few *blacks*. I am one of them but I think there are some very smart blacks as well as whites but the learning center usually leaves the blacks out and I think you should start including them in the Learning Centers computer programing.

Murray is always telling lies on children and i hate him.
Roach is all that Bad sometime he accuses you of something you didn't do.
Stone is the Best teacher in the school.
I don't like the lunchroom.
And sometimes halls are too noisy.

Why don't the teachers throw out that teacher? You know that the principal would not, do you? because they run over him: if someone done wrong in school he would not do anything because he's scard.

Jackson is always talking about room 6 and not paying attention to his own room.
Phillips keeps saying [the basketball team] is going to get uniforms cause we're gonna raise money but he hasn't taken any steps to raise money.
We need more, better, hotter food in the lunchroom.

When the statements were translated into the instrument that follows, an analysis of the items made it possible to divide them into ten subtests that made it easier to understand the students' responses. The subtests may be summarized briefly:

1. General Climate.   The responses were surprisingly favorable, considering the rather loud complaints that had been received. The students were very critical of themselves and, while they conceeded that the school was better than it was a year previously, they pointed out that it still had ruffians and there was still racial prejudice.

2. Student Power.   The students agreed strongly that they should have more say in what is taught and done at the school. But they were not asking for control; they were asking to be part of the action, to be listened to, to have more discussion about rules and problems.

3. School Administration and Rules.   Because strong objection might have been expected to strict rules, it was important that the objection was relatively mild. Since it is practically mandatory for students to hate an authority figure, it was a fine tribute to Mr. Allen and to the students that so many of them thought him a good principal.

4. Student Behavior.   Again, students showed a strong sense of selfcriticism; they were not being defiant and anarchistic. They were being honest with the staff in their criticisms, and were asking to be heard.

5. Teacher Behavior.   Almost half of the students said that the teachers did not give *enough* supervision; about three-quarters said that some teachers were afraid of the students.

6. Curriculum and Special Programs.   The responses showed that the students were thinking about the academic and extracurricular program; they thought the language arts period too long, they wanted more attention paid to black studies, they would have liked an individualized program, with those students who needed more help receiving it.

7. Physical Conditions.   The children were obviously sensitive to their physical surroundings and, even if the best the staff could do by way of improvement would be to talk to the students more realistically about the actual limitations of the budget, they should, and would possibly get more cooperation.

8. Lunchroom.   Food matters to children and they were unhappy about it.

9. *The Learning Center.*   The Center received considerable support from the students. Even in agreeing that the staff should see that the equipment and materials were not misused, stolen or wasted their protective attitude toward the Center was revealed. Staff and students should have reached an understanding about such supervision since the Center staff had tried to build independence and responsibility, and to avoid a highly structured, closed, supervised environment. Learning Center staff and classroom teachers needed to take more care in selecting students for individual referral.

10. *Gym, Sports and Social Center.*   Boys would have liked more sport; girls were less enthusiastic. Students would have liked more time in the Social Center, and thought that more kids should participate. The students were interested, and the staff might have used their interest to channel youthful energy and to improve school morale.

On the report for each subtest, all of the items are included, together with the percentage of students who agreed with the statement; the student groups are differentiated by grade and sex.

1. *Attitudes Toward the General Climate in the School*

| | | Girls | | Boys | |
| | | \<\>Grades | | | |
		7th	8th	7th	8th
1.	I hate school.	36	36	43	34
2.	I think the Irwin School children should like Irwin and not fight unless there's a reason.	76	80	83	73
3.	I think the school is good.	48	54	62	63
4.	School is boring.	56	60	60	57
5.	The students don't help keep the school clean.	71	78	65	59
6.	I feel safe around the school.	23	34	83	90
7.	Irwin is a well-behaved school.	31	37	37	43
8.	This is a bad school.	31	30	43	40
9.	There should be more social activities.	95	87	92	76
10.	There are ruffians in the school.	82	79	82	88
11.	I think it would be real fun if we had a hobo day for dressing real messy and a dress-up day for dressing up real good.	82	69	78	64
12.	Irwin School is a nice school.	66	71	63	70
13.	There is racial prejudice in Irwin.	82	77	76	69
14.	Irwin School is better this year than it was last year.	86	73	73	86
15.	Irwin needs more supplies and books.	82	94	88	87
16.	I wish I could go to another school.	31	39	30	27

2. Attitudes Toward Student Power

		Girls		Boys	
			Grades		
		7th	8th	7th	8th
1.	Students should have more control of school rules.	77	89	78	63
2.	I think I want to be able to pick some of the classes I should go to.	76	83	79	73
3.	The school should give kids more freedom to do what they want.	81	76	83	72
4.	Students should have more say in what is taught and done in the school.	86	80	79	72
5.	I think the children should run the school for one day.	83	84	90	78
6.	Students should have a part in planning graduation ceremonies, songs to be sung, etc.	94	77	100	81
7.	Teachers and staff should listen to the Student Council.	94	94	92	84
8.	We should have more discussion for the whole school about rules and problems that the kids feel.	79	92	88	77
9.	Having a voice in the administration of the school is not as important as the academic program.	51	55	67	42
10.	It wouldn't be good if students had as much freedom as they want in school.	47	42	46	53
11.	The faculty and students don't communicate well enough.	77	83	86	80
12.	The school should run democratically, with the principal as president etc.	34	51	50	50
13.	Students should have some part in planning the school curriculum.	84	84	98	76
14.	The Student Council should have more power.	79	85	86	70

3. Attitudes Toward the Administration and Rules of the School

		Girls		Boys	
			Grades		
		7th	8th	7th	8th
1.	I think when we are walking down the halls and in between classes we should be able to talk and walk down the hall relaxing, not walking to the right and mouths shut.	84	83	91	79

		Girls		Boys	
		Grades			
		7th	8th	7th	8th
2.	We should have five minutes between classes so that we can go to lockers.	88	83	98	67
3.	Our school has a discipline problem.	58	61	54	55
4.	The principal is too strict.	44	53	60	32
5.	The new dress code makes girls late for being prepared in gym.	20	24	23	27
6.	They should let us in in the mornings in the winter because we get very cold waiting outside.	98	96	94	81
7.	The girls and boys should be allowed to play together on the playground.	72	75	69	81
8.	The school rules are too strict.	59	63	70	38
9.	You should not have to pay anything to be allowed to graduate.	89	84	88	77
10.	Mr. Allen is a good principal.	71	78	77	75
11.	It should not be mandatory to salute the flag and say the pledge and sing the national anthem if you do not believe in it.	67	83	78	53
12.	Some students are allowed to fight and don't get suspended.	71	62	83	82
13.	When you get in trouble, teachers put you on trial. The principal acts like the judge. Most of the time you are guilty.	77	72	80	66
14.	We should be able to get water when we want.	86	85	92	94
15.	We should be able to go to the washroom when we are in class.	17	50	20	46
16.	The principal suspends too many people.	56	50	70	27
17.	There are too many restrictions in the school.	70	63	81	55
18.	The principal doesn't listen to students.	48	45	65	35
19.	The principal is all right.	76	65	70	78
20.	Thanks to Mr. Allen for the new dress code! It's a good idea.	95	92	80	67
21.	Children shouldn't get suspended because when they're out they miss a lot in school.	76	65	83	73

4. Attitudes Toward the Behavior of Students

		Girls		Boys	
		Grades			
		7th	8th	7th	8th
1.	There are too many fights.	50	54	45	37

		Girls		Boys	
			Grades		
		7th	8th	7th	8th
2.	I wish some of the students wouldn't act the way they usually do.	73	76	79	75
3.	Most kids don't care about school problems or world problems.	57	51	60	50
4.	I am afraid I won't be able to function as an adult.	16	12	17	24
5.	I am scared of other kids, who pick on me.	18	19	25	28
6.	The big problem is that most kids aren't interested in what they are learning.	86	82	69	63
7.	Other students laugh at you because of what you believe.	40	60	53	47
8.	Children blame their problems on teachers.	53	43	57	45
9.	Classes should be nicer to subs.	69	87	63	81
10.	I don't understand why I get the grades and test scores I get.	49	61	49	41
11.	Pregnant girls should not have to drop out of school.	70	81	88	74
12.	The older kids at Irwin aren't friendly with the younger ones and won't let them play ball or something we could come together and play.	66	40	59	39
13.	Students should help keep the noise down in the hall.	71	68	73	60
14.	I am afraid to walk home by myself.	34	10	4	12
15.	A lot of kids act like babies and the teachers treat them like babies.	90	92	74	75
16.	I don't think you would even need to have a lock on your locker if people would be honest.	90	69	69	59
17.	I think that children should obey the teacher.	79	77	82	76
18.	I don't think it is right for kids to "run all over a teacher" even if you don't like her.	79	82	66	78

5. Attitudes Toward the Behavior of Teachers

		Girls		Boys	
			Grades		
		7th	8th	7th	8th
1.	Some teachers are unfair to some students who are trying hard.	81	78	84	69
2.	My teachers like me, at least one does anyway.	75	69	60	69
3.	I feel some teachers play favorites.	81	73	79	64

		Girls		Boys	
			Grades		
		7th	8th	7th	8th
4.	Some teachers are too emotional.	84	82	92	79
5.	Some teachers keep you late when it's time to get out for lunch which makes a big problem because the lunch period is so short.	90	90	90	81
6.	Some teachers like girls better than boys and aren't fair to boys.	35	27	76	53
7.	We have real good teachers in this school.	43	58	50	53
8.	Some teachers are racially prejudiced.	79	77	80	73
9.	The teachers are out in the hall supervising their classes every day.	65	62	56	68
10.	Some teachers ought to quit acting like we're babies and let us act our age.	92	96	99	87
11.	Teachers should be able to take things away from their students when the things are dangerous or if the kids shouldn't be fooling with them.	75	67	65	75
12.	Some teachers should teach us something instead of giving us free periods.	17	50	20	46
13.	Teachers make you feel inferior.	70	63	73	50
14.	Most teachers are fair.	51	69	59	72
15.	We have Departmental because teachers want to get rid of you.	51	26	37	50
16.	Teachers don't give you a fair chance and other teachers always believe teachers.	83	79	88	87
17.	Many teachers don't give enough supervision to their classes.	51	53	47	32
18.	Some teachers are afraid of students.	65	76	78	75
19.	Teachers give grades according to race or how well they like you.	46	41	47	40
20.	Most kids are scared of teachers threatening to take graduation away.	67	65	69	63
21.	Teachers put down things kids feel and say.	75	70	67	71
22.	Some teachers don't expect enough out of the students and then students don't get their work done. There is no pressure.	53	53	64	53
23.	I think that teachers should have more respect for the children.	86	94	94	81
24.	Teachers are not strict enough.	27	16	20	29

6. Attitudes Toward the Curriculum and Special Programs

	Girls		Boys	
	Grades			
	7th	**8th**	**7th**	**8th**
1. The classes should go on more educational and fun field trips.	99	99	98	82
2. Language Arts class is too long.	75	63	79	82
3. We should have Black Studies.	96	84	90	72
4. There is not enough individual help in the classroom.	59	61	63	55
5. History is not being taught properly, because it leaves out about the contributions of black people and doesn't tell about the prejudice of famous whites, such as George Washington owned slaves.	85	86	72	77
6. We should have more library periods.	57	49	65	42
7. Students who are not skilled in a certain subject, like math for example, should have a longer math period than other students, and the same for language arts, etc.	50	56	58	54
8. We should have more individual subjects like in college.	74	83	76	69
9. When you have three different teachers, sometimes they require more homework at the same time than we can do.	94	76	92	70
10. I think the library is very good but they need more good books.	77	75	76	66
11. Mr. Moore should take the students on a camping trip.	90	75	88	81
12. There should be more fashion shows showing fashions for boys and girls both.	84	82	86	78
13. I wish we had more assemblies and plays put on by children.	90	94	84	81
14. There should be one party period a day for each child.	82	86	80	90
15. There should be more emphasis in subjects other than language arts & math.	79	87	83	72
16. We should have television and more movies in the school.	91	84	92	91
17. I think we should have a longer math period.	22	29	19	19
18. The French program should be grouped according to how much French someone knows rather than by classes.	67	77	65	57

7. *Attitudes Toward the School's Physical Facilities*

	Girls		Boys	
	Grades			
	7th	8th	7th	8th
1. I don't like the locks on the bathroom doors.	71	88	73	67
2. I like the washrooms that have been fixed up but others need fixing too.	96	88	90	79
3. There should be soap in the washrooms.	99	98	97	88
4. It is always too hot or too cold, so when it's too hot and the window is opened it's too cold, and if the window is not opened, the room smells.	81	66	83	65
5. The school needs to be redecorated.	91	92	97	84
6. There are not enough things on the playground to play on.	86	85	89	76
7. There are roaches and ants in the school.	40	60	54	42
8. I am glad Irwin is going to get a new playground this year.	98	90	98	77
9. The washrooms smell.	75	79	90	81

8. *Attitudes Toward the School's Lunchroom*

	Girls		Boys	
	Grades			
	7th	8th	7th	8th
1. The food in the lunchroom is not hot enough.	78	94	68	62
2. The lunch period for the upper grades should be an hour.	87	93	89	91
3. The lunchroom is better than it was last year.	47	47	60	70
4. The lunchroom menu needs more variety.	89	91	94	87
5. There ought to be more supervision in the lunchroom.	53	39	60	43
6. I don't like the lunchroom food.	72	88	57	57
7. The lunchroom looks kind of sloppy.	86	88	81	70
8. The lunchroom serves good food.	20	10	28	28
9. The milk in the Canteen should be cold.	98	98	92	83
10. They don't give enough food on the lunch.	94	89	84	90
11. The lunchroom's food is improving.	67	37	64	41

9. Attitudes Toward the Learning Center

		Girls		Boys	
			Grades		
		7th	8th	7th	8th
1.	More kids should be given an opportunity to use the Learning Center.	89	87	93	79
2.	I don't know what the purpose of the Learning Center is.	32	33	19	34
3.	The Learning Center should be in Irwin School until the school breaks down.	78	80	83	81
4.	The teachers in the Learning Center do not watch to see if people put away the materials they were using or watch to see if the students wreck or steal something or waste keypunch cards.	71	62	77	50
5.	I wish I was allowed to go to the Learning Center more.	66	63	89	56
6.	The Learning Center needs more materials for advanced students.	75	81	73	70
7.	I like the Learning Center because you get to choose what you want to do and somebody isn't telling you what to do all the time and what not to do.	65	80	90	74
8.	I don't like the Learning Center because it doesn't have enough equipment.	30	33	30	23
9.	The computer terminals and key punch machines are neat and I wish there were more.	78	82	90	90
10.	I am glad all classes get to go to the Learning Center.	84	78	92	71
11.	I like the Learning Center pretty much!	77	88	94	80

10. Attitudes Toward Sports, the Gymnasium and the Social Center

		Girls		Boys	
			Grades		
		7th	8th	7th	8th
1.	We should have gym every day.	57	49	79	82
2.	The best players and biggest kids use the basketball stands and don't let anybody else play and that's not fair.	72	64	77	56
3.	The gym period should be longer.	67	56	89	82
4.	Students should be able to do what they please when they have outdoor gym.	84	88	99	78
5.	Social Center should end at 5:45 instead of 5:00.	88	77	80	74

	Girls		Boys	
		Grades		
	7th	8th	7th	8th
6. We should have a football and a baseball team and a hockey team to play other schools.	86	66	89	90
7. There should be an organized program in the large playground.	78	74	83	77
8. We should use the gym equipment more.	89	90	100	82
9. More kids should participate in Social Center.	62	70	82	84
10. Mr. Phillips said he would get the basketball team some uniforms and he did and I am glad.	87	86	90	69
11. Gym should not be required of students.	40	53	29	28
12. The home backgrounds and cultures of one group of kids should not be imposed on other students, such as the social center music for dancing.	65	81	64	65
13. There should be nets on the basketball rims.	91	86	94	91
14. We need more sports activities.	84	76	92	90
15. Gym should be held outside whenever possible.	95	98	90	80

APPENDIX II

Evaluation Questionnaire for the Woodsville Workshop

This instrument was administered to a group of trainees in human relations skills, to help them resolve a situation that threatened to wreck the group. Degrees of response are indicated by:

A = strong agreement
a = agreement
d = disagreement
D = strong disagreement

The numbers in the response columns indicate the number of group members responding to each category.

		Response		
	A	a	d	D
1. The Woodsville episode has created ill will among participants and between some participants and staff and was an unnecessary, destructive intrusion on the purpose of this workshop.	4	4	9	8
2. A lot of this trouble dates back to the Monday when staff failed to deal directly and immediately with the protest by Group A and just let everyone flounder.	4	6	6	13
3. I feel concerned.	17	5	2	1
4. The selection was on the basis of black/white.	2	11	2	5
5. I think that the group sent their best participants to Woodsville in achieving their goals. The black/white issue is important—and the maximum possible number of whites went.	9	4	4	7
6. We should discuss the feelings of people not selected for the Woodsville workshop.	13	10	0	1
7. I am concerned about the group that stayed—feeling toward the ones that went, and I would like to hear from *all* that were not selected.	13	9	3	0
8. As small group leaders we sometimes have to be more concerned with our clients' feelings than we are for our own feelings.	17	8	0	0

	Response			
	A	a	d	D
9. I am concerned about the feelings of the workshop participants who did not have [the] Woodsville experience.	11	13	1	0
10. An additional concern is selection by participants of the activities they have chosen at other locations and why.	2	12	10	2
11. I am concerned about hurt feelings, feelings of inadequacy on the part of those not selected and the creating of more division among this so-called "group."	14	6	4	2
12. I wonder why we cannot deal with those concerns that continue to divide us.	19	7	0	1
13. I felt that the white staff members, because of their experience, would be better able to handle the black/white issue, if it came up, than the white trainees and I wanted to spare them a bad experience.	6	6	7	5
14. I didn't care as much about the white staff members—whom I wasn't as close to—I really didn't consider them at all!	1	7	8	8
15. I am unable to deal with the Woodsville situation because I was denied the privilege of dealing with it. I feel rejected, by both groups, and unwanted. I am operating on an emotional level because feelings about *self* are threatened.	5	4	7	9
16. The issue may fragment the group and this is a late stage for this to happen.	6	6	7	5
17. I am concerned with the lack of openness on part of participants in large group in regard to feelings that they voiced in subgroups.	16	7	2	0
18. I am concerned about the feelings generated by not being accepted, and the failure to understand the causes, including specifically the unwillingness to complete the *process*.	10	12	2	1
19. I was disappointed.	5	7	5	8
20. The feelings of the people who were not selected are real and they should be dealt with honestly and openly.	20	7	1	0
21. I feel that the group should be kept together as a *total* team although *every* member can't participate in an activity. That is, everyone should take part in *briefing, pay, critique*, etc.	12	0	3	10
22. At least *two* white participants should have been included in the Woodsville workshop.	3	6	8	6

	Response			
	A	a	d	D
23. *Openness is essential.*	18	4	0	0
24. The fragmentation of the group affected the Woodsville experience.	6	4	6	7
25. I would like to discuss it in a large group setting. Let's discuss the whole thing, starting with the method of selection. Let's not ignore James and his possible input into this situation.	14	8	2	1
26. I am apprehensive that some whites have feelings of guilt at being left out and are wondering if they are deliberately segregated.	9	7	4	5
27. The weak whites were unable to accept black rejection of them and their personal inadequacy.	8	4	7	6
28. I am concerned that the selection of Woodsville staff forced the workshop participants into a competitive structure which has caused a schism as yet unresolved.	9	8	5	3
29. The resolution of the present schism could be a useful learning experience.	20	4	0	0

APPENDIX III

Evaluation Questionnaire for a Curriculum Change in a Suburban High School

In the following instrument the range of responses is denoted by: A = strong agreement; a = agreement; d = disagreement; D = strong disagreement. The numbers in the response columns indicate the number of faculty members responding to each category.

		Response			
		A	a	d	D
1.	I fear that many of our students will not take the responsibility necessary to make the program work.	36	12	13	7
2.	I am very concerned about resistance from some colleagues and hope they won't doom our experiments before we start.	56	31	10	1
3.	Problem: Communication between students, parents, teachers etc. is necessary if we are to overcome the selfish desires of each individual group.	22	19	19	1
4.	I feel that too many students will choose the lesser path—doing nothing—unless driven to learning through guidance. I fear for our future unless we can start this approach at an earlier level than secondary school.	30	52	18	1
5.	We need a strong vocational educational program at Lowell in order to serve the needs of the non-academic student.	33	32	23	3
6.	The problem that most bothers me is how do I get on a one-to-one basis with my students in the time allowed and with the number of students I still must handle.	43	30	16	0
7.	We ought to stop talking about the future and begin to implement it now.	46	39	9	0
8.	I am a loner, dislike working in groups and jealously guard my autonomy.	4	18	32	52
9.	I wonder how I will be evaluated, and by whom?	13	31	38	23

	Response			
	A	a	d	D
10. Most helpful to me in making change will be a feeling of confidence that professionally I can survive in the face of uncertainty, mistakes and failures I am bound to encounter.	33	51	16	3
11. The closer contact of student and teacher will break the old conception of the teacher as an unapproachable automaton.	53	40	7	2
12. I would like to feel that the mutual interest and support of my peers help me to take risks and to accept and deal with frustrations and failures I will encounter. I would like to work in an atmosphere with more *joy*, excitement, and stimulation—more optimism.	67	29	7	1
13. The greatest difficulty I anticipate is on the question of the administration's preparedness for *real* change.	17	26	39	20
14. I am most afraid of students taking advantage of a liberal atmosphere.	18	36	31	19
15. One goal would be to train teachers and students to deal with their new environment.	49	51	3	0
16. To live in this changing environment we would have to cope with noise.	10	41	40	10
17. We need in-service programs for both teachers and students to help them through this period of change. For example: teachers need to know *how* to provide more experimentation and good guidance. Students need to know *how* to take more responsibility for their education.	62	34	5	2
18. The thing that bothers me the most is that in my own subject area some things should be changed in a *different* way from the changes that are being planned, e.g., I need more *individual* space along with the wide open space.	28	44	22	5
19. More vocational trade areas and less emphasis on the saving of the world—*College*.	43	44	6	5
20. Will the contact with students be increased or will [the change] in effect lessen personal contact with students?	8	23	30	9
21. The thing that will help me most is more workshops teaching me how to work with students individually.	35	37	21	7
22. The apparent "chaos" that is likely to develop in a changing school must be accepted by staff, students, and community.	31	54	15	2

	Response		
	A	a	d	D

23. Facilities must be provided to give students and faculty the opportunity to select from several different kinds of "learning areas" in which communication can occur.   53 44 1 0

24. Students have a difficulty in budgeting time and using time and will waste it.   28 35 30 6

25. Students should not be required to come to class.   22 33 29 11

26. I fear that many faculty members change only in their rhetoric and not in their behavior.   30 43 23 2

27. Discussions in small groups composed of students, teachers, and parents would be helpful.   47 47 4 2

28. I fear that I would no longer be able to plan and direct my course/s the way I want to—that I would not be able to keep the same overall objectives that I have had (and which I believe are good ones), and thus I would not be accomplishing what I really want to accomplish.   11 16 48 24

29. Teachers should be placed on a differential pay scale according to ability (as per Dr. Field's talk).   18 25 24 29

30. Parents should be encouraged to visit the school at any time—to just drop in and pass the time of day; to observe.   44 44 12 4

31. Students don't need passes to remember their names or where they are going—it's the teachers who probably do.   27 36 20 18

32. We need more in-service training—at least one day a month.   50 37 13 5

33. If we are not ready for change as professionals we cannot expect parents or students to be ready. We're the ones who are *supposed to know* about educational matters.   42 48 10 4

34. Teacher counseling or psychological evaluation of my individual mental stability (as it pertains to my work) is or should be everyone's major need. Am I still fit to teach after five years of teaching?   16 41 28 13

35. One of the greatest problems I foresee is the cultivation of this "personal rapport." I am basically more of a quiet person and have found difficulty in establishing these. Other more outgoing people seem to have large groups of followers. Will I be able to help?   10 27 41 18

36. The administration must make a commitment, on class size, etc. to *each and every* department, that will ensure that no one or two departments will be

	Response			
	A	**a**	**d**	**D**
favored or given more priority than any other department in this school.	38	32	17	17
37. Students should be allowed to select their teachers and to initiate courses which to them (students) appear relevant to their roles as young adults.	39	41	15	7
38. I need a voice and the satisfaction that my ideas about the change are not being dismissed as being "in the way." This crap about if you don't like it leave doesn't settle with me. If I don't like the change I should have some vote to change the change.	40	49	7	2
39. We need a much more realistic method for assessing a student's educational needs.	49	49	6	0
40. The attainment of *honest* intellectual intercourse rather than self-serving manipulation of personnel will solve all other problems.	28	41	25	2
41. The "hard-sell, negative attitude" method that prejudges all criticisms as the reaction of "fear" or "insecurity" precludes an honest evaluation of the program.	25	45	24	3
42. Staff personnel will verbalize change, but their behavior will not be consistent with their beliefs.	18	40	40	1
43. I feel we have a great need for more facilities such as accommodation for automotive and printing trades and more *on the job training*.	58	40	4	2
44. We need to have good research into how much freedom will be creative for a student, taking into account maturity. (Some students are not emotionally ready for some kinds of responsibility.)	48	51	2	3
45. I thought I detected a touch of rigidity in some remarks, "Be flexible our way, or else." Is only the student, and not the parent or teacher to be an individual? There is more than one way to regiment people—the group way seems democratic.	24	47	22	4
46. Vital to me as I approach new situations is the belief that I can affect them; I need to feel absolutely able to state opinions on the situations without fear of personal loss or threat to my position on the staff.	49	47	4	0
47. Students need places to go to eat, sit, talk, be alone, even sleep, *whenever* they want to and as long as they want to.	30	39	24	9
48. The above statement also applies to teachers and other living things.	40	34	22	7

	Response			
	A	a	d	D
49. Periodic meetings with teachers, students, and parents to discuss the changes, as they are put into effect, will help in adjustment and evaluation.	47	48	5	1
50. One thing is being said and quite another done—I have trouble seeing how we can expect a "media center" to function when I have my students sent out of the library every day because they whisper too loudly.	34	35	27	4
51. We teachers have been educated under the present school setup. I feel myself that I would need to be reeducated about just what we are trying to accomplish when we speak of change.	36	43	20	7
52. The most helpful thing to me in meeting change would be to know where we are going.	36	48	15	4
53. More interest areas will strain our facilities and/or teacher training and/or existing knowledge of present or future teachers.	11	40	42	5
54. Large open spaces do not make education any more personal than do the large open spaces of factories encourage human personal relations.	23	44	30	4
55. Damn it, I need more time and more money—to relate to other persons, to study, to participate in our culture, to read in areas of my own interests for my own personal fulfillment, to diminish my own incompetence as a teacher and person.	35	41	17	3
56. I am in the field of communication. In the new setup I hope to increase the areas of human communication—intonation, shared laughter, body language—all the things that radiate from a vital, living, human being. Success in these areas should provide the stimulus that leads to the solution of problems of core communication.	29	58	1	10
57. Teachers need time (blocks of time) to communicate ideas and frustrations as they prepare for change.	53	43	0	4
58. I would most like to see the elimination of students having to study within a field they do not judge to be necessary for their progress or education.	34	37	5	23
59. I feel a problem for us will be to try more to take risks thereby leave ourselves open to criticism.	15	39	8	41
60. We need to give the students freedom with *responsibility* rather than allowing them to do as they please. *Accountability* for all!	40	43	4	6

	Response			
	A	a	d	D
61. The most difficult problem I believe will be living with increasing diversity, without becoming frustrated, suspicious and defensive.	15	47	29	6
62. Students should be involved in setting up the curriculum. This would mean that some teachers might have "their" courses undermined by having a book or topic covered at a different level.	35	39	15	4
63. I imagine it will be a lot more difficult for the older teacher to make these changes than for the younger teacher because we have been living with the old traditions for so long.	23	27	28	20
64. I think it will be one hell of a mess.	8	13	42	33

REFERENCES

Helmer, O. *Social Technology*. New York: Basic Books, 1966.

Naisbitt, N. Report of Teacher Learning Center Questionnaire. Mimeographed. Chicago, February 1970.

Rossi, P. "Evaluating Educational Programs." *Urban Review* 3, no. 4 (February 1969): 17.

Thelen, H. A. "New Practices on the Firing Line." *Administrator's Notebook* 12, no. 5 (Chicago: University of Chicago, Midwest Administration Center, January 1964).

Wille, L. "Room for Miracles." *American Education* (August-September 1969): 7-10.

4

A CASE STUDY OF AN
EVALUATION PROJECT

HARRIET TALMAGE

"But what if the final report isn't favorable to us?" a harried
assistant superintendent asked an evaluation consultant. The superintendent represented a prominent suburban school district plagued,
in addition to the usual concerns, by threats of a federal review of
the system's neighborhood policy practices.

BACKGROUND

Three decades previously the school district had been a model
suburban system. Its population, white and mainly blue collar, included a good number of lower level executive and professional
people. Despite the district's diverse ethnic composition, including a
small black community, many people held common values: they had
strong church affiliations, a high regard for education, for the role of

the school in providing education, and for home ownership. For a few years the school system had had a forward-looking reading program that attracted the attention of outside educators, but, apart from this program, the school system made no waves, except that, long before other suburban school systems in the area were comfortable with the idea of professional unions, the teachers had worked for the recognition of the American Federation of Teachers as the negotiating body between themselves and the School Board. Unionism, with, for a time, higher salaries than those in the surrounding areas, gave the district an adequate pool of teachers, even during the fifties and early sixties, when teachers were in short supply.

During and after World War II, the suburb's composition was changing and changes in the older section, the southern portion of the school district, differed radically from changes in the northern section. In the south the black community was increasing in number as well as spreading out. Executives and professionals in this section of the school district were leaving, to be replaced by more blue collar workers, newly arrived Appalachian whites, and Spanish-speaking people who filled the schools to overflowing. The northern section consisted of an older, established, stable, and well-maintained Italian community with close family ties. New houses, built on what had been prairie, were being occupied by Italians who had been displaced in the city by black inmigration, younger Jewish apartment dwellers who were leaving the city to buy homes in the suburbs, and younger Greek families, most of whom had recently attained their higher economic status. An attractive new school was built, but apart from that, the shift in population composition went unacknowledged, at least by the area's institutions.

This movement created a divergent rather than a homogeneous value system. The school had not had to cope with pupils who felt their ethnic identification so strongly. In the northern section, the Jewish and Greek parents showed an intense, overt interest in the schools. They demanded to know about the curriculum, the teachers' qualifications and the school's philosophy of education and administration. When it organized its first Parent-Teachers Association, the school was unprepared for the fervor created by the PTA presidential election. PTAs had been docile in the past; now the election took on the dimensions of a full scale political battle. One side wanted the new math, transformational grammar, and a full-fledged science program. The other wanted "excellence" through the traditional curriculum. The school continued its traditional methods throughout the furor. When the new school and the others in the district made preparations for the usual Christmas program the administrators were once again unprepared for the avalanche of protest: "Why Christmas songs?" "Religion doesn't belong in the schools." "We want half and half." Several years later new protests were heard: the black community wanted the school to recognize its ethnic heroes, its cultural contributions, and to appreciate its mores and customs.

The school district had established and maintained a monolithic administration system. Superintendent Rogers had presided over the School Board for over twenty-five years. He had worked out power relationships with the various sectors which permitted each a minor role without disturbing the equilibrium or threatening the autonomy of the superintendent's domain. To the old, stable, Italian community, the superintendent turned over control of building and ground maintenance in exchange for complete support on all bond issues. With the teachers, the superintendent exchanged direct negotiation with the Board for minimal union demands, which seldom went beyond questions of salary increments.

Waiting to assume more direct leadership was the highly respected assistant superintendent, Mr. Davidson, well known in the state for his theories on curriculum and instruction. Although he set the tone of academic excellence throughout the district, many of his ideas had to bide their time until he could take over the superintendency. When Mr. Davidson assumed total responsibility for the administration and curriculum of the schools, in the early sixties, the monolithic style of administration was no longer in tune with the times. New power alliances, with different channels of accountability, needed to be developed.

By the mid-sixties the school district was a microcosm of the large urban system. Political lines were identifiable: neighborhoods established their boundaries of influence; white liberals, uneasy about losing their new affluence, supported the policies of neighborhood schools and ethnic identification. The school administration faced many of the problems that are now so characteristic of changing communities: lower reading scores, increased behavior problems, increased vandalism to the school buildings, and low teacher morale. The parents blamed the teachers; the teachers blamed the school administrator, the central office, and the parents; the administrators blamed the financial support system and an uncooperative and unimaginative staff. The village government supported the school administration as long as it upheld the policy of academic excellence within the status quo. A civic group, labeled "the bird watchers" by school personnel and composed of concerned residents, had for many years tried to keep the central office administrators account-able to the taxpayers. Formerly the group had simply attended board meetings and asked embarrassing questions in public. Now they demanded access to account books and records, and were supported by a court order maintaining that the materials were public records. The various ethnic groups were consolidating their lines and positions on major educational issues. The administration responded by put-ting the administrative staff through a human relations workshop which merely helped to face up to some pressing racial and social concerns but did not provide the staff with the skills to carry out any changes.

Concurrently, the sheer numbers of new students kept bringing unpleasant matters before the public. How should these children be housed? Each alternative solution had its detractors, whether the option was to enlarge the present school, shift boundaries, build new schools in the immediate areas of need, or locate new buildings to assure a better ethnic mix. Few used the term segregation to describe what had been happening, or integration to describe what most meant by a "better ethnic mix." In some schools the site was expanded; in others mobile rooms were added; in others the boundaries were shifted slightly. Each of these changes was swal-lowed without too much disturbance.

By the late sixties the district had two all-black schools in the southern section, four all-white schools in the central and northern sections, and five integrated schools in the center and at the south side of the district. Integration was only a chance and passing phase in schools whose composition was rapidly changing. So it was in the mid-sixties that the administration was forced to go beyond make-shift solutions, and to grapple with the problems of space, race, and academic achievement.

The central administration submitted two innovative plans. In the first plan they proposed building a new middle school; in the second, creating an experimental school in renovated premises. By the first suggestion the administration hoped to be able to solve the shortage of space, to assure an adequate ethnic mix, and to raise academic standards; by the second they hoped only to solve the problem of academic standards. The first plan met with instant and violent resistance. Every social-action group, every organization, religious, social, political, and economic took up arms. A centrally located middle school would mean the demise of the neighborhood policy. In two referenda the proposal of a middle school was presented to the public and defeated: in the first by a vote of two to one; in the second by a vote of somewhat less than two to one, but a large margin nevertheless.

The idea of the second plan was to establish an experimental school as a source of ideas for other schools in the district. The school would be a small, innovative, vehicle for testing new curricula, instruction methods, and in-service programs. The school would be characterized by ungraded groups of all ages, personal instruction, team teaching, parental involvement, an innovative use of space, and the creative use of a wide range of instructional materials. The students would be selected from a representative random sample of those children whose parents had volunteered to have them attend the school. Thus each school in the district could send a given number of students chosen according to sex, race, and degree of overcrowding in the school. The selection process, ostensibly random, dispatched a disproportionately large number of difficult children—children with behavior problems, disgruntled parents, or feelings of alienation—to the experimental school. In some cases, the principals persuaded the parents of difficult students to volunteer.

With money coming from the building fund, no referendum was necessary to establish the new school. The students were selected from volunteers in the third and fourth grades. This required some form of bussing, at which point several communities balked. Some people feared that the administration was putting something over on the public, others were skeptical about so much money being put into experiments that were merely frills and would coddle the children. Still others saw it as the first step toward the elimination of the neighborhood policy. Amid the hue and cry, the newly acquired apartment building was remodeled and the staff selected.

It was in this atmosphere that I was called in as an evaluation consultant on the experimental school. At the first meeting, with the evaluator, Superintendent Davidson, the assistant superintendent, Mr. Rheeder and the principal-designate of the experimental school Mrs. Kahn, Mr. Rheeder's remark quoted at the opening of this chapter was made: "But what if the final report isn't favorable to us?"

THE EVALUATION DESIGN PLANNING SESSION

Four weeks before the new school opened, the initial evaluation planning meeting took place. It was apparent that Superintendent Davidson was deeply committed to finding workable solutions to some of the academic problems and had great confidence in the ability of the experimental school to help him. He saw in the experimental school a chance to demonstrate his belief that, given a racial and ethnic mix, a dedicated staff using imaginative materials, and educational methods that permitted freedom to learn on an individual basis, the children's learning ability would be enhanced and their behavior and attitudes toward the school and toward others would improve markedly. He was putting a solid reputation of many years service to the school district on the line in taking this stand, and, indirectly, he was putting to the test his own convictions on integration, to such an extent that he willingly agreed to a full-scale evaluation research plan involving experimental and control groups, assessment before and after the school was established, and access not only to the children but also to the parents.

His assistant superintendent, though less dedicated to evaluation research, proved in time to be the more astute politician. He questioned the composition of the tentatively defined control group, and suggested that we compare the experimental school children with the third and fourth graders in the schools that had the worst performance record. Thus "the new school is bound to look good." Gently Superintendent Davidson and I explained that a substantial amount of the taxpayers' money, about $600,000, was going into this school and that we owed it to everyone to help make the school effective. This could be accomplished through formative evaluation, and, through summative evaluation, by getting some evidence on whether the larger objectives were being met. Mr. Rheeder was not convinced, but held his fire until he could review the entire plan.

After discussing the objectives of the school with the principal-designate Mrs. Kahn, we agreed that within two weeks the school staff would review and rewrite their own objectives and, on the basis of the restated objectives, I would submit an evaluation research plan. None of the objectives was to be concerned with race or ethnic mix. The emphasis was to be on cognitive and affective growth of children within a flexible school environment.

At the next meeting the evaluation plan was discussed. Mr. Rheeder became more outspoken. He maintained that whatever occurred in the school would be criticized, so the evaluation plan had to reflect a 'low posture.' Superintendent Davidson, though still in command, appeared weary of the argument. He looked like a man who had made a moral decision—to choose the path of good education over that of expedient politics. He was supported by Mrs. Kahn. At this point I was mentally formulating a plan of transactional evaluation, an adjunct essential to the total evaluation design if formative and summative evaluations were to be carried out.

The staff of the experimental school and the district administration agreed on the school's objectives, which depended on a flexible environment. The objectives were:

1. To view each child as a unique learner and to use many types and levels of instructional material so that each child could achieve at his own level of success.
2. To teach the children in various ways: in small or large groups, by personal instruction, in multiage and multigrade groups, by independent study, and in interest groups.
3. To develop the staff as a team so that the strengths of the staff members would be available to all the children.
4. To develop each child to take the initiative and responsibility for his own learning and behavior.
5. To have the staff accountable to the parents and the school community.

It was hypothesized that, by striving to carry out these objectives within a flexible learning environment, the cognitive and affective learning of the children would be enhanced. Mr. Rheeder, considering that the objectives were innocuous enough if not taken too literally, accepted them.

The intention would be to stimulate the children's positive attitudes toward others, their positive self-concept, and their cognitive development. It would have been impossible to separate each input variable in the flexible environment in order to measure its possible effect on the children's development, so the independent variables, use of space, instructional methods, curriculum, the teachers' behavior, were subsumed under the term "flexible environment." The dependent variables were the children's cognitive and affective behavior, and the parents' attitudes toward the school. The assistant superintendent could accept all but the last. He was leery of parental participation, indicating the can of worms that it could release. Table 1, below, shows in summary the evaluation plan. Having had the plan explained to him, Mr. Rheeder voiced his reservations. Neither the school building principals nor the School Board would permit data collection on the parents' attitudes toward the school. The teachers would decline to collect data from the children on their schools. The teachers' union would object to the time taken by the teachers to collect continuous data on students' social and personal traits. The evaluation plan, placing too much weight on pupil growth, did not "preserve the flanks." Politically, insufficient pupil growth at the

TABLE 1

Summary of the Evaluation Design Plan

MEASURES / SUBJECTS	Attitudes Toward School	Classroom Behavior	Biographical Data	Cognitive Learning	Aptitude	Unobtrusive Measures
Experimental Students N = 160	Pre- & Post- Hoyt's *Describe Your School*	Continual measurement of 4 personal and 4 social traits	Age Sex Grade etc.	Pre-& Post- Stanford Achievement Test	Pre- Otis-Lennon	Observations Records Informal interviews
Control A Students N = 240	"	" (random selection)	"	"	"	Records Teachers' reports
Control B Students	"		"	"	"	
Experimental Parents	Pre- & Post- *Parents' Questionnaire*					Reports Informal interviews
Control A Parents	"					
Control B Parents	"					

Note: Experimental = 160 volunteer students selected to attend the experimental school.
Control A = 240 students whose parents had volunteered to send their children to the experimental school but who were not selected.
Control B = balance of 3rd and 4th grade students in the school district.

experimental school would be its death knell. There was no assurance in the plan that any of the results would make the experimental school look good.

Superintendent Davidson recognized the validity of these reservations but he was buoyed up by the enthusiasm of the principal-designate. Mrs. Kahn felt that nothing should stand in the way of a forward-looking educational stance. Actually Mr. Rheeder was not opposed to good education, but he was attuned to political realities. He was reading the new power alliances and the extent of opposition to change more accurately than the superintendent was. The established Italian community was no longer prepared to support the administration in exchange merely for control over maintenance jobs; it was demanding a reaffirmation of the neighborhood policy. Because it felt that its demands were being thwarted, the community organized. The mood of the blacks had changed. They were demanding the power to make their own decisions, and so they organized. The more affluent Jews and Greeks, disturbed by the racial trouble in the local high school, were looking around for new allies. They found them in the organized Italian sector.

In retrospect Mr. Rheeder, the assistant superintendent, was doing everyone a service by dragging his heels on the evaluation. Although Rippey had not at the time coined his term Transactional Evaluation, indirectly this was what the assistant superintendent was meaning. The best laid evaluation plans can come to naught if the support of the parties involved is not elicited early. So the remainder of the second evaluation planning session was devoted to transactional evaluation. We had to encourage everybody who was concerned with the school to become involved in the evaluation program and to support it.

The building principals and other central office staff were most concerned about the parent attitude measurement. After some pressure from the superintendent, they revised several of the items on the *Parent Attitude Inventory,* changed the title to *Parents' Questionnaire,* and arrived at an understanding about the use of the data. All the data from the various schools would be categorized by groups: Experimental (consisting of 160 students selected to attend the experimental school), Control A (consisting of 240 students whose parents had volunteered to send their children to the experimental school, but who were not selected), and Control B (consisting of the remainder of the third and fourth grade students in the school district). The only data identified by school were the postexperimental data. When the principals were reassured about the analysis of the data, they agreed to distribute, collect, and deliver the question-naires, in sealed envelopes, to the central office before the experimental school opened and again at the end of the academic year.

The parents, by contrast, were most cooperative. They were only too happy to present their views on the schools without having to do so in an open forum, so the rate of return was unusually high. Most parents also took the opportunity to express additional remarks on several open-ended questions; many used the back of the questionnaire to get an idea across. The teachers were concerned about the use of data collected from the students' questionnaire, *Describe Your School*. Again, the data were to be used only to compare the Experimental, Control A, and Control B groups; data would not be analyzed by classroom. The teachers did not wish to use the data as feedback information for their classes. What came across clearly at the meetings of the teachers, the superintendent and the principal of the experimental school was the resentment the teachers felt toward the experimental school and how threatened they felt their own status to be because they were still associated with the traditional schools. Their feelings were summed up in the remark: "Of course they'll do better than we will! Who wouldn't with a new building, carpets on the floor, and all those materials?" (No extra monies were given to the experimental school beyond the remodeling expenses, and Superintendent Davidson had been careful to make this known.)

The teachers' union did not present a problem. As an organization it had taken no stand on the experimental school, because several active union members had volunteered to teach in the experimental school, and because some members personally supported any experiment that might help the district face its problems, while others felt themselves threatened by any change.

The Political Aura Surrounding Implementation

The School Board, at this point, gave its vote of confidence to Superintendent Davidson by agreeing with the evaluation plan.

The collection of initial pretest data took place as scheduled. The students moved into their experimental school and the problems both expected and unexpected were met by the principal and her staff with extraordinary patience and dispatch. Fortunately for the experimental school, the principal had shaped the staff into a close working team several months before the school opened. They needed all the inner support they could muster.

The second referendum on a new middle school was defeated. There were many open attacks on the idea of the experimental school and its implication for the neighborhood policy. The referendum was followed by a bitterly campaigned school board election. The terms 'racist,' 'segregationist,' and 'integrationist,' took the place of more polite rhetoric. The residents in the northern section mobilized a political machine that could serve as an example to many a large city machine. They reaffirmed their commitment to the neighborhood policy, totally opposed the idea of a middle school, and in moments of real heat, pledged to dismember the experimental school and scalp the superintendent. The black community and what remained of the white liberal community proved no match.

The new Board represented almost entirely the northern section of the school district, either in actual geographical location or in point of view. Superintendent Davidson asked the Board if it would prefer him to resign. His question went unanswered, leaving him with no alternative but to resign at the end of the academic year. His resignation also left the experimental school with no strong support from the central administration.

Mrs. Kahn and her staff carried on without support, knowing that any mistakes would open them to direct attack. Problems with the buses, with children who had to learn to work in an open environment and peers so different from themselves, with dissatisfied parents and so forth, had to be worked out internally. Although no data were collected about the teachers' morale, it was evident that without the first, fairly secure, three months in which the staff developed the school and organized themselves into a team, any one of the pressing problems could have closed the school.

One of the last things Superintendent Davidson did before leaving was to see that the necessary post data (the *Describe Your School* questionnaire, the *Parents' Questionnaire,* and the achievement test) were collected at the end of the school year. The principal, fearing that something might happen, removed the data from the central office to her school vault. Also in his last months in office, the superintendent had another consultant visit the experimental school once a month for five months. The consultant's observational report to the new Board was cautious and avoided the racial issue. It was ignored. Parents of children in the experimental school and some liberal residents of the southern end of the district asked the Board about the possibility of setting up more experimental schools. They too were ignored.

Dissemination

During the summer the data were collated, tabulated, and analyzed. A preliminary report on the *Parents' Questionnaire* was submitted to Mrs. Kahn, who hoped to share it with the Board. It did not appear to have reached the Board's agenda. The final report, a short statistical report, was also submitted to the Board; there is no record that the Board was aware of this report. However, as Mrs. Kahn had used the report as formative evaluation data, she was able to make some changes in the school during the following year.

At the start of the next school year, Superintendent Madden was appointed; the first superintendent appointed from outside the system in over thirty-five years. Mr. Rheeder retained his position as assistant superintendent. There seemed to be a new attitude toward the experimental school: everyone now was happy to keep it in 'low profile.' Even the other school principals were not disturbed by its existence. It was evident from the records that some principals were using the experimental school as a dumping ground for their behavior problems. An inordinate number of students with social, emotional or academic problems were sent to the experimental school, and the number increased during the second year. The principal persuaded Superintendent Madden to carry on the evaluation program for another year, and Mr. Rheeder was put in charge. Apart from agreeing to have a committee of parents and community members review and revise the *Parents' Questionnaire,* he assumed no further responsibility for assisting with the evaluation.

The experimental school began the new year with many new and inexperienced staff members selected by the central administration without consulting Mrs. Kahn. Many of the former teachers had left because they felt that the oppressive climate within the school district made innovative approaches to education almost impossible. It took the greater part of the school year to teach the new faculty the necessary skills for personal learning approaches, flexibility and nonjudgmental pupil evaluation. Data collected the previous year helped.

A committee was convened to revise the *Parents' Questionnaire* for the second year. The revisions confirmed the importance of transactional evaluation. Represented on the committee were parents of children in the experimental school, a resident of the community who was not affiliated directly with the schools, the principal of another school in the district, Mrs. Kahn, and the evaluation consultant. The previous year's questionnaire had been distributed to the committee a week before the meeting. The data obtained from it were discussed. The principal showed us how she was using the information to make changes and how her staff had studied responses on the various items to determine new instructional emphases. The committee's suggestions revealed clearly what the parents wanted from their schools. They were very interested in 'discipline' (taken to mean a reduction of noise level and movement), and the childrens' behavior toward one another and toward school authority. The evaluation consultant rewrote the questionnaire, revising items and adding new ones suggested by the committee. The revision was reviewed before the next meeting. Out of this session came the final *Parents' Questionnaire,* which is reproduced on p. 83.

The school district administration office reviewed the final instrument and found one item, about the effectiveness of the School Board in providing an adequate education for the children in the district unsuitable. Therefore item 32 was eliminated, although items 29 and 30 were not, possibly because, while they too were about the services and management of the school, the bodies accountable were the school administrators and the central office, not the School Board. The percentage of positive responses to items 29 and 30 was the lowest, in the entire questionnaire, from the Experimental and Control A groups. A very small percentage of the Control A group responded positively to item 37: "Is the instruction your child receives as good as in other school districts?"

TABLE 2

Item	% Positive Responses	
	Experimental Group	Control A Group
29	40	41
30	14	11
37	72	14

No data could be collected from the Control B group (those children whose parents did not volunteer to send them to the experimental school), because of transactional evaluation problems. Because the experimental school was kept out of the public eye, the principals of other schools could not share the trials and rewards inherent in innovation or participate in the decisions of the evaluation. Consequently, they looked upon any type of comparative data as a threat to their administrative autonomy and as an indirect evaluation of their administration. However, the principals did cooperate in obtaining the data from Control A, the matched group.

As the end of the school year rolled around, Superintendent Madden resigned. The assistant superintendent, Mr. Rheeder was elevated to the superintendency of the school district. Apparently the 'low posture' game had political merit. Since the first unacknowledged report, no evaluation report was recognized by the Board, or disseminated by it to its constituencies.

Positive responses in four categories of the parents' perceptions of the school milieu, which were elicited in the Parents' Questionnaire were tabulated (see Table 3 below) to enable the responses for each of the years to be compared. The observations on the comparison illustrate, perhaps, why the Board felt that it should ignore the evaluation:

TABLE 3

Parents' Questionnaire

Mean Percentage of Positive Responses on Four Categories

| | -----------------1968-69----------------- | | | | --------------1969-70------------- | |
| | Experimental Group | | Control A Group | | Experimental Group | Control A Group |
CATEGORY	Pre*	Post†	Pre	Post	Post	Post
1. Teacher affective influence	70.6	90.4	73.2	58.9	85.4	30.4
2. Teacher cognitive influence	55.7	87.1	58.9	47.8	84.6	27.7
3. Administrative influence	46.5	79.0	47.4	39.9	75.1	21.1
4. Learning environment‡	...	...	...	...	66.5	27.3
a. Teacher mediation	...	...	...	...	68.0	28.8
b. Home attitude	...	...	...	...	65.6	26.2

Note: An explanation of the categories will be found on p. 83.
* Data gathered before the experimental school was opened.
† Data gathered after the experimental school was opened, and at the end of the school year.
‡ This category was added to the questionnaire in the second year.

Observations
1. While the mean percentage of positive responses of the Experimental and Control A groups was initially alike in the 1968-69 data in the first three categories, the Experimental Group's post mean percent increased sharply; conversely, the Control A Group's post mean percent declined.
2. In each of the first three categories the gains in the Experimental Group's percentage of positive responses are statistically significant.

3. The differences in the mean percentage scores in the Experimental and Control A groups for the 1969-70 data in the four categories are statistically significant.

4. Positive attitudes of the parents in the Control A Group declined sharply between the post scores of 1968-69 and 1969-70.

5. The mean percentage increase between the Experimental Group's pre and post 1968-69 scores might have been attributed to a Hawthorne effect. However, the post scores in 1969-70 indicate that the gains in the first three categories were maintained.

With or without the dissemination of evaluation reports, the experimental school is still receiving support, is growing stronger each year, and is gaining a reputation outside the school district as an educational innovation that might be duplicated in other districts. However, it has not fulfilled its purpose as a testing ground for new workable educational practices in the school district. The political climate does not permit it, although it does not permit the closing of the school either. With the latest Supreme Court ruling on desegregation and the ambiguous position of government officials, administrators can be none too sure what stand to take. To do nothing at times proves the most expedient action.

There are sufficient hard data to document the school's value to the children who attend the school, to the parents who were formerly highly dissatisfied with the schools, and to the staff who have found new professional roles which make them more effective teachers and more accountable to the pupils and their parents. Analysis of other data indicates that, on cognitive measures, the gains made by the experimental students were similar to those made by the Control A and Control B groups. On the measures of overt social behavior in the classrooms, the experimental students made notable progress, in spite of the number of children with social or behavioral problems who were in the school.

Unfortunately, all the formative and summative evaluation in the world can end up as mere exercise if avenues for dissemination are not carefully prepared at every phase of the evaluation. In retrospect it is obvious that a number of steps could have been taken to make the evaluation program more than the manipulation of quantitative data in an ivory tower. First we should have recognized that the process is as important to evaluation as the product. Second, we should have made a case study, planning any evaluation to identify all the factors that needed consideration. Third, we should have gone beyond our stated objectives because they focused too narrowly on the defined object or characteristic under study, and rarely took into consideration the many external factors that impinged upon the objectives. Fourth, we should have contacted all affected groups and provided each with an opportunity to define its role in the planning, collecting, interpreting and disseminating activities. Fifth, as the evaluation consultant I should have been prepared to be the fence mender and help different groups to communicate with one another.

"When the roll is called up yonder (Rippey 1970)," this evaluator might not make it in. The case study may, however, help open the gates for the next consultant.

THE PARENTS' QUESTIONNAIRE

The responses to this questionnaire were organized into four categories to indicate parents' perceptions of the school milieu:

1. *Teacher-Pupil Affective Influence:* Parents' perceptions of teachers' affective behavior toward their children. *Items* 3, 14, 17, 25, 26, 35 and 38.

2. *Teacher-Pupil Cognitive Influence:* Parents' perceptions of teachers' cognitive influence on the children through the instructional program. *Items* 7, 12, 13, 19, 20, 21, 22, 23, 25, 36 and 37.

3. *Administration-Pupil Influence:* Parents' perceptions of administration's effectiveness in providing support for the children's learning. *Items* 1, 4, 9, 10, 11, 16, 18, 29 and 30.

4. *Learning Environment Influences:*
    a. *Teacher Mediation:* Parents' perceptions of the learning environment as it is affected by the teacher's behavior. *Items* 2, 3, 5, 31, 38, and 39.
    b. *Home Attitude:* Parents' perceptions of the learning environment as it is affected by the home attitudes of parents and children toward the school. *Items* 6, 8, 15, 24, 26, 27, 28, 33 and 34.

The Questionnaire
Directions. If you feel that the school is adequately performing the tasks described below, check the space that has been provided. *Adequate* in this checklist means that conditions are satisfactory, but they may not necessarily be perfect. There are no right or wrong answers. What is important is *how you feel,* as a parent, about each question.

1. Is the condition of the school building adequate for your child's education?
2. Are the classes quiet enough so that each child can learn undisturbed?

3. Are the children expected to respect one another and their teachers?
4. Does the school provide the type of supervision of children that prevents accidents to and from school?
5. Do the teachers enforce the school rules?
6. Do the children accept one another's cultural differences?
7. Do the teachers make an effort to help your child with individual learning problems?
8. Do you feel your child enjoys school?
9. Do you feel free to talk over a problem with your child's teacher?
10. Do you feel free to talk over a problem with the principal?
11. If your child needs extra help (such as medical, psychological, social) does the school provide you with the information?
12. Is the instruction your child receives helping him to learn?
13. Are you satisfied with the type of teaching your child receives?
14. Do the teachers show respect for the individual differences among the children?
15. Would you rather have your child remain at his present school than attend another school in the neighboring school district?
16. Do you feel free to visit the school at any time?
17. Are the teachers interested in personal problems your child may have?
18. Do you feel the library in the school is adequate?
19. Is your child able to read easily the textbooks and other learning materials assigned to him?
20. Are the teachers helping your child to be more independent in his learning?
21. Have the teachers helped your child learn how to study?
22. Does your child seem to understand the school assignment?
23. Do you feel the teachers are doing their very best to give your child a good education?
24. Are the children accepting the socioeconomic differences among their classmates?
25. Does your child get involved in a learning project that was started at school?
26. Does your child look forward to going to school each day?
27. Are the children careful with the school property?
28. Do the parents show enough interest in how their child behaves in school?
29. As a taxpayer, do you feel your school district (the main office administration) is doing all it can to help your child learn?
30. As a parent and a taxpayer, do you feel you have enough to say in the management of the school?
31. Would you describe your school as an orderly, disciplined school?
32. [1]
33. Do the children respect each other's property?
34. Do the children show respect for the teachers?
35. Have the teachers shown an interest in the children?
36. Has your child been showing steady improvement in his learning?
37. Is the instruction your child receives as good as in other school districts?
38. Do the teachers respect the cultural and racial differences of the children?

39. Does the school program make an effort to help children understand and accept one another?
40. Check the subject areas in which you feel the school is doing a satisfactory job:

Language Communication

Writing (composition)	Grammar
Spelling	Penmanship
Reading for skill	Reading for enjoyment

Science and Mathematics

Arithmetic reasoning	Science information
Arithmetic computation	Science experimentation

Social Studies

Current news events	Social studies as information
Social studies as stimulating	about countries and people
thought	Learning relevant to the
	child's own world

Physical and Artistic Communication

Art program	Music program
Physical education program	Literature program (poems, famous
	short stories, classics)

41. During this school year, what part of the school program was unsatisfactory?
42. During this school year, what part of the school program was most beneficial for your child?
43. What suggestions have you for the teachers and principal that would help in planning next year's program?

For The Experimental School Parents Only[2]

44. Do you think the Experimental School should have some type of parent organization? (Parents' Club, PTA, etc.) Circle below:

YES   NO

45. Are you satisfied with the parent conferences as a substitute for report cards? (Explain)

FOOTNOTES

1. Item 32, on the effectiveness of the school board in providing an adequate education for the children in the district, was deleted by the school district administration.
2. Items 44 and 45 did not apply to the other schools.

REFERENCE

Rippey, R. M. When the Roll is Called Up Yonder, Will Evaluators Be There? Paper read to Phi Delta Kappa, University of Chicago, Illinois, 1970.

5

THE EVALUATOR AS TRUTH SEEKER

GORDON HOKE

In a statement prepared for the Report of the National Goals Research Staff, Daniel Moynihan (1970) cited the need for an evaluation that "predicts results rather than simply measuring them." The use of evaluation as a means of prediction is obviously difficult. Certainly the growing trend for subgroups to seek some form of separatist autonomy and demand acknowledgement of the values of cultural diversity indicates the task that faces program developers and evaluators in the years ahead. "Measurements are new seeds of doubt," Stake (1971) declared. However, he continued, they are vital to this world, "not because they tell us what is truth but because they keep the other sides of truth alive."

BACKGROUND

In my activities as a combination change agent-evaluator for a school and community study during 1970/71, I have tried to use the information obtained in the project as baseline data for predicting forthcoming patterns of school, community, and regional development in rural oriented areas.[1] I was constantly reminded of the axiom that what one finds is not "truth" but, indeed, "new seeds of doubt."

The Place

Located about seventy-five miles south of the University of Illinois in Urbana-Champaign, at the intersection of highways I-70 and I-57, Effingham, Illinois, is the county seat, with a population of approximately ten thousand, in a region where German Lutherans and Catholics abound. It is one of the few rural communities to show a steady gain in population between the census of 1960 and that of 1970. It is also one of the even rarer small towns in the United States where *two* interstate highways converge. There are three school systems in the district: two supported by Catholic parishes; the third, the public school system. The town, a handful of tiny hamlets and several farms form an unusual population mix within the boundaries of School District No. 40, which encompasses a large expanse of territory and, like its surrounding districts, represents a compromise made between religious forces generations ago. Several of the chief problems confronting schools in Effingham county today, particularly the staggering complexities of bussing, are the end results of those earlier compromises.

Legislative debates and Supreme Court decisions on the constitutionality of using tax funds to support parochial education tested community bonds in the past year. Dual-enrollment programs were expanded as the school and community issues take on additional stature.

Field Requirements

I have viewed the Effingham area as a field laboratory in which to appraise the dynamics of social, political, and economic change affecting a community, its public school district and its Catholic educational institutions. Barker's research on the analysis of settings (Barker et al. 1964) has guided my efforts in Effingham. Defining settings as places "where most of the inhabitants can satisfy a number of personal motives, where they can achieve multiple satisfactions," he concludes that "a setting contains opportunities." He also notes that "the primary link between settings and behavior is via the inhabitants' cognitions of the relations between goals and the routes the setting provides." The studies conducted in the field station in Kansas by Barker, Gump, and their associates have been extended recently, not only by the original group, but also by Sarason at Yale. To a degree, the basic issues were anticipated by Hunt's stress on the importance of the "match" between intellect and environment (1961). To date my efforts in Effingham suggest that settings may not be as stable as Barker asserted, although there is no doubt about the myriad opportunities presented by a changing environment such as that currently found in Effingham.

The central theme of my study was the issue of talent development. One of the key variables, it appears, is the amount and quality of information that people—adults and children—receive within their respective settings. Sarason's emphasis (1971) on the interplay of various roles in settings indicates the potential for disruption that is created when forces of change acting upon those settings alter perceptions of traditional roles.

Work in the field calls for more reliance on interviews, observations, descriptions and, ultimately, judgments than experimental researchers are wont to accept. The task of building generalizations (predictions) on a foundation of examples collected and assembled inductively exerts its own price, makes its own demands. Normally I try to operate as unobtrusively as possible. However, in Effingham, primarily because I hoped that the residents and students would approach me, rather than the officials of the school systems, with their complaints, questions, and so forth, I tried to get my name and face closely identified with the operation. Consequently the physical, intellectual, and ethical requirements were even more significant.

Interviews, for example, can become exhausting, particularly if they consume the greater part of the day. Interviewing the reluctant or uncertain, I had to be particularly alert for cues from their voices, bodies, and facial expressions that would help me redesign the questions, seize apparent leads and the like. In some cases, wives insisted on interviewing me before agreeing to let me return to conduct an evening session with their husbands. I deliberately chose to make little use of the phone: conversations and discussions on important issues, in my opinion, require face-to-face exchanges. Part of this belief, admittedly, is a personal uneasiness about intruding into people's lives without giving them a chance first to react to me. Overall, I believe in and act on intuition. Hunches, first impressions, the way I feel about people and events—these are the elements that guide much of my activity. I trust my perceptions and believe that my biggest mistakes occur when I fail to honor them.

My greatest concern on the eve of the assignment in Effingham was whether or not I could still talk to students. I left the public school classrooms in 1963 and had had little contact with adolescents since then. It was quickly evident that an open display of honesty was essential for my relationships with high school students. Almost ruthless honesty was demanded throughout the year, particularly during the trying weeks of collective bargaining (I tried to serve as a resource for both the adversaries: the teachers on the one hand, and the administrators and board members on the other, as well as a troubleshooter for the entire district).

A climate of trust and openness is not the only essential for working in the field. An ability to adapt to local conditions without sacrificing personal and professional integrity is vital. Much of the literature on change deals with it in elementary schools, and my activities to date—in Effingham and elsewhere—strongly suggest that it is easier to function as a change agent in such schools, principally because the institutional structure of a high school is vastly different and the emphasis on specialized subjects is so much greater. Also it is extremely difficult to win acceptance from administrators or teachers if one has not actually had public school experience. Thus, my ability to act as a substitute teacher was invaluable for satisfying informal entry requirements and providing an avenue to the students.

I am convinced that my teaching background made it possible for me to enter the school-community arena, and that much of what ensued would not have taken place had I not had the experience. I revised my Vita, stressing the public school experience, for the board members and administrators to review before our first meeting.

To be effective, changes must be accepted, not imposed, and so the *process* of acceptance must be accorded a high priority (see, for example, Gallaher 1964). Efforts to change the schools cannot be effective without the participation of staff, students, administrators, and the community. Schools are pivotal social institutions: unless the moment of their central place in modern society is grasped there is a real danger that praise and criticism, problems and possibilities, will all be misunderstood. Fiscal difficulties and social changes are combining to furnish new leverage for reform in Effingham schools, and in their counterparts across the nation and throughout the world.

It is necessary, if one is to have the change accepted, to know about and to respect the system of values of the community. Such knowledge requires work—hard, enduring, but exciting work. My experience in Effingham left me with the indelible impression that knowledge of value systems: mine, others', the schools', can be acquired only through long hours of observation, discussion, and reflection. For me, it meant arriving early at school to drink coffee with janitors and other employees, skipping lunch to rap with students in their rec-room, participating in late afternoon sessions at the Elks Club bar, and spending my evenings writing notes, reading from local sources, meeting parents, or talking to Effingham's hippies, who congregate on the county courthouse lawn.

Work is a prized ethic in rural Illinois. I was born and raised about fifty miles north of Effingham, in an area which held to the same code. My visibility in the community, especially my substitute teaching, helped to convince residents that I was busy. Appearances before local civic and service clubs added credence to my efforts, and the newspaper accurately and comprehensively covered the entire project. My roots in central Illinois gave me credibility as a person apart from my university affiliation; the University of Illinois still commands respect despite the dents in its image that campus riots caused. I attempted to serve as a resource for teachers, administrators, students, and residents in ways that would convince them of my genuine interest in assisting the schools and the community.

In the original Statement of Purpose prepared for school officials it was stressed that:

> We are seeking the privilege of working *in the community of Effingham in association with its school personnel.* We believe the study would provide extremely valuable information for decision-makers in both the parochial and the public school systems (italics in original).

Tomorrow's Uncertainty

The changes in Effingham are portents of the future, for the area seems certain to become a prototype of the rural communities that will emerge as stabilizing points to guide development in the closing years of the twentieth century. The issue facing local residents is similar to the challenge confronting the nation at large: is it possible to harness the forces of technological change, to use rational powers in planning, development, and execution that will enable communities to seize the initiative rather than simply to react to seemingly omnipotent elements of economic and political power?

Major developments in Effingham, especially those precipitated by new means of transportation, represent a massive intervention, and I endeavored to judge the reactions of individuals, groups, and certain institutions, chiefly schools, to this intervention and others. In the long run people in Effingham will make many of their decisions in terms of certain values, just as, for instance, value choices are implicit in the construction of interstate highways rather than other forms of transportation and communication.

Moynihan called for an evaluation that could predict results in advance. I finished the year in Effingham convinced that institutional arrangements for what we have chosen to call secondary education will not much longer endure in their present form. High schools, as institutions responsible to communities, today's adolescents, and a technological society, whose future is threatened by neo-Luddite revolts and destructive battles over issues of the environment, are hopelessly outmoded.

"Measurements are new seeds of doubt," Stake warned. Granted that my "measurements" were less scientific and more subjective than many noted authorities would care to accept, I found much evidence to confirm his judgment. For example, I discovered that my professional background presented formidable obstacles to effective work in the field. It caused me to forget that literacy is not an infallible badge of intelligence. Wisdom is derived from sources other than books and the printed page. Many residents of Effingham read less than I, rarely write, and most do not hold college degrees. Years ago, before the advent of television and transistor radios, reading and writing were essential to communication. Today, the media make it possible to bypass the traditional channels and give new power to the spoken word and the visual image.

Are educators sufficiently aware of how much people learn out of school? and in ways the school does not esteem? I doubt it.

FOOTNOTE

1. Copies of two mimeographed interim reports are available from the Center for Instructional Research and Curriculum Evaluation (CIRCE), College of Education, University of Illinois, Urbana. The final report of work completed during 1970-71, entitled *Goodbye to Yesterday: Talent Development in a Changing Era,* is available from the same source.

REFERENCES

Barker, R. G., Kounin, J., and Gump, P. V. *Big School, Small School: High School Size and Student Behavior.* Stanford, Calif.: Stanford University Press, 1964.
Gallaher, A., Jr. "The Role of the Advocate and Directed Change." In *Media and Educational Innovation,* edited by W. C. Meierhenry, pp. 33-43. Lincoln, Nebr.: University of Nebraska Press, 1964.

Hunt, J. M. *Intelligence and Experience.* New York: Ronald Press Co., 1961.

Moynihan, D. P., Counsellors' Statement. In *Toward Balanced Growth: Quantity and Quality,* Report of the National Goals Research Staff, pp. 14-15. Washington, D. C.: Government Printing Office, 1970.

Sarason, S. B. *The Culture of the School and the Problems of Change.* Boston, Mass.: Allyn and Bacon, 1971.

Stake, R. E., Informal memorandum, Center for Instructional Research and Curriculum Evaluation, University of Illinois, Urbana-Champaign, April, 1971.

6

TRANSACTIONAL EVALUATIONS IN FIELD SETTINGS: ROLES AND DESIGNS

MAURICE J. EASH

With the advent of heavy public funding for social programs, there has been a demand for evaluation, a demand that has wrought changes in the role of the evaluator and in the design of evaluation.

Evaluation in the broad sense of rendering a judgment and staking out choices has been an ancient human endeavor. The concern that these judgments be more than expressions of prejudice and subjective bias is relatively recent. Canons governing designs for evaluation have been largely devised to guard judgment against those biases that are characteristically human, chiefly the construing of causality toward personal predispositions. The practice of restricting evaluation settings to arenas where variables were easier to control enhanced measurement and increased attribution of causality. Particularly in social sciences, this practice also restricted the usefulness of findings because the context of the investigation was artificial and the range of phenomenon that could be studied narrow. As long as rigor and scholarship were defined as obedience to set canons of investigation, and admission to the camp of science judged on one's compliance with these canons, much social science research was concerned with technical manipulation. In a newly developing discipline, building on borrowed traditions from the natural sciences, but tackling new variables that posed problems in stability of measurement and coherence of theory, strict attention to the definition of a workable domain through laboratory-oriented research may have been necessary. But the increasing propensity of our society to intervene actively into social ills has spawned a demand for evaluation that calls for different designs and a vastly expanded range of activity, principally in the field. Usually, intervention has meant using investigative techniques and research designs in more open settings. Thus, the area of evaluation research has emerged as a union of the field evaluation of social programs using modified research designs, and the techniques that were originally developed in the laboratory investigation period of social science. But the problems facing evaluation research have not been exclusively the problems of adaptation of research techniques. An accompanying demand has been for the expansion of the usefulness of evaluative data, chiefly through bringing it to bear on actual problems within on-going programs.

The investigator must adopt new methodologies and new roles. The use of evaluation data throughout the project rather than as a final judgment on the project's worth will redefine the relationship between the project developer and the evaluator. Transactional evaluation's birth is a result of this new relationship. The break with use of evaluation findings solely in a summative manner, as a final judgment, and the substitution of their use as formative data, to shape the program, has shifted the focus of the evaluation design and the working relationship between the evaluator and the evaluated. Since the use of transactional evaluation requires a managed relationship between evaluator and evaluated, and incorporates different paradigms of investigation into evaluation designs, these two preconditions will serve as the organizing foci for the major sections of the chapter.

EVALUATOR AND EVALUATED: A RELATIONSHIP

A British wit once evaluated the contribution of economists to a current fiscal crisis with the remark, "If all economists were laid end to end, they could not reach a conclusion." Similarly, evaluators disappoint when their reports do not provide the information that project sponsors and directors are needing. Usually, such reports have not dealt with the critical problems, the internal dynamics, and have dealt merely with past events. One of the leading causes of this problem is the relationship between the evaluator and evaluated, a relationship defined by the role, in the past, of the researcher. From that role, the main problems in evaluation were seen as problems of design and measurement which, in the open settings of field projects, strained the formal requirements of design. But, as the tension between evaluator and evaluated, and the dissatisfaction with the results, grow, evaluation must become more than a technical matching of designs to projects. Evaluation must be linked to some of the concepts emerging from the field of organizational development, whereby information is seen as an integral part of the decision-making process. However, it is not enough merely to collect information. First the information needed has to be identified, next garnered, and then fed back into the project through a process that the project agents would recognize and accept.

The evaluator's job is further complicated by the confusion that frequently surrounds the field project. Few projects, if any, have sufficient lead time to plan, staff, and secure the multitude of arrangements that accompany complex projects. Thus, frequently evaluation deadlines must be met before the project is underway, and both evaluator and evaluated become anxious. Often, the field project is not sufficiently organized so that a formal design of pre- and posttests, random treatment assignment, and prespecified measures of treatment can be inaugurated. In these circumstances the evaluator has to bring order into an apparently disorderly situation.

A Case Study

In one field evaluation I was asked to head a team of evaluators on a project that involved twelve innovative, educational, demonstration projects that were to receive support, training and evaluation from a single consortium. Before the evaluation we read descriptions of all the projects, the original proposal, and all current reports on the projects. We also asked for a set of questions from the project staff which would guide us in setting up a temporary evaluation plan. Upon arriving at the site, we found that the twelve projects were in very different states of development: some were functioning; others were not started. Those that were underway, we soon found, were deviating markedly from the original descriptions.

One of our first tasks was to help the project staff order their goals, define the unique characteristics of each demonstration, and arrange internal evaluation. A model of social organizations was used to sketch in the manifest characteristics of each project. We held asymmetrical interviews with the participants in each of the twelve projects, with samples of the subjects, and with the consortium administration. In the interviews we would look for the answers to a number of questions:

1. What are the primary goals being emphasized? What are the secondary goals?
2. Who is performing what tasks in the project?
3. What rewards do the different groups see from their participation in the project?
4. What constraints are felt in working and developing the project?
5. Are there visible or expressed conflicts among the participants within the project, or between the project staff and the consortium?
6. What routines or procedures have been established to provide data on operations and their effects?

These questions elicited information on goals, methods of operation and evaluation. They also served to order a large number of disparate bits of data. These data were subjected to a congruence analysis with the original program and feedback went to the central administrators, the project directors and the internal evaluators. From this initial first year evaluation, goals began to firm up, aphorisms that passed as goals diminished, and evaluation procedures could be formalized. At this point the feedback was mostly formative, except for one project which was discontinued on the recommendation of the evaluation team. As the result of the team's direct feedback, the current stage of each project was identified and an internal evaluational procedure instituted. We recognized that projects just beginning needed different evaluation data from those projects that were operating. In this case study, my role, as chief evaluator, moved considerably beyond my simply gathering data and processing it. I became a design consultant to those projects that were in the early stages of development.

From our findings we had to design projects that, in some cases, were largely intuitive activities and unformed models when first evaluated. Therefore, there had to be extensive interaction between the chief evaluator and the administration in planning the evaluation, during the data gathering, and in the feedback. In this process I was pledged to lay bare my design, demonstrate how I believed that the data gathering procedure related to the information desired by the client, and to package the findings into information that could be readily used. Moreover, the transactions between us shaped the evaluation design, making it more directly useful in preparing the demonstration projects for more advanced development.

Schematically, the evaluation changes. In figure 1, it takes the form of a separate, outside judgment. In figure 2, it takes the form of a reciprocal relationship, between the study and its findings, in which each is shaped by the other and produces results different from those originally envisaged.

FIGURE 2

Traditional Evaluation Design

Evaluation Design   **Demonstration Project**

measures — — — — — — — — — — — — — ➤goals

+   +

judgments — — — — — — — — — — — ➤outcomes

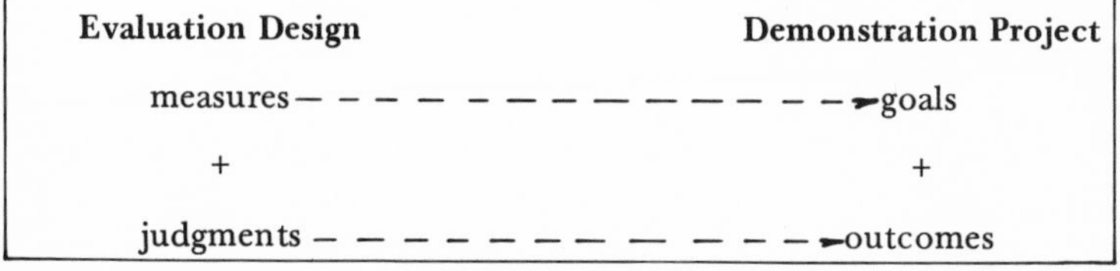

FIGURE 3

Transactional Evaluation Design

Evaluation Design   **Demonstration Project**

measures— — — — — — — — — — — — —goals

+   +

judgments — — — — — — — — — — -outcomes

x

x — — — — — — — — — — -Evaluation findings

x   redesign projects

and evaluation

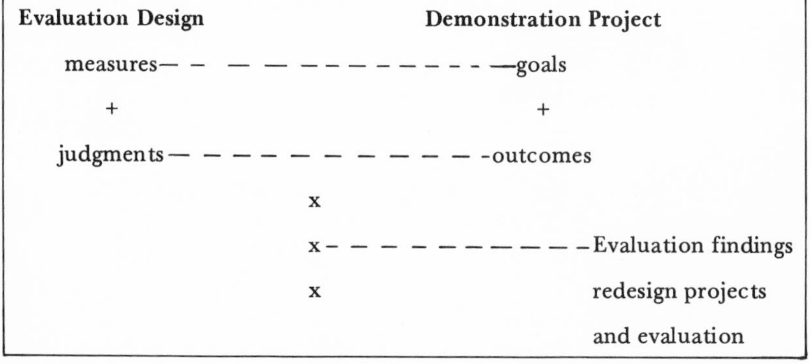

If evaluators are willing to interact with project planners early, before project models become rigid and their sponsors defensive, evaluation and project design may be interwoven. But this function will require of the evaluator a different role and stance. The assumption that the evaluator has a packaged design that he can implement without consulting the project teams is to be rejected. A more sustained relationship, which will provide a channel for mutual exchange of information must be formed, so that the evaluation design can be mutually built and carried out.

In the second and third years, evaluation of this project, which was funded under Title III of the Elementary and Secondary Education Act, became more formal; the team served largely to check the inside evaluators, and assess those elements that were not accessible to the internal evaluators, for example, the internal evaluators could not assess the chief administrator, or evaluate their own functioning as a unit servicing the twelve projects. The data they gathered and the designs they used in aiding project evaluations were judged by the outside evaluators. In the second year, the evaluation was a combination of formative and summative findings; however, decisions on the evaluations were reached by both the evaluator and evaluated. In the third year, the summative evaluations of the projects were deemed more important as the federal funding would end and the model projects would have to terminate or become a part of a regular program in the school district.

For successful transactional evaluation to be undertaken over a longer range in a field project, it appears that four conditions must prevail:

1. The evaluator must be willing to merge his scientific skills and arts with the project planners' needs. He cannot expect to bring in a ready-made design built outside the context in which the evaluation is to be conducted. Where a project is vague and intuitive, he must help frame the demonstration models by clarifying goals, identifying means, promoting reliable feedback, and resolving conflict.

2. The evaluator must be willing to plot a longer range evaluation that accepts a variety of goals. In certain instances the evaluative data will be so formative that it will merge in with project planning data. This is the case particularly when the project is untried and evolves from theoretical or intuitive suppositions that have not been empirically tested.

3. The evaluated must be willing to support evaluation for the information it develops and not for the defense of current practice. Where the evaluator can be involved early in the project, the directors will find it easier to be flexible to accepting options. Administrators who advocate projects and procedures because their own egos are involved and they are exposed to the limelight, tend to regard evaluation as a threat rather than as a useful corrective to open up other options. This is probably the single most difficult

hurdle in accepting evaluation from an outside source. An early transactional relationship between evaluator and evaluated, with some understanding of how broad evaluation can contribute to a project's future, can save a school system and project director from becoming trapped in their own biases.

4. To be successful, transactional evaluation in field projects must be supported by key administrators, who believe in the disclosure of findings and the corrective virtues of accurate information. Evaluation by external agencies can become a diversion and a subterfuge, as happens when evaluators are requested to work on parts of a project and to avoid others. Since few aspects of education are isolated from larger entities, a partial, fragmented assessment can be misleading. It is probably impossible to do transactional evaluation with any degree of success and accept restrictions that, for instance, permit one to evaluate subordinates but not administrators, or look at processes but not at goals. The process of establishing a relationship and mutually developing the evalution design that is at the heart of transactional evaluation will indicate to any skilled evaluator the constraints that are being imposed and provide him with sufficient information to decide whether he can ethically and professionally accept the constraints. Mutually planned evaluation is educational for both parties, and the evaluated is in a far better position to understand and implement results. When a ready vehicle for implementation is a part of the evaluation design, the danger that results will be relegated to the shelf, unread and unwanted, is on the way to being eliminated.

The evaluator, to make transactional evaluation effective, must be able to fuse the design of evaluation research and the needs of the program. These two demands assume a technical base of knowledge. As evaluation becomes closely linked with accountability, appropriate designs must be used in field settings lest educational innovations be stifled rather than assisted by evaluation.

Transactional Evaluation in Field Settings

Evaluation has become a code word for a pervasive public sentiment that expenditure, whether in material goods such as automobiles or social goods such as education, should return due value. That bumpers do not fend off bumps or education does not educate is viewed as failure. Producers are being held responsible for making good on the promised performance of their goods when the consumer has made a commitment of good faith in the producer's initial claims. Evaluation enters into this dispute as the process which checks the goals obtained in a program against the goals promised.

However evaluation is more than a comparison between goals, just as consumer protection is more than a haggle over fair prices. In the large, evaluation objectives culminate in philosophical differences, the necessity of ordering values along some priority, and the expansion of considerations of whether the goals were worth pursuing. How goals were selected, what shifts were made from the initial formulation and what trade offs were made in selecting these goals against other possible alternatives become evaluation questions of concern equal to that of the question of whether the goals promised were delivered. But evaluation as conventionally conceived is severely limited.

Field evaluations of projects extending over several years pose special problems of accountability. Accountability, like evaluation, needs trustworthy data that agree with the reality they represent, thus the resolution of central issues in both evaluation and accountability is a major consideration in the long range funding of programs which allocate resources and obtain educational goals. The transactional evaluator in a field evaluation faces three major issues that normally do not confront other investigators: he must ascertain the appropriate framework for field evaluation as it relates to the particular program; he must establish an evaluation methodology that is comprehensive and recognizes the necessity for several levels of evaluation; he must determine his own role in making the relationship between broad areas of accountability and the evaluation more intelligible so that accountability becomes a valuable and generally accepted constituent of every program.

Field programs, often innovative, and developed outside a controlled environment, present problems for program administrators, project evaluators and funding agencies, problems which, if not reconciled, seed conflict and sabotage efficiency.

Innovative programs often lack the specific definable objectives that are deemed necessary in evaluation research. Thus, if the evaluator or the funding agency insists on ready-made specific objectives to serve as the criteria for the program, innovation becomes sacrificed, program developers and evaluators tend to deceive one another. Therefore, innovative field programs must be free to evolving further objectives and clarify initial objectives as they proceed. Flexible program requirements demand that evaluators help clarify objectives and trace their evolution as well as design the evaluation of the objectives stated at the beginning of a project. In this respect the framework of a field evaluation differs most from a laboratory research project, which has comparatively fixed goals, and the researcher's task is to prove or disprove previously hypothesized relationships. In most innovative programs the state of knowledge permits some conjecture on relationships; however, it is not usually possible to specify precisely the variables and their relationships. The program evaluator must recognize the differences (a process of differential evaluation), use a conceptual scheme to select appropriate evaluative procedures, and guide the collection and analysis of data. The program must, therefor, be placed along a continuum determined largely by the objectives that specify the relationship of variables, the clarity of these relationships, the interaction of theoretical constructs, and operational descriptions.

On such a continuum three models may be described: the initiatory model, the developmental model, and the integrated model. In the initiatory model, the major process consists in planning goals, specifications and operations; in the developmental model, in the actual construction and testing of a field program; in the integrated model, in generating evaluation data for internal adjustments, for the program's goals are clear and its outcomes reasonably accurately predictable.

Programs for Gifted Children Modeled at Three Levels: Initiatory, Developmental, and Integrated

1. Initiatory Model

Initiatory models are vague, intuitive in effects to be achieved. Objectives are stated as general outcomes and social goods to be achieved. There is much concern with theory. The debates on alternatives are theoretical rather than operational or based on data. Justification of the program may be drawn from analogous programs in other contexts or be based on philosophical assumptions. Details for executing the proposals are sketchy.

Précis.   A special program for gifted and talented children is drawn up. Decisions on the form it will take, special classes, enrichment, independent tutorials, or a mix of these, are still open. There is a lack of agreement on definition of clients. Who is a gifted or talented student? How should he be educated? Should he be identified? At what grade? By whom? Will extra monies be allocated to his education? Will a separate administrative unit need to be established for this program? What type of research will be conducted? When will parents be involved?

A committee has been set up to resolve some of the issues.

Administrative responsibilities and money for planning have been allocated. The committee has been meeting for a year. A set of minutes, a list of consultants, and a description of the field trips to visit other programs for gifted children exist.

2. Developmental Model

Developmental models are characterized by a mixture of objectives. Macro-objectives give some general guidance, and some micro-objectives are defined. Objectives still seem to be shifting and the model still takes different forms in various descriptions. There is more concern with operational alternatives than with a given alternative. While the program is operating there are many unknowns and, frequently, considerable improvisation.

Précis.   One special program for gifted and talented children has been underway for two years. Fifty children are involved. In some cases, teachers nominate students for the program, in others they are selected on the basis of test scores. In the first year, students spend four hours per week in the program; in the second, six. The program has focused on scientific interests though there is concern about including more humanities. One teacher arranged for twenty-five of the students to see the Old Vic perform at the local college. Some data, mostly descriptive, has been collected on the students, their achievements and the program. Teachers do not have a fixed style for instruction; the instruction reflects their personal teaching styles.

3. Integrated Model

Integrated models have specific objectives. Procedures are monitored for consistency of operation. Relationships of treatment (what is done educationally) and effect (outcomes) are specified, and replication is made easier by the elaborate descriptions of the model in operation. Logical relationships are explicated, and empirical data collected. The outcomes are assessed and the range of effects can be attributed to the program treatment.

Précis.   A program for gifted and talented students has been in operation for five years. Instruction is open-ended and teachers and students plan the curriculum cooperatively for three months at a time. The Director of Research for the school district monitors the program through teachers' records, interviews with students and regular classroom visits. Program outcomes are investigated through their effect on students' achievement and interest. A control group of students who are not in a special program, in a neighboring school district, which has a similar student body, is supplying comparable data on achievement and interest. The study also supplies data on the influence of special programs on the regular program. At the end of the five years a summer workshop, composed of teachers and pupils in the program, and administrators and university consultants, will draw up the program description for the next three years. Decisions will be made on the program organization, the selection and retention of students, and the research to be conducted.

An evaluator will need to recognize the stage that the program has reached and frame his evaluation questions and methodology accordingly. He is obliged, as always, to feed back the evaluation data into the program.

Differential Evaluation

Once the various models are recognized as being distinct phases in program development, the evaluation designs needed to collect and compare data can be drawn. As the descriptions in the program models reproduced above indicate, the evaluation, while important at each stage, does present different issues and, subsequently, shifting demands on the evaluation design. In a program in the initiatory stage, for instance, an evaluator would be more concerned with analyzing the committee's functioning and making recommendations for its future work than with gathering data on the program that, even on paper, is still tentative.

To recognize the varying emphases and demands on evaluation, and to link that evaluation to a model of program development, one must use differential evaluation, rather than merely apply a standard set of tools to the situation. Representative, specific questions that an evaluator would raise in attempting a differential evaluation of three categories—effort, effect, and efficiency—of the programs for gifted children mentioned earlier, are illustrated below:

Differential Evaluation of Programs for Gifted Children Modeled at Three Levels: Initiatory, Developmental and Integrated

1. Initiatory Model
EFFORT
1. What have been the main directions of the committee's efforts?
2. How much have the committee members participated?
3. Has the committee broadened its constituency and recognized the sociopolitical aspects of its efforts?

4. How much time has been spend on certain phases of the program?
   EFFECT
1. How much does the committee know of special programs for the gifted and talented?
2. Are the committee members conversant with issues, trends and programs?
3. What is the present stage of the plans? Are they almost in operation?
4. What are the main impediments to a developmental model program
   EFFICIENCY
1. Does the committee have an organized working plan, with deadlines and completion schedules?
2. Is the committee aware of its responsibility to the Board of Education and the superintendent?
3. Given the amount of time and money invested, has a useful product emerged? How far are they from an operating program?

2. Developmental model
   EFFORT
1. What have been the program's main efforts?
2. What objectives have received most attention?
3. Who has been involved in the program?
   To what extent?
   Voluntary or mandated? Honorary or paid?
4. Where has the support for the program emanated from?
   What have been the developmental costs—financial and physical?
5. How much total time has been spent?
   What parts of the program are most time-consuming?
   EFFECT
1. What data on the functioning of the program have been or can be collected?
2. What have the effects been on program students, other students, teachers, parents, and administrators?
3. Has the data on effects been used to modify or shape the program, or to explore alternatives?
4. Can the effects on students be attributed to the program?
5. Have there been any unexpected effects?
   EFFICIENCY
1. Are there records or other evidence that problems with the program are being systematically resolved?
2. How does the cost of this program compare with that of other programs in the district and in other districts?

3. What goals seem attainable?

    What goals have not been attained?
4. Given the findings of the program, what will be the approximate cost of an integrated program?

3. Integrated Model

EFFORT

1. What are the major goals of the program?

    Who is involved?
2. What percentage of staff and student time is committed to the program?

    What is the total time spent?
3. What data are available for a historical account, and for planning future developments?
4. What areas of effort are perceived as worthwhile by the different role participants?

EFFECT

1. What are the program's short-range effects on students in the program, students not in the program, teachers, parents, administrators?

    Are data available to study the effects of both process and product?
2. Is any provision made for studying long-range effects?
3. Can the desired effects stated in the original goals be attributed to the program?
4. Have there been any unexpected effects?

EFFICIENCY

1. Are problems systematically studied?

    Are the participants conversant with the decision-making process?

    Has it been scrutinized?
2. What is the cost of this program, compared with that of other programs in the district, and with similar programs?
3. What is the future projection of such costs, now that developmental costs have, largely, been met?
4. What has been the cost of attaining certain effects?

    What concessions were made in the interests of cost?

The evaluation questions on each of the three dimensions of effort, effect and efficiency should lead to a coherent picture of the model, its main constructs, and its functioning. One question by itself is not decisive, but, together, the questions enable an evaluator to make comparisons and decision makers to judge accountability. Each dimension of evaluation has some characteristics in common, but seeks different data according to the stage of the program model.

Effort.   Within the dimension of effort the evaluator should know how time is spent, time being one of the costly ingredients in program development. An especially critical matter, in developmental and integrated models, is the allocation of time for delivering services and procuring results.

Effect.   Product evaluation has usually concerned itself with effects, but the initiatory model has no product, so the questions will deal, instead, with the development of the model, and there will be few outcomes to study. As the model becomes more integrated and fully developed, the evaluation of products and other outputs will increase. In an integrated model, the evaluation questions deal with the attainment of goals and their congruence with original goal formulations—the more conventional focus of evaluation.

The evaluator will also be required to attribute effects to specific parts of the program. To do this, he must delineate a program model and be able to guarantee a degree of consistency of functioning, which is usually possible in the developmental model where the definitions and descriptions of the main constructs are distilled from the experience of operating the model and observing results. Without the specification, consistency of functioning, and agreement on the reality of the basic constructs, any attribution of effects will be largely speculative. For example, in the developmental model described above, the program is going to be improvised by the teachers, so that any study of the specific instruction given to gifted children is ruled out. Any exploration of student aptitude and instructional treatment interactions on achievement is precluded until the teaching in the developmental model is defined and stabilized.

Because field settings lack the controls of a laboratory, a program produces unexpected effects, obvious and subtle. The staff, through long association with the program, may accept the effects without being aware how they have redirected the original aims of the program. In one instance, in a program to establish learning centers for remedial work in elementary schools, evaluators found that the students had, over a period of time, rearranged their schedules so that they were spending more time on self-programmed activities in the learning centers than on any other single classroom subject. One may applaud their management, but their records showed that the students were using the learning center not for remedial work but for their immediate interests.

Efficiency.   Efficiency relates the efforts and resources committed to the effects achieved. Usually these relationships are recorded in some cost-benefit statements. As in the other two dimensions, the focus of the evaluator and the data collected will depend on the stage of the progam model. In the initiatory model the emphasis will be on the process of planning; as the model becomes operational, the evaluation for efficiency shifts toward an assessment of the relationship of effort and effect as reflected in the model's output.[1]

Evaluation is frequently defined as a fair comparison. Within each dimension the data is eventually compared with other data to form a basis of judgment. Sometimes comparisons are made of the same groups over a period of time, much as one might compare income tax returns to chart one's economic progress over a period of years. Sometimes one group is compared with another group, just as one might compare one's own income with that of a group of people with a similar education, place of residence, or occupation. In the example we have illustrated, the program for gifted children is compared with other programs within the same school district and with similar programs in other school districts.

Conventional rather than transactional evaluation often causes evaluators to misjudge the data needed. In the development of new programs in education, integrated models are rare. Typically, federal funding for innovation has been used to stimulate initiatory or developmental models and often the funding has been terminated before integrated models were produced. Development has suffered further from a failure to distinguish between the three models: evaluation designs have subjected initiatory and developmental models to evaluations appropriate for integrated models. Thus, what the evaluation data deemed deficiencies may only have been growing pains; the models were not at the stage where the effects as product outcomes were ready to be assessed. If evaluators will recognize and make allowances for stages in educational program models, the designs will correspond with the particular stage of the model and they will not have to rely only on product outcomes to assess the entire program. Testing a model at the initiatory stage is, in transactional evaluation, a matter of formulating and carrying out an evaluation design that will demonstrate the process and progress of the venture and permit comparison with similar efforts. The client, at this stage, is the group building the model. Testing a model at the developmental stage is a matter, apart from evaluating the individuals responsible, of collecting data on the operation. Testing an integrative model is a matter of evaluating those data that will assess the outcomes, in terms of the original intent, and in terms of the outcomes of similar programs. By linking evaluation findings to the project staff's efforts, transactional evaluation maximizes the usefulness of its findings to the program development. The results will be, in some cases, that goals are clarified, or resources put to better use; in others, that conflict among the participants is resolved.

Accountability in field projects cannot be divorced from evaluation and, to the extent that the evaluation is appropriate, will be decreasingly a matter of subjective judgment. Evaluation data that are not directly useful to the practitioner tend to foment suspicion; evaluation comes to be seen as a coercive weapon to structure behavior. Yet, decision makers at all levels, gatekeepers and field practitioners, need accurate evaluation to help form their judgments. Transactional evaluation used with a series of models of program development helps to resolve some of the issues that prevent evaluation from improving educational programs. As evaluation becomes more useful to its clients with the application of transactional evaluation and evaluation designs, the participants, be they school boards, professional practitioners, or the recipients, will become more directly accountable for the educational programs.

FOOTNOTES

Portions of this chapter were originally prepared for the United States Office of Education, Special Programs Division.

1. For their explication of the concept of differential evaluation, I am indebted to Tony Tripodi, Phillip Fellin, and Irwin Epstein, *Social Program Evaluation: Guidelines for Health, Education and Welfare Administrators*. Itasca, Ill.: F. E. Peacock, 1971.

7

TRANSACTIONAL EVALUATION IN THE WOODLAWN EXPERIMENTAL SCHOOLS PROJECT

ROBERT M. RIPPEY

Transactional evaluation is particularly important where roles are threatened. In the Woodlawn Project such role threats not only were common, but also were considered by some members of the project to be a key to the improvement of instruction. It was sometimes postulated that if teachers had closer contact with parents and their anxieties about school, they would be motivated to make a effort and show more concern.

THE PROJECT

The Woodlawn Experimental Schools Project was a federally funded effort to improve education in a small area of Chicago by means of annual injections of over a million dollars. The project terminated, at the end of the traditional three-year run, in 1971.

Three schools, Wadsworth Elementary School, Wadsworth Upper Grade Center, and Hyde Park High School were the focus of the attention. The initial aim of the project was to bring students, parents, and teachers into a new working relationship. This new relationship would then determine new goals and new programs. To accomplish this, a project staff (with three constituencies: community, in-service training, and research and evaluation) was added to the regular school faculty.

In the community, the staff was to organize and direct the energies of the community toward solving the problems of the schools, which problems can be summarized by the phrase: "Not enough of anything." The community had too few teachers, not enough food and clothing, not enough room at home or at play, not enough hope. The in-service component was to assist teachers develop new programs once needs had been indicated by the parents. The research and evaluation component was to keep the usual records of achievement, and to record the temperature and blood pressure of the project at least through gestation.

Although the role of the research and evaluation staff was plotted carefully on paper during the early stages of project planning, many changes occurred along the way. In the trade, project evaluation is often seen as the less than noble, or at least the less than scientific job of reassuring federal agencies that tax monies are being well spent. There are more legitimate aims for evaluation that run the gamut from providing basic research into learning disorders to being a super ego for the project in hand. To function in any of these ways, one must survive.

The School

Wadsworth School lies in the middle of Woodlawn. One block south of the school at 65th and University is Dead Man's Corner—a conglomeration of deteriorating and abandoned stores—the site of numerous shootings and beatings connected with recruitment for the local gangs, the Rangers, the Disciples, the Gonzatoes, the Falcons. Directly east of the school is a new home for the aged—built on the Rangers' former shooting lot. One block to the east is Woodlawn Avenue, the dividing line between two of Chicago south side's largest and most powerful gangs, the Rangers and the Disciples. The older students in the school represent each in about equal numbers. The school has been declared neutral territory by the gangs; the zone of neutrality extends fifty feet beyond the limits of the playground.

A walk around the neighborhood demonstrates immediately the

diversity that makes up the microcosm of a ghetto block. Neatly kept homes with flowers in profusion stand next to burned-out tenements. A modern fourteen-story apartment stands next to a battered dwelling sprayed with a painted message that the Maniac Disciples run it. A vacant lot, filled with rubble, is identified by a sign: "Another civic improvement for the City of Chicago—Richard J. Daley, Mayor." And everywhere one sees broken glass, broken bottles, on the playground, on the streets, and on the sidewalks.

The school building itself was built over a period of three generations. The first building, for an upper middle class school, was built in Woodlawn at the end of the First World War; the third and last addition to the school was only partially completed in 1962 when the present principal took over. The new addition lacked glass in many windows, tiles on the floor, and had not been accepted by the architect when school opened. For this reason, maintenance men refused to enter the building.

The school did have plenty of children and too few teachers. As his first official act, the principal demanded more teachers. He also salvaged a truckload of obsolete textbooks from the school incinerator to buttress his meager supply. It took longer to get the windows installed—until November. Many parents still remember those first difficult months. The school, in spite of its situation and its difficult beginnings, was at the median level of achievement for Chicago. Many children had parents and brothers and sisters who cared for them; many teachers wanted to help the children succeed and to know a richer life.

The Plan

The project's history really began in 1964 when the University of Chicago proposed a laboratory school, near the Illinois Central tracks and the Midway, as a part of its plan for developing the south campus (described by the residents south of 60th Street as the University's plan for "Negro removal"). Parts of the history of the proposal have been detailed by Silberman (1964) and Congreve (1968). The new laboratory school was to provide the University with a resource for studying urban education problems, and the Woodlawn Community with a new, exemplary school.

It was hoped that the laboratory school would lower community resistance to the new Kenwood High School that was to remove most middle class black and white students from Hyde Park High School. The Woodlawn community felt that the new Kenwood High School would cause Hyde Park High School to deteriorate further. In addition, the presence of a laboratory school that used Woodlawn children as guinea pigs was considered demeaning and intolerable.

It was no surprise to many when the Reverend Arthur Brazier, leader of the Woodlawn Organization, appealed to the Office of Education, asking that funds for the University's experiment be approved only conditionally until the community could participate to a greater extent. He cited the government's policy of requiring community involvement in such projects. As a result, a small planning grant was awarded to the University along with an invitation to submit a new proposal when more community planning had been incorporated into the proposal. Willard Congreve, then Principal of the University High School, Lorraine Levigne, from the Chicago Public Schools Administration, and Anthony Gibbs, from the Woodlawn Organization, were appointed to explore the possibility of a collaboration among the schools, the community, and the University. The new proposal (Woodlawn Experimental Schools Project, 1968), quite different from its predecessor, called for the establishment of an experimental program in existing schools using existing resources. Substantial funds were to be made available for program changes once parents and teachers could agree on the changes they wanted made. The objectives of the program covered some seven pages in the Title III Proposal. The key ideas were: "to restructure the school as a social system in terms of its community through mutuality of effort, and to improve the quality of teaching and learning."

The three institutions, the University of Chicago, the Woodlawn Organization, and the Chicago Board of Education had too much to lose if the project failed and much to gain if it succeeded. The University could not be an island of enlightenment in a sea of poverty without risking the fate of Athens. The Chicago Public Schools Administration would not wish to risk the political consequences of another battle with an angry, organized Woodlawn community. The Woodlawn community could not reach its aspirations without the technical help and opportunities for training that both the public schools and the University afforded.

The Woodlawn Community Board

The three groups worked together through the Woodlawn Community Board, which was an advisory board to the Board of Education, made up of representatives from the Chicago Public Schools, from the Woodlawn Organization, and from the University. Although starting with seven representatives from each group, its composition changed throughout the history of the project to provide greater representation from the community. Recommendations from the Director of the Project were passed by the Woodlawn Community Board before being submitted to the Chicago Board of Education for final approval. Thus, the Woodlawn Community Board had great power to initiate ideas, but considerably less legal authority over such crucial matters such as finances and personnel. Many of the severe problems encountered during the first year resulted from well-intentioned but unrealistic efforts of the project to operate occasionally beyond the intricate web of regulations, roles, and agreements that surrounds the school system.

To the people of Woodlawn, the project was often perceived as a pioneering effort at community control. To many in the public school heirarchy, the project was a new, federally funded, Title III Project undergoing a few birth pains. Both views had their elements of truth, but such disparate perceptions magnified the difficulties. The the Woodlawn Community Board had a long history of disagreement. The Woodlawn Organization was instigated by Saul Alinsky about fifteen years ago. Its first goal was to thwart the University's expansion south of the Midway. The Chicago Board of Education, attempting to digest two critical reports by Phillip Hauser and Robert Havighurst as well as numerous lesser research hors d'oeuvres, was suffering from dyspepsia. Nor did the University look upon the impending wedding feast as an occasion for conviviality. As Congreve described the situation:

> We have used the word "collaborate" advisedly and have avoided the term "cooperate." We dislike the term cooperation, not because we feel the literal meaning of cooperation and collaboration are not fairly synonymous but rather because the term cooperation immediately suggests giving up something to get along ... Each time the conflict was faced squarely, we progressed. When we attempted to avoid disagreement we lost ground (1968).

Of course, not all of the action was at the board level. To the leaders of the project, to a majority of its participants, and to many of the parents whose children attend school within the boundaries of the project, peripheral involvement was anathema. Yet, while it is important that the project be successful, not all involvement is fundamental to its goals. Although many teachers cooperated fully, some, threatened by the new role of leadership expected of them, were fearful. Some transferred to other schools; others maintained a knowing silence in teachers' meetings. Some spoke out openly in disagreement; others covertly prepared grievances for the union representative.

The Woodlawn Organization

The Woodlawn Organization likewise had other fish to fry. An unsuccessful campaign to get a black principal for Wadsworth School was at times more political than educational. Nor was it easy to weld together the diverse factions in the community. The Woodlawn Organization is acknowledged to be one of the largest, most powerful, and most effectively organized black community-action programs in the country. Yet, being a loosely structured federation of many small community and business organizations, it had identity problems. Its members did not hesitate to attack its leaders. Rumors of a sellout to the University or to the white honkies were easy to find or revive. The Woodlawn Organization's position has been stated explicitly by Brazier (1969), who felt that black people must solve many of the problems of today's black America. He proposed that this be done, not through separatism, and not through unfocused violence, but by sharply focused, organized attacks on individual, critical issues— issues that would mobilize the energies of the members of his community:

> [I] urge and plead for immediate action and a visible strategy to promote the security and solidarity of black people in Woodlawn and throught the nation. It is an appeal for a truly genuine, unbreachable racial solidarity plus a racial strategy that is workable and makes sense. I emphasize solidarity and strategy because without them, we can forget about any kind of security.

The University of Chicago

The University was ambivalent about participating and did not reap much good will from its participation. A vocal segment of the community and the student body of Hyde Park High School demanded that the University withdraw. Few persons at the University used the project as a resource for either training or research. The project director initially opposed the presence of university-based teacher trainees in the project; later, the policy was changed. If the project was not much used for training teachers, it was still less used for research, and the community's attitude towards the researcher was, at times, justifiably antagonistic. They talked about "hit and run research." They were wary of the student from North Dakota who spends a few months in the community writing a critical paper, which they may never see. On my first day in Woodlawn, two Rangers asked me what I was doing. I said, "Research." Their reply was, "Oh, a tourist. Would you like us to show you around?" The same sentiments surfaced at a public meeting. The first question I was asked after introducing the research and evaluation staff to the parents and teachers of Wadsworth School was, "What we really want to know is which one of you is going to write the book?"

During the first week of the summer, a sensitivity training group of parents, teachers, and project staff told me that my being white was not going to be nearly as much of a handicap as my being from the University of Chicago. One of the research assistants came in the following day wearing a University of Chicago sweatshirt and was persuaded, in light of the climate of opinion, to exchange it for one saying Lake Forest College.

Of course neither the University nor Woodlawn had any patience with "absentee landlord" research. In his commencement address for the winter quarter of 1965, Edward Levi, then University Provost, encouraged a greater commitment to the study of local problems. Throughout this and other projects, the University has tried to adapt itself to Brazier's policy of self-determination. As Julian Levi, Professor of Urban Studies, commenting on a press conference on a housing project organized by the University and the Woodlawn Organization, said,

> It's not the business of the University to run anybody's life or to run anybody's community ... the housing will be owned, operated, managed, and controlled by [The Woodlawn Organization], not by the University. The University sees its own role as a very limited one. Now as far as Hyde Park-Kenwood is concerned, and this is often lost sight of, the plans which were carried out were part of a conservation program in which there was and is a neighborhood conservation council, which has to approve everything which has occurred there as a result of public action, and where there were something over nine public hearings involving thousands of people over the years (September 4, 1969).

The idea of self-determination was a guiding principle for research and evaluation. The subjects of the research were to have a hand in both planning and executing the research connected with the project. Such participation is a basic tenet of transactional evaluation:

everybody affected by educational change—not just the project directors and his hired man, the professional evaluator—should have a hand in monitoring and criticizing that change.

RESEARCH AND EVALUATION

Research and evaluation were included in the design of the project. As well as the descriptive, instructional, and transactional functions of the research team, they had also to provide feedback to the clients and to make a final evaluation of the results. As well as a director, the research staff consisted of nine part-time students of psychology, comparative education, measurement, evaluation, sociology, and anthropology. Several research staff members lived in Woodlawn; several had attended both the elementary and high schools that were part of the project. Most were under thirty years of age. Four were white, five were black. One research assistant spent three months in one of the schools and was able to convince the students that he was a student, the teachers that he was a substitute teacher, albeit one without a heavy class load. However, the staff had its comeuppance when we discovered that one of our own team, who was with us for only a short time, was doing his own research for the Federal Bureau of Investigation.

Research Team Functions

Initially, the descriptive function consumed much of our time. Using field notes, observations, and checklists, observers reported what happened, who did what to whom, and why. Because our independent observers came from separate disciplines, the reports themselves differed, both in content and in interpretation. These reports were ultimately classified according to basic questions formulated before the project began, questions such as, What are the effects of the project on teacher morale and turnover? What new programs are underway? Are there more parents in the schools? Are the students getting more out of school?

The second function of the research team, to provide feedback, was accomplished through discussions with the project director and staff members, through occasional meetings with teachers, and the use of newsletters. Research assistants reported on their observations to the groups or classes they observed. They conducted small scale surveys, assisted teachers to evaluate their students, and helped develop plans for the evaluation of new programs.

The instructional function was not noticeably successful. A few students were trained to keypunch our data. Two students helped revise instruments, others helped administer tests. Research seminars for parents and teachers were planned. Computer programming courses were taught at Hyde Park High School.

Our fourth function, the transactional role of evaluation, seemed to promise some solution for problems of conflict and confrontation. As a service to the project administration, evaluators tried to engage conflicting groups in the design and implementation of an evaluation plan that represented their concern and apprehension. The transactional evaluation of a program would occur, when for example, as teachers developed a new program for teaching reading, the teachers and parents would agree in advance to an independent evaluation of the effects of the program on both teachers and students. This independent evaluation would suggest modifications that might improve the program. Such a procedure does not remove any initiative from the group proposing the change, but it does provide the initiators with a powerful tool for gaining effective support and acceptance for proposals that, having the power to modify roles, tend to be threatening. This service of evaluation, perhaps its most important use, has seldom been employed in public schools—perhaps because some administrators tend to emphasize the necessity to suppress or avoid conflict. The transactional use of evaluation has a sound basis in theory. Its importance was, perhaps, first called to the attention of educators by Coffey and Golden, who suggested, in their model for change within institutions (1957), that

> unless there is resistance, it is doubtful whether institutional change can endure or individual change can go very deep. Change is less threatening and, indeed, may be more validly tested if, in the beginning, while involving all levels within the institution, it can be placed upon an experimental basis to be evaluated as a part of an action-research program.

At the end of the evaluation time-line, final or summative evaluation (our fifth function) described the changes which took place.

The Role of Parents

From the description of the program, it can be seen that there were many opportunities for role conflicts to develop. Evaluation made it possible to examine some of the conflicts in detail, and to deal with them as they developed. It was a situation ideally suited to transactional evaluation. There was another point of view within the project that suggested that teachers were too sheltered from the heat in the community. Thus, transactional evaluation was not fully achieved because its aim of reducing role threat was antithetical to confrontation, which thrives on role threat. This is not to say that transactional evaluation was not used, it is only to point out that transactional evaluation played a minor role in a many-faceted program.

One of the earliest transactional surveys of the project, made in 1968, showed that, in spite of overt expressions of conflict, teachers and parents agreed in general on many of the goals of the school. Parents wanted more emphasis on subject-matter and discipline. Parents and teachers agreed that the inner-city child needed to improve those skills that would get him out of his restricted environment. In fact, in response to one of our interview questions, almost all the teachers and parents agreed that they did *not* want the curriculum to follow too closely the life of the community: they do not want it to emphasize the poverty, deprivation, and violence. They did want it to offer every child realistic encouragement and the best possible development of his skills to enable him to assume his rightful place in the world. Direct, intense, and continuous interaction among children, parents, teachers, and service agencies was critically important, but not always possible. Interference came, not only from passing trucks and elevated trains (the classrooms were not soundproof), but also from the emotional static of gang conflict and insufficient living room. The groups themselves were not used to working with one another.

There are important things for parents to do in schools; there are areas where parents are particularly capable, as evidenced by their insights about children, their ability to communicate with children, their intimate knowledge of what is reinforcing and rewarding to children, and their ability to discipline; in other words, parents can help explain ideas to children, encourage them, console them, and, on occasion, even spank them. For example, the first day that the parents came to the high school, an immediate calming effect could be noticed. As a teacher said one day, when some of the parents were absent from their work session, "I just don't see how we can get along without the parents."

It is fairly clear, though, that there are many barriers that have been set up to inhibit the parents from participating in the school. A barrier that was not foreseen at the outset was thrown up by the students themselves: Some were not certain that they wanted their parents in school, and would occasionally discourage them from coming. One student, overheard in the hall on noticing his own parent coming into the school, asked "What's she doing here?" Since parents are likely to exert a disciplinary influence in the school, it is debatable whether all the students will want them there.

The parents might well be discouraged from coming to the schools by the cavalier treatment they receive in the halls, or by the fact that the administration asks them to come only in times of trouble. Discouragements such as these can be avoided if a little trouble is taken to clarify, for the parents, their particular functions in the school. Role clarification is often necessary on the opening day of school. One of our research assistants was assigned to sit in the upper grade center office and observe how the parents were treated. She reported that many parents were treated brusquely, and that some students were sent home for forms that, it seemed, might just as well be brought in the following day. Some retraining of the front office staff followed her report, and one clerk, nicknamed "The Dragon Lady," was moved to a desk away from the counter. The situation improved greatly. Soon after, parents were employed in the project to help other parents feel more welcome, and to see that they received the information they needed. Probably most important of all was the need to make the parents aware that their contributions were valued, even indispensable. This required more than an invitation: it meant getting involved with them; it meant involving them in situations where they could make decisions and see the decisions implemented fairly rapidly; it meant encouraging them and responding to their requests and their new ideas.

A lack of communication, verbal and nonverbal, tended to fix a gulf between parents and teachers. In field notes, written in July 1968, the first month of the project, Morgan, observed:

"All this time there's a lot of jargon, just big words. Uproar increases, and people begin to leave. Parents are bored, people are shouting in the microphone, and the din is deafening.

"Mrs. F. stood up and proceeded, she said, 'I didn't understand, absolutely didn't understand a single thing that was going on.' Mrs. W. several times managed to oil the waters and to explain that what the communication gap consists of mainly is that the parents don't understand 'teacher-ese' jargon. She expresses the fear that we're going right back where we started from—the same old problems handled in the same old way.

"The seating is awfully separated—parents always sit on the left."

However, the entire picture was not negative. In field notes for July 1, 1968, Procter reported a small group session:

"When I came in the group was discussing whether teachers should be given paid time during the day to visit parents. One teacher talked about the time she had visited a child who was in the hospital—the point was that she never thought of asking for pay for it. (Teachers perhaps have internalized society's expectation of dedication beyond monetary considerations.) Somebody said something about the union contract.

"The one white male in the group said, 'We could give them (the parents) a time that we will be here—they could come to the school—the PTA tries to do this—we're all equals in the school; no one knows how the other lives in their home.' (Interesting logic; ignores the school as 'the teacher's domian,' etc.) A parent says, 'I don't feel that way,' and the teacher says, 'No, no, not *you* . . . I'm just suggesting this . . .' (This happens frequently—people talk about 'some teachers,' or 'some parents,' not *you*—good way to handle grievances without personal attacks.)

"A parent gave her views. She talked about one teacher who used to call her. Some comment about taking time off of work to come to school. This teacher made her feel really a part of the school. X commented that we have some very good teachers, and the parent said, "I had to get to know this." The other parent talked about her experiences going to the school, and commented that children behave well when a parent is there. Also that she is proud when a teacher comes to her home (or would be). The other parent said the teacher should do whatever it takes to reach the individual parent (whether calling, or visiting, or whatever). Y said, "In the final analysis, you should give teachers time to do this."

Not all the teachers were welcoming, as Procter observed in reporting a planning meeting held in January:

"Parents, more often than not, sat in positions peripheral to the large circles which were formed. When not sitting peripherally (i.e., on the outside of the circle, or as eruptions from a perfect circle), they sat as adjacents and in small knots. The seating resulted in parental isolation. Many of the problems reflected in seating may be seen emerging from the chair's failure to engage in cohesive structuring. There were no set times or patterns for the opening and closing of meetings. Both students and teachers tended to exit immediately at the sound of the bell. Entrance to meetings was marked by 'bell drift,' people entering casually and over an average ten-minute time span. Preparation for the day's task, or that of the day to follow, was not easily communicated under these circumstances. Holdover seating (usually restricted to parents), but also to students occasionally, gave clear evidence of the distance between the (groups). As teachers entered, they would sit either alone or in pairs. When greetings were extended to parents, one-to-one, conversation rarely followed. Establishment of cohesive structures could have begun with the holdover group; they could have been given the responsibility to take attendance as people entered, this would have served as mechanism for contact communication and monitor of attendance."

The Role of Students

Student sessions showed a similar pattern, the students often forming a second circle around the teachers. Even when sitting in the circle, students sat isolated, seldom speaking to one another or with the larger group. The teachers' own conflicts over identity and commitment deflected energy away from the problems of the children. Such conflicts probably need to run their course, and any plan for change within the schools that does not account for internal pressures will have small chance of success.

Time

Beyond the role-related concerns, which apply primarily to the scene of the action, are four other concerns, which go beyond boundaries and roles; two are concerns of time; two of space.

The first issue of time is the timing of funding. Funding was approved only a few weeks before the start of the Woodlawn project, thereby delaying the procurement of staff, an initial obstacle difficult to overcome.

The second issue of time is the duration of funding. To produce any appropriate findings, the Woodlawn Experimental Schools Project would need at least one year of planning and shakedown, several years of operation, and perhaps, an additional year for the final analysis of the outcomes of the project, especially if delayed effects are to be sampled. Longitudinal data, including postgraduation follow-up, seems to be essential to the evaluation of any large-scale intervention program. One might suggest the need for separate funds for evaluation and research, with the funds being made available before the project begins (and lasting for some time after the project itself ends).

Space

The first issue of space is that of an experimental school district. The idea of an experimental subsystem within a large city system is by no means new (Rippey 1969). A number of models are available; perhaps the most ambitious is that for the Community Council for Educational Development in Boston (1969). In the Woodlawn Project, the concept of an experimental subdistrict was not realized during the first year. Although informally recognized as a district superintendent, the project director was not, and could not have been, accorded full authority. The operation was not as flexible as it should have been for an experimental district. The restrictions placed upon the project by the legal and extralegal requirements of the subsystem might well be compared with those on such projects as Boston's Boardman School (The Staff of the W.L.P. Boardman School 1969).

The purpose of an experimental school district is to allow for the flexibility necessary for innovation. Perhaps essential for this flexibility is the ability to recruit personnel committed to and helpful to the new program—personnel who agree in advance to the scrutiny required to develop a new program. An experimental school district encourages the development of alternate solutions to the problems of education. Our confining the experimental district to a single project when there were other projects successfully operating within the city weakened rather than strengthened both the idea of an experimental district and the project itself. The subdistrict structure of the first year was not only dysfunctional, but actually operated as a barrier between this and other projects in the city; the Woodlawn project was competing for funds against other Title III Projects.

The second issue of space is that of transferring the findings of this project to other schools, of using the project as a model for other inner-city education efforts. The suggestion violates both science and good sense. If I have learned one thing this year it is that each school and its surrounding community has a unique character. One school may well learn from another, but it will be necessary to temper information with a knowledge of local conditions. Perhaps the three most salient characteristics of the Woodlawn Experimental Schools Project are the existence of the Woodlawn Organization, an organization with influence not easily matched in other communities; the proximity of the University of Chicago and its resources; and the nature of the gangs. The Blackstone Rangers are no ordinary street gang; their organized adult leadership sustains an influence different from and perhaps more pervasive than that which many of the other gangs exert.

The Woodlawn Experimental Schools Project was a fascinating arena to test many assumptions. The project was not conceived in consensus, although the concept of change based upon the planned evaluation of contending positions was reasonable and productive.

The project is now terminated. The final research report (Hughes 1972) has been completed and reviewed:

> One of the conclusions that emerges from the report of the Woodlawn Experiment is that the very deep differences in outlook, method and style which characterize universities, community organizations, and public schools can indeed yield to shared decisions and shared power, *when* the commitment to change is greater than the rivalry and jockeying for power, and *if* the dedicated individuals on all sides have the skills, patience and persistence (as well as the commitment) to see the job through.
>
> Not only is change difficult to bring about, it is far more difficult than most people imagine. The often heard assertion that "if we can go to the moon, we can clean up this dirty planet, feed every hungry mouth and see that every child learns to read, is well housed, etc., etc." is based on the misunderstanding that all that is required is vast sums of money and a "reordering of priorities." In fact, the great element lacking is a consensus on the part of members of the system on the means and direction of change. The change agent entering the system with the best of intention, goodwill and expertise, perceiving himself as a bringer of aid and assistance, is typically perceived by members of that system as an alien, a threat, a new problem to be faced. This was dramatically put by a teacher during the first summer workshop who, in response to the questionnaire item "What are the three greatest problems that you as a teacher face in doing your job?" declared: "The University of Chicago, the Woodlawn Organization and the Chicago Public Schools."

I would agree with this conclusion and point out that lack of consensus is a prime target for transactional evaluation. The concept of transactional evaluation itself may not be accepted by agents of change and is at times honored more in the breach than in the observance.

REFERENCES

Boston Committee for Community Educational Development. "Summary of Present Proposal." Mimeographed. Boston, 1969.

Brazier, A. M. *Black Self-Determination: The Story of the Woodlawn Organization.* Edited by Robert DeHaan. Grand Rapids, Mich.: Erdmans, 1969.

Chicago Board of Education. "Woodlawn Experimental Schools: Title III Proposal, February 1968." Mimeographed. Chicago: Chicago Public Schools Administration, 1968.

Coffey, H. S., and Golden, W., Jr. "The Psychology of Change Within an Institution." In *In-Service Education,* Yearbook of the National Society for the Study of Education. Chicago: University of Chicago Press, 1957.

Congreve, W. J. "Institutional Collaboration to Improve Urban Public Education, with Special Reference to the City of Chicago." Mimeographed. Office of Education, Final Report on Project No. 7-0346, March 31, 1968.

Fortune, A., and Rippey, R. "Research Report." Mimeographed. Woodlawn Experimental Schools Project, Chicago Public Schools Administration, October 1968.

Hughes, H. "The Vicissitudes of Change." *Education and Urban Society* (May 1972).

Morgan, M. Field Notes—Woodlawn Experimental Schools Project. Chicago Public Schools Administration, July 1968.

Procter, M. Field Notes—Woodlawn Experimental Schools Project. Chicago Public Schools Administration, July 1968.

Rippey, R. "Becoming Involved in Educational Research and Evaluation—Why and How." *Illinois Journal of Education* (January 1969): 3-8.

Silberman, C. E. *Crisis in Black and White.* New York: Random House, Vintage Books, 1964.

The Staff of the W.L.P. Boardman School. "The Developmental Classroom." Mimeographed. Boston Public Schools Administration, 1969.

II TRANSACTIONAL EVALUATION IN CHANGE
The Perspective

8

TRANSACTIONAL
EVALUATION IN
PROFESSIONAL EDUCATION

HERBERT J. WALBERG

Transactional evaluation, as defined in this chapter, is the acquisition and feedback of information and values into an ongoing social system to assess goals, means, and their match within and outside the system. It is distinct from traditional evaluation in education in two ways: its focus is on social and organizational relations rather than on educational materials and techniques; and its emphasis is on diagnosis and improvement of a system rather than on establishing the superiority of one system over another in the manner of an agricultural field experiment or a horse race. It seems most appropriate in the large part of education about which there is little consensus or rigor of definition and operational specification of goals and alternative means, especially in the arts, humanities, and social sciences, and also in professional schools of education and social work. This chapter is a case study, from the perspective of transactional evaluation, of our experiences in system development of a project conducted by a consortium of graduate schools of social work who were trying to bring about integrative teaching and learning.

BACKGROUND

The Project on Integrative Teaching and Learning was supported by a grant made by the Office of Juvenile Delinquency and Youth Development, U.S. Department of Health, Education, and Welfare to the Council on Social Work Education, the national accrediting body for professional social work schools. The project staff consisted of Louis Lowy and Leonard Blokesberg, professors of social work at Boston University, and myself, as education and evaluation consultant.

We tried introducing cooperative, innovative changes into professional education for social work and studied the presumed effects of our efforts. Our goal was to promote integration (the relating of ideas) in the student's mind as a result of his professional education. We attempted to accomplish integration by: asserting our own judgment of its values, analyzing the concept in philosophical and psychological writings on education, tracing some of the underlying factors that may prevent it, generating a set of educational arrangements and methods likely to bring it about, and gathering opinions from the students and faculty of eight graduate schools of social work on the actual use and value of the arrangements and methods of integration.

Our original intent was less ambitious—the incorporation into the curriculum of instructional materials and case studies to be viewed from a number of diverse perspectives, which would lead to greater integration. We soon realized that new teaching materials alone are not likely to change graduate education. Bureaucratic fiat, administrative charisma, and individual faculty initiative are unlikely to change the curriculum and teaching fundamentally. Professors are busy; they have little time and energy for educational reform unless they are given convincing reasons and strong incentives. Accordingly, much of our effort went into developing a rationale for integration, specifying the ways it might be brought about, developing means of enabling faculties to carry out and evaluate them and, finally, theorizing about our study of these processes, especially with respect to promoting change in professional social work education by simultaneously implementing concepts of organizational development and human relations.

Concerning the scientific credence of our findings, we were able only to offer the tabulated opinions of the participants, and our own observations and interpretations. We were inclined to agree with the physician's advice: "When in confirmation to doubt, and when in doubt to refrain." At the same time, we realized that, in most professional fields, the engaged practitioner can never afford the luxury of waiting to act until unequivocal experiments are performed and duplicated (if indeed they are possible). Physicians will continue to condemn or condone cigarette smoking on the basis of the uncertain probabilities and noncausal evidence yielded by thirty years of extensive, expensive, and as yet inconclusive research. Still more uncertainty resides in the social sciences and their applications; yet, the social worker, psychotherapist, and professor must make minute-by-minute decisions affecting equally important aspects of their clients' or students' welfare.

POSTURE REGARDING CHANGE

At the outset, we dissociated ourselves from those who, simply advocating change for its own sake, dismiss tradition and the present state of educational affairs. There is danger in resorting to abstract generalities, such as "advocating change" and "moving in a new direction"; it obfuscates rather than sharpens substantive issues. Taken to an extreme, such a position leads to anarchy and anti-intellectualism. Nor could we bring ourselves to agree with the mindless eclecticism that sometimes seems to characterize the applied social sciences. We could not accept the myth of the detached academic observer who picks flowers of social science theory to present a bouquet to the student. For dialogue in debate or teaching, one must have a systematic position, no matter how crude and tentative, and an emotional commitment, no matter how weak. Without personal identity and perspective neither the professor nor the student can engage in true dialectic. In a Hegelian sense, there can be no synthesis without antithesis and no antithesis without thesis or hypothesis. Those who gratuitously combine, for example, Freud, Skinner, and Lewin in psychology, or Weber, Marx, and Durkheim in sociology, without recognizing their deep and far-reaching ideological clashes are deluding themselves and their students. Those who uncritically apply these kinds of conflicting ideas in practice are technicians rather than liberally educated professionals.

At the same time, it was not enough for us to build our own case upon the rejection of a straw man; in rejecting we had to advocate something that might turn out better. We shared the change-advocate's desire for reform and, specifically, the change we attempted to bring about was the greater integration of teaching and learning. And also we had come to recognize our own values, ideas, and strategies in the process of promoting integration. We renewed our regard for democratic decision making within the framework of the rights and responsibilities of academic freedom. We tempered our rational planning with empiricism, pragmatism, and the realities of the political process. We limited our professional autonomy to the confines of accountability to sponsors, peers, and clients. We now feel that, among the factors needed to promote organizational change, there is much to be said for university consortia to combat institutional parochialism, for the contract method to assure rational planning and execution, for conceptual frameworks to promote comprehensive thinking about the curriculum, and for human relations techniques such as cooperation, competitiveness, and conflict resolution to encourage constructive, responsive, responsible change.

THE PROJECT PLAN AND EXECUTION

Table 4, a Procedural Time Chart, depicts the major task components of the project and their scheduling. The idea and funding of the project was a response to the disparate qualities of professional education for social work. The integration of course work and field work has been difficult. Social work, an applied field, has drawn on the behavioral sciences and other more basic fields in which there are a great many unrelated, sometimes conflicting, ideas and methods. The teaching and practice of social work have evolved into distinct branches: individual case work, social group work, community organization, research, and public planning and policy. The basic premise of the project was that changes in the educational delivery system could improve the integration of the diverse ideologies and practices.

The executive officer of the Council for Social Work Education wrote to the deans or directors of the seventy-two accredited schools of social work in the United States, Puerto Rico, and Canada. The letter described the the goals of the project and requested indications of interest in participation. Twenty-three schools expressed interest, and eight were chosen to provide a representative sample in terms of size, age, geographic location, and control (public, sectarian, and independent): the schools of social work at Atlanta University,

TABLE 4

Procedural Time Chart

TIME / PROCEDURE	1967			1968					1969				
	Spring, Summer	Sept., Oct.	Nov., Dec.	Jan., Feb.	Mar., Apr. May	June– Aug.	Sept., Oct.	Nov., Dec.	Jan., Feb.	Mar., Apr.	May	June– Aug.	Sept.– Dec.
Creative idea and funding; selection of schools and Project staff	x												
Field Visit I and contract with schools; selection of Project faculty by schools		x	x										
Conceptual framework supplied		x					x	x					
Curriculum materials supplied				x				x	x				
School proposals due					x								
Workshop I: San Juan						x							
Selection of Project students													
Experimental semester							x	x	x				
Log reporting by schools							x	x					
Field Visits II and III							x	x		x			
Newsletters and other contacts	x	x	x	x	x	x	x	x	x	x	x	x	x
Questionnaire administered by schools									x	x			
Final school reports due First draft:										x			
Final school reports due Final draft:												x	
Workshop II: Atlanta											x		
Staff reports to field (oral and written) due									x				x
Follow-up by schools													x

SOURCE: Lowy, Bloksberg, and Walberg, *Teaching and Learning*, p. 98.

Adelphi University, Indiana University, the University of Puerto Rico, Syracuse University, the University of Toronto, the University of Utah, and the Case Western Reserve University School of Applied Social Sciences. The project consultants visited the selected schools, informed their faculties of their roles in the project, and requested that faculty committees be formed to plan and implement each school's participation. During these visits, the consultants realized that the schools required a great deal of conceptual input to help formulate their plans. The transactional evaluation provided was perhaps the most important facet of the consultants' work.

Accordingly, four major position papers were prepared and mimeographed, three by Herbert Walberg, *The Integration of Learning; The Dis-Integration of Learning;* and *Can Educational Research Contribute to the Practice of Teaching?;* the fourth by Louis Lowy and Leonard Blokesberg, *Integrative Elements in Teaching and Learning.* The first paper presented to the participants an analysis of the three philosophical perspectives (Plato's, Aristotle's, and Whitehead's) and two psychological perspectives (James's and Brunner's) on the integration of knowledge. Perhaps an "iconic representation," to use Bruner's term, will summarize the major concepts of the views and afford comparisons among the orderings of concepts (See figure 4). In all five views, the lower levels are tied most closely to the perception or experience of the particular and concrete. Ascending to higher levels, a process logicians and psychologists have come to call "induction," experience is transformed into knowledge, which becomes first general, then abstract, and finally integrated. Emotion intrudes to help or hinder the process; the ascent is difficult and proceeds step by step since, as Aristotle held, the most universal knowledge is generally the most difficult. We offend some practical advice on how difficulty might be overcome and concluded with the observation that, for these philosophers and psychologists, cognitive integration in education is of the utmost significance and value.

The Dis-Integration of Learning dealt with Weber's concepts of bureaucracy and collegium, and their possibly unfavorable effects on the organizational development of the university. There is much opportunity for the two forms of organization to conflict, and Abraham Flexner's insight (1930) was prophetic: "Efficiency in administration and fertility in the realm of ideas have in fact nothing to do with each other—except, perhaps, to hamper and destroy each other." Indeed, there is grave danger that the modern university has combined the worst of both. Let us exaggerate for a moment to sharpen the issue. The university preserves the Ph.D. as a "union

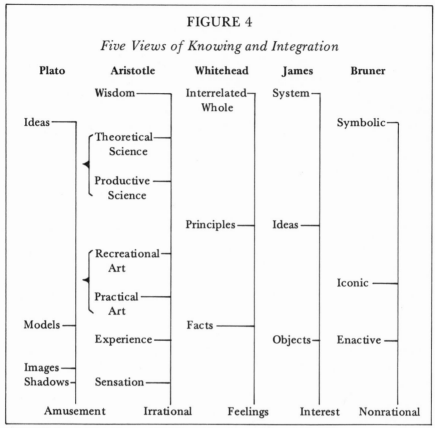

FIGURE 4

Five Views of Knowing and Integration

SOURCE: Lowy, Blokesberg, and Walberg, *Teaching and Learning*, p. 50.

card" for membership in the craft guild. As an institution it is characterized by protectionism and the lack of further accountability of the members; rival virtuosos, elites, cliques, and coalitions; struggles for leadership; and, seemingly, endless committee deliberations and debates yielding ad hoc compromises satisfying no one. Like the medieval apprentice, the modern academic invests his talents, not in his workplace but, as Myrdal noted (1966), in

> negotiable wares—publications and other more or less quantifiable contributions to his field—which can easily be transferred to other employment situations that are widely and easily negotiable throughout the academic marketplace—much as a sojourner in a hostile country often converts his assets from real estate to jewels in order to facilitate a quick getaway across the border.

The lecture, recitation, notebook, pedantic teaching and vicarious learning; the thesis, dissertation, and oral defense— all can be traced straight back to the sixteenth century university collegium. Yet the university has acquired the undesirable aspects of bureaucracy: hierarchic power structures, refusal to accept the buck, resistance to social change, insensitivity to student needs (which have now escalated to demands), insistence on procedures rather than principles, impersonal standards and credits, fragmentation of knowledge, and, to hold it all together, a flurry of mimeographed paper preserving records, rules, and resolutions. Perhaps the caricature is not so exaggerated—perhaps it is true in part. If so, what becomes of the vital center, the Idea of the University? As the classic philosophers and a few modern psychologists have asked, how shall universals be sought? As Newman asked (1947), how are students to "apprehend the great outline of knowledge . . . [with] freedom, equitableness, calmness, moderation, and wisdom?" In short, how can learning be integrated?

The third paper, *Can Educational Research Contribute to the Practice of Teaching,* was a response to the participants' request for an analysis of recent pedagogical theory and research on the psychology of learning. The content of the paper would be familiar to most readers of this volume, but we found interesting the demand for advice on educational research from professors of social work and the request for publication rights from the Council's journal, *Education for Social Work.* The published paper could not treat the psychology of teaching and learning comprehensively, but it did provide a bibliographical guide for further reading (Walberg 1968).

The fourth paper, *Integrative Elements in Teaching and Learning,* provided a comprehensive list and description of the activities the consultants believed would lead to integrative education. As shown in Table 5, the twenty-three activities were grouped in four major categories: interactional, curricular, temporal, and institutional elements. Also shown in Table 5 are the patterns of elements chosen by the eight schools.

Given these four conceptual inputs and a selection of curriculum materials supplied by the consultants, the project faculties began planning their integrative innovations. As contracted with them from the start, they were to write, according to an outline supplied, a detailed proposal of their goals and activities with an appropriate rationale. The elements they chose to employ could be freely selected from the framework supplied. They were also free to draw on the consultants' ideas and on material other than that supplied by

TABLE 5

Integrative Elements Used by Project Schools

Category	School								Fre-quency
	A	B	C	D	E	F	G	H	
Interactional Elements									
Faculty-to-Faculty									
Team teaching	x	x	x	x	x	x			6
Faculty meeting	x	x	x	x	x		x	x	7
Systemal information sharing						x		x	2
Faculty-to-Student									
Faculty-student advising		x			x			x	3
Informal integrative seminars		x	x	x			x	x	5
Charismatic leadership								x	1
Student-to-Student									
Peer task-force grouping		x		x	x	x	x	x	6
Curricular Elements									
Structural Devices									
Classroom arrangements	x	x	x	x	x	x	x		7
Field arrangements		x		x					2
Delivery Devices									
Media									
Lecture/discussion group		x		x	x			x	4
Role-play		x							1
Heuristic device							x		1
Integrative conference							x		1
Technology									
Core record	x		x	x			x	x	5
Audiovisual aids	x	x					x	x	4
Conceptual matrix				x	x	x			3
Simulation			x			x			2
Bibliography		x		x		x			3
Evaluative Devices									
Examination and									
Assignment					x	x		x	3
Time Elements									
Contemplative Time		x		x		x	x		4
Arrangement of Courses				x	x				2
Institutional Elements									
Ecology					x				1
Organizational structure		x		x	x	x		x	5
TOTAL	5	13	6	13	11	10	9	11	78

SOURCE: Lowy, Blokesberg, and Walberg, *Teaching and Learning,* p. 107.

the project. They also knew that they would be presenting their plans to their professional peers at a national planning conference to be held in San Juan, Puerto Rico. This expectation and newsletters describing what the participating schools were doing generated constructive competition among the eight faculties. During this planning period, a committee of eminent social work professors was appointed to advise the project. The visibility of each faculty member and each faculty as a team tended to channel energies into the project and build administrative support from deans and others in each school.

During the conference in San Juan, each group distributed copies of its proposal, described its overall plan to the other groups, answered their criticisms, and responded to their suggestions. During the conference, there was a healthy stealing of ideas, which delighted the consultants. The ambiance of the island helped us get through the heavy schedule of meetings, but there were tense moments that culminated, in the late evening of a hard day's work, during my presentation of a modest plan of evaluative research (which depended largely on a student questionnaire and other data to be provided by the project faculties), in five professors rising, one after another, to make angry comments about the presumptiousness of evaluating professors, the inadequacies of educational research, and our scheduling of the conference. It is difficult in retrospect to know exactly what troubled the sixty or so participants. Admittedly we had already put them on the spot for several sessions and had unwittingly allowed competitiveness among faculties to rise possibly dangerously. We had tired them out. Later we came to believe that the root cause was the professorial anxiety that permeated academia at the time about student unrest and hostility. I had tried to make it clear that all data would be grouped, and any reports would identify the school-aggregated responses by a letter code to preserve anonymity (a promise, of course, we kept). A quick-thinking colleague consultant rose and, with great passion, gave a magnificent impromptu speech that completely changed the spirit of the group. He also announced that one or two sessions for the next morning would be canceled so that the participants could restore themselves with *Piña Coladas* (a local rum-laced drink) and other entertainments that evening. It was perhaps inhumane of us to schedule meetings with only a few short breaks for two and a half days. My colleague, a specialist in group relations, later confided to me that he had always experienced such crises in constructive groups. The session was a moving one for me and, since then, I have always paused before calling or attending meetings that last more than an hour or two. The conference ended on a positive note. We made a number of warm acquaintances; the participants felt a part of an important project. The faculties went back to their schools, rethought and revised their plans according to suggestions their peers had given them, and readied themselves to implement their plans.

During the experimental semester, the consultants visited each school twice, as indicated in Table 4. We prepared for these visits by reviewing the proposals and reading the logs sent in weekly by each faculty. By the time of our visits each school seemed to have developed a distinctive "personality" and to be facing a unique set of challenges in implementing its project plans. In some schools tensions had arisen between the project faculty and the other faculty members who had not participated and felt left out or threatened. (The project budget permitted only six professors from each school to attend the conference.) In some cases the project was being used (constructively, we believe) by deans to reorganize their schools and to press for a number of reforms, not all of which were related to the project. In perhaps all the schools, but in some more visibly, there were tensions between the faculty and students.

Our job, as we saw it, was to help the project faculty to change strategies of goal attainment or to rethink unattained goals. We were called upon to help diagnose difficulties in the school and to share our perceptions of its strengths and weaknesses. The schools would ask us to meet different subgroups: students, administrators, senior and junior faculty members, faculty in special subject matter areas and, occasionally, entire school faculties. We identified a number of group conflicts and communication gaps, but were cautious about revealing all. We were careful to preserve anonymity for those who would prefer it, and attempted to sort out and transmit organizational intelligence that would have a constructive effect on the school. My two colleague consultants, both professors of social work who specialized in group processes, were far more adept and experienced than I in this sort of work, and I learned much from watching them and discussing our experiences on the way back to Boston. Moreover, the school faculties seemed reassured and grateful at the end of our visits, and it became apparent that all three of us had certain advantages in our roles as they evolved. We were all professors, that is, peer consultants to our clients, rather than representatives from an accrediting agency there to enforce its standards. Yet we had the sanction of the Council on Social Work Education and the aura of "experts" (which we jokingly defined as anyone who comes more than a hundred miles to consult). We had attempted to master some of the literature on conceptual integration, and we knew better than anyone else what was going on in all eight schools. Moreover, social workers work well with consultants; in practice, they continually work with different agencies, consult one another, and refer their clients back and forth to specialists in medicine, psychotherapy, and many other areas.

My role was somewhat different from those of my colleagues in that I was a purely educational consultant among practicing social work professors. I enjoyed it, although I was often troubled and uncertain about the best counsel to give. I liked my work in the schools because of the obvious sincerity of the educational questions that were asked of me. It was pleasant to be able to give advice without facing dissent from another expert. My associates and students at the Harvard Graduate School of Education have always, as good colleagues should, fought me at every step of any complex analysis and brought out every rival hypothesis and critical assumption. My sense of liberation when among social workers turned to hesitation when I had to grapple with such simple and perfectly reasonable questions as: What is the ideal class size? Is discussion better than lecturing? Should students have more power? Do objective tests breed conformity? Is this lesson plan a good one? Should we try some team teaching? On several occasions, many answers or no answer at all would come to mind. Rarely did it seem possible to give a simple straightforward recommendation. Although we seem to have done much research on these kinds of questions, it has produced conflicting findings and implications. To have rolled out a series of empirical findings and the opinions of "great educators" would have been easy enough for me, but pedantic, tedious, and useless for our clients.

Often I had to admit that many of the questions are still unsettled in the educational field and for the present will be answered best through experience and value judgments. As best I could, I gave a very brief summary of the literature on the question, referring the questioner to the best resource material I could recall. I sometimes spoke about my own teaching experiences that might relate to the question. Perhaps the best answer I gave was the suggestion that the question was important enough to answer with some informal field research, since there was little evidence available in the teaching of social work. I was glad to learn that several professors did carry out evaluation studies and later reported on them at our final conference; one began a doctoral thesis related to his work on the project. I also learned to perceive a question behind the question, such as: Am I doing something foolish? Am I a good teacher? Often the questions would come from the younger faculty. Unless I had a very good reason on educational grounds for discouraging them (one would avoid, for instance, intensive sensitivity training in classes), I generally reacted enthusiastically and tried to reinforce innovative teaching practices.

At our second project conference for all the schools, held in Atlanta, Georgia, a sense of accomplishment and finality pervaded our work. The schools reported to one another on their successes, failures, and future plans. I described the student questionnaire findings, which were generally favorable to the project. My colleagues gave their impressions of the project as a whole and spelled out how the findings would be used by the Council to promote further work on integrative learning. The conference lacked the excitement, expectancy, and tension of the first conference in San Juan; but we felt the spirit of friendship among those who have worked hard and, in spite of difficulties, attained a measure of success.

ONE ALTERNATIVE FOR ORGANIZATIONAL RENEWAL

The plan we developed during the project has a number of organizational features for promoting institutional renewal and innovation that merit further testing on other groups attempting broad changes. Although the success of the project is ambiguous, and I can be even less assured about future trials, I believe the project model would be most promising in organizations in which: the members are autonomous, as in the professions; the ultimate goal is general and abstract, for example, integrative learning; and the best means to attain that goal is not defined, as in team teaching or independent study. As I have argued elsewhere (Walberg 1970), the traditional method of curriculum building, consisting of the statement of goals, the provision of learning experiences, and evaluation, provides nearly insuperable theoretical and practical difficulties at every step. I believe it has been tried extensively in areas where it would seem most applicable, for example in science and mathematics, and has failed. With enough resources, it might work, but there seems little reason to adhere to it in efforts such as that outlined here. A number of the project's mechanisms seem to deserve further testing. Those most worthy are, we feel, the mechanisms by which:

1. We sought and organized, with the sanction and support of a higher agency, a group of separate institutions whose members

were committed to a single, though perhaps ill-defined and un-measurable, goal;
2. We provided an *a priori* conceptual framework and specific alternative means to attain the goal;
3. We had a written contract, between the school and the peer consultants, stating the roles of each, and giving definite dates for completing tasks;
4. We had the groups expose their plans and evaluation to one another, thus making them accountable to their professional peers; and
5. We could ensure that certain goals and means judged outstanding were reinforced by immediate colleagues, regional and national peers, and the consultants.

The Transactional Evaluator

Benne and Chin (1969) specified three basic strategies of purposive organizational change:
1. Empirical-rational, through fact and reason;
2. Normative-reeducative, through cultural and social standards and emotional commitments; and
3. Power-coercive, through political and economic sanctions, as well as through psychological incentives and disincentives, such as praise and guilt.

During and immediately after the project, we believed we were employing the empirical-rational and normative-reeducative bases of change. Three years later and after rethinking at least my own role, as I have tried to in this essay, I have come to the conclusion that actually we used the third, power-coercive, strategy and that this strategy was necessary to the project's goals. Indeed, it would have been an evasion of responsibility not to use it.

To rely, as a consultant, on reason alone is to play the disinterested technician, the traditional educational evaluator. To rely, like a sensitivity trainer, on the often conflicting emotional commitments of group members can mean that the group will become preoccupied by processes rather than outcomes, and so be no better than one found it. Even the combination of these two strategies appears to result in a leaderless pseudodemocracy and an irresponsible consultancy. Alone, power is autocratic. It seems to me that the responsible transactional evaluator must combine all three strategies as a wise parent or teacher does. He must bring to bear the best that reason has to offer. He must assess individual attitudes carefully and help sort out desirable, feasible goals. In terms of power or coercion (*management* or *goal setting* might be better terms to use in this period of distrust of authority), he must develop a framework of responsibility for himself and his clients to ensure the timely accomplishment and evaluation of specified tasks.

FOOTNOTE

The Project on Integrative Teaching and Learning was very much a collaboration by the three staff members, Louis Lowy, Leonard M. Blokesberg, and myself. Credit for any success of the project is due to my colleagues; any shortcomings of this retrospective account and reevaluation of the project are my own.

REFERENCES

Benne, K., and Chin, R. "General Strategies for Effecting Changes in Human Systems." In *The Planning of Change*, edited by W. Bennis, K. Benne, and R. Chin. New York: Holt, Rinehart and Winston, 1969.

Flexner, A. *Universities: American, English, and German.* New York: Oxford University Press, 1930.

Lowy, L., Blokesberg, L. M., and Walberg, H. J. *Integrative Teaching and Learning in Schools of Social Work. A Study of Organizational Development in Professional Education.* New York: Association Press, 1971.

Myrdal, G. "Broadening General Education." In *The University in the Future*, edited by T. Stroup. Lexington: University of Kentucky Press, 1966.

Newman, J. H. *The Idea of the University.* New York: Longmans, Green, 1947.

Walberg, H. J. "Can Educational Research Contribute to the Practice of Teaching?" *Journal of Education for Social Work* 4 (1968): 77-85.

Walberg, H. J. "Curriculum Evaluation: Some Problems and Guidelines." *Teachers' College Record* 71 (1970): 557-570.

9

TRANSACTIONAL EVALUATION IN A NATIONAL STUDY OF HEAD START

VICTOR G. CICIRELLI

Program evaluation used today is frequently classified into two broad types: summative and formative. Formative evaluation is conducted while the program is being carried out, it is continuous and diagnostic, concerned with improving the component parts of the program while it is developing, and is carried out by the original planners or operators of the program. Summative evaluation is conducted at the end of the program to determine whether program goals have been attained, it is concerned with the effects of the program as a whole, with comparisons with other programs or with some standard and with whether the program should be continued or modified, and is usually carried out by outside experts.

Evaluation is nearly always a threatening concept, particularly when it seems that the program may be changed or cut back as a result. Administrators and program personnel, along with outside supporters of the program, can become quite defensive if they expect any negative evaluation of their efforts. This defensiveness can provoke serious resistance when the evaluators are carrying out their study, when their findings are published, or their recommendations implemented. Many an evaluation has been relatively successful technically, but has produced no real change in the program because of such resistance.

The problem, generally ignored in the past, has more recently been recognized under the rubric, "transactional evaluation." Transactional evaluation is a process of program evaluation that involves individuals who support a program innovation as well as individuals who oppose the change, identifies and assesses the resistance to any possible change from those who would be affected by the change, and reduces the resistance of those who oppose the change by encouraging them to participate in the evaluation. Resistance may be identified and dealt with at each stage of the process of change: when a program innovation is set up, when the program is being evaluated, when the findings or results of the evaluation are accepted, and when further changes in the program are recommended.

Transactional evaluation resembles formative evaluation in its local scope and its concern for the continuous diagnosis and improvement of a developing program, but differs in that it involves a larger group of concerned individuals and accounts for the group's resistance to evaluation and change. Transactional evaluation thus may easily be applied to many situations in which formative evaluation is used.

Summative evaluation, particularly large-scale summative evaluation, seems to be less suited to the process of transactional evaluation. Although it is conceivable that a group might plan a formal summative evaluation when a program or change is instituted, it is rarely done. In the typical case, the government (or other institution) will begin a program innovation, and then decide, later, to conduct a summative evaluation of the program outcomes. The result is usually a retrospective summative study conducted by outside experts. Whatever the technical disagreement with this kind of study, there are compelling practical and political reasons for its continued use, reasons which have been ably presented by Evans (1969), and Evans and Schiller (1970).

Although program innovation will have been in effect for some time before a retrospective summative evaluation is begun, the evaluators will still be faced with resistance to their study, their findings, and their recommendations for change. Such resistance can come from administrators, staff, and program users at the local level, from government administrators of the program at the national level, and from "outside experts" who may be acting as consultants to the program at any level.

In this chapter I explore the question of whether transactional evaluation might profitably be applied to the problems inherent in a large national summative evaluation. My subject is the Westinghouse/ Ohio University evaluation of Head Start, an ex post facto summative evaluation of the effects of the program on children's cognitive and affective development.

WESTINGHOUSE/OHIO UNIVERSITY
NATIONAL EVALUATION OF HEAD START

Head Start was begun in the summer of 1965 as part of the Johnson administration's "War on Poverty," to remedy the disadvantages of poor children throughout the nation, and by 1967 about two million children had participated in the program.

In June, 1968, the Office of Economic Opportunity (OEO) contracted with the Westinghouse Learning Corporation and Ohio University to evaluate the success of the Head Start program. Most previous evaluations of Head Start had been carried out by the program's own Office of Research and Evaluation and its thirteen Evaluation and Research Centers in universities throughout the United States. While many studies reported gains in the children's performance while they were attending Head Start programs, few studies assessed longer-term outcomes and, in those that did, there was little evidence that the gains persisted into the elementary school years. Most previous studies were local or regional, and it was difficult to compare the separate and independent studies, owing to differences in design, instrumentation, schedules of testing, and so on. The Westinghouse/Ohio study (1969) was larger in scope than previous studies, in that it included a national sample, comparison groups of children who did not attend Head Start, multiple measures of cognitive and affective development, and an evaluation of effects up to the third-grade level.

Objectives of the Study
The basic question of the study was:

> Do children in the first, second, or third grade who have had Head Start experience, either summer or full year, differ significantly in their cognitive and affec-

tive development from comparable children, in those grades, who did not participate?

The study did not attempt to evaluate the medical, nutritional, or dental aspects of the program, nor the influence on the children's parents and the community. As important as these aspects are (and they were being evaluated in other studies), we felt that the basic thrust of the program was toward the improvement of the children's cognitive and affective development. Should the program not be fulfilling its basic aims, its other objectives might be attained more efficiently in other ways.

The study was limited in another way: it was intended only to determine the overall or average success of Head Start. Some centers and school systems might well have been more effective than others, but our purpose was not diagnostic—it was not to identify the better centers, or to recommend possible improvements in the program, or to determine relationships between gains in Head Start and earlier or later experiences. Our purpose was to obtain information that policy makers could use for their decisions: whether to continue to support the program as it was, to drop part of it, or to make a vigorous effort to modify the program, which would then involve further diagnostic studies. (The Westinghouse/Ohio study was only part of a larger OEO evaluation effort in which were planned a number of studies to assess other objectives.) Finally, because of the concern for overall assessment, the objective of the study was rigidly adhered to rather than modified during the study because the concern was with overall analysis (rather than subgroup analysis), and because of limitations of time and money.

The study was to assess what were felt to be essential common objectives of all Head Start programs rather than objectives unique to local implementations of Head Start. In the cognitive domain, improvements in language facility and school achievement were considered to be among the essential common objectives; in the affective domain, improved self-concept, more positive attitudes toward school and community, and increased desire to achieve were considered to be the essential common objectives of all Head Start programs.

Results of the Study

The major findings of the study were that summer Head Start programs were not effective, and that full-year Head Start programs were marginally effective. There was a statistically significant difference in favor of the Head Start children over the children in the control groups but the difference was too slight to have any practical relevance. The major recommendations were that the summer programs be phased out and that the full-year programs be continued and made more effective. The many detailed and minor findings and specific recommendations need not be mentioned here. The interested reader is referred to the report itself (Westinghouse 1969) or to a summary by Cicirelli (1969).

The Field Study

Many problems were encountered in the process of carrying out the field work, especially many logistics problems in managing a study in 104 far-flung communities. However, only problems of resistance to the study will be discussed here, with, we hope, enough descriptive background to enable the reader to place the problems in perspective.

Selecting the Sample of Head Start Centers. The Head Start centers included in the study were selected by a computer random sampling procedure from an OEO listing of 12,927 centers in operation in 1966/67. We communicated with the officials of selected centers by letter and by telephone to obtain their permission for carrying out the study and to insure that adequate records would be available. The permission of school officials in the target area was also sought so that we might carry out the testing phase of the study within the schools. In most cases, complete arrangements for the participation of a center (and its target area schools) in the study were made before field workers were sent to the area. In some cases, however, the inclusion of a center in the study was not confirmed until a field worker had actually been sent to the site. Of the 225 centers originally selected, 104 were ultimately confirmed, the remaining 121 investigated but subsequently excluded, twenty-eight of them after our first field visit. Of the 104 centers finally selected, six were in the New England area of the country, seven in Middle Atlantic, twenty-one in East North Central, twenty-three in South Atlantic, fifteen in East South Central, four in West North Central, five in Mountain, and twelve in the Pacific area. Fifty of the 121 centers we eliminated because we could not find enough children to meet the criteria for controls. Twenty-one centers originally considered were dropped because they had had Head Start programs for one year only. Eight centers were excluded because they lacked the staff for the summer phase of the program. Nineteen centers were dropped because the associated schools in the target area declined to participate in the study for various administrative or scheduling reasons. Their disinclination might be viewed as one form of resistance to the Head Start evaluation. Certainly some of them had valid reasons for not participating; others may simply have been defensive about the evaluation.

Problems of Field Interviewers. The recruitment and training of field interviewers was undertaken concurrently with the selection of centers to be included in the study. Fifty-five interviewers who had studied sociology, education, or related social sciences at college were given a week's intensive training. Spanish-speaking interviewers were assigned to certain areas; workers with diverse racial backgrounds to areas suiting their qualifications.

Once in a target area, the field interviewer first interviewed the Head Start official and secured a master list of pupils who had attended the center in the specified program and year. He then went to the local schools and identified all Head Start children still enrolled, to make the Head Start population list, from which he drew the required random samples at each of the grade levels represented. After selecting the Head Start samples, he consulted with Head Start and school officials and studied all available records to identify a control population. A sample of individual control subjects was drawn in random sequence and each Head Start subject was matched with a control subject on the basis of sex, race, and kindergarten attendance. After all the children who were to be included in the study were identified, and an oversample of two added to each category, the field worker interviewed the parent or guardian of each child. Before leaving a target area, he made tentative arrangements with school officials to test the pupils in the fall. Field operations were supervised primarily by telephone and by written reports, although some supervisory visits were made. Follow-up telephone calls were made to local officials and to parents participating in the study. At the end of the field operations all field reports were reviewed, and interviewers answered a questionnaire on their field experience.

The field interviewers dealt with three groups of people affected by the study: local Head Start officials, school administrators, and the parents of the children. Local Head Start officials offered no resistance to the study, even though we might have expected some resistance from them, since their own programs were under evaluation. They had already given permission by telephone for the study, and all of them cooperated with the field workers. The interview questionnaire was long and detailed, but field workers reported that center directors went to considerable lengths to provide accurate information. The only difficulty encountered was the occasional center that had poor records.

Similarly, school officials had already given permission for the study by telephone and most were highly cooperative. The field interviewers encountered ten local school systems that were uncooperative, and complied with the study only grudgingly, by being elusive, making the interviewers wait several days to gain access to the school records, and generally creating an unpleasant atmosphere for the field workers. In two cases, the field worker found himself in the middle of a feud between Head Start officials and the school administration. One school principal told his staff, "Don't cooperate any more than you have to." Other difficulties with the schools were minimal. Some schools kept poor enrollment records, but the cooperation and knowledgeability of the school administrators made it possible to establish a sample of children. In some places the school officials were highly sensitive to racial problems that might be stimulated by the field interviews or by the fact that only certain children were tested during the school year. Such situations required exceptional diplomacy of the field interviewer.

Parents of both Head Start and control children were quite cooperative. The parent interview questionnaire contained eighty-two items (plus a vocational aspirations instrument of between fifteen and eighteen items) and required about an hour to complete. Hardly any parent refused to be interviewed as most of them recognized that the interviewer was there on school business. After the interview the field worker rated the parent's cooperation on a five-point scale. Less than three percent of the parents were rated as "Uncooperative" (they were tense and defensive in answering questions) or "Very uncooperative" (they offered explicit resistance to the interview). Fifty-five percent were rated as "Very cooperative" (they were friendly and relaxed, volunteered information readily, and showed interest in the study), and another thirty-six percent were rated as "Cooperative" (they, too, were friendly and relaxed, and answered questions readily, but did not volunteer information beyond that requested). Six percent were rated as "Slightly uncooperative" (they answered questions readily, but may have shown some defensiveness, or maintained some distance from the interviewer).

While black interviewers were sent to centers known to serve mainly black children, Spanish-speaking interviewers to Mexican-American centers, and so on, nearly all interviewers met parents who were not of their own race. Some interviewers were apprehensive on the first of such interviews, but reported no problems. The most difficult interviews were reported to have been with some poor whites in the south and with some ultraconservatives in small towns in the midwest. The most serious problem the field workers had was to find the parents. Frequently the parents had moved and the schools did not have the right addresses. In some cities, urban renewal projects had wiped out entire blocks and streets. Rural areas were particularly difficult since there were often no addresses or road markers. (In Appalachia, one field worker searching for a parent was mistaken for a "revenue" agent and was shot at.)

The field workers spent approximately three and a half weeks at each of the two centers they visited. A substantial number of interviewers indicated that they felt isolated and lonely in their work, and suggested that more frequent communication with project headquarters might be helpful or, better still, that they be assigned in teams. In small towns, many field interviewers found it difficult to obtain suitable accommodations. Some field workers were greatly inconvenienced by the late arrival of paychecks and interview materials. On several occasions it was necessary to wire money to field workers. In spite of such problems, the field interviewers managed to select the required samples of children, complete the interviews with Head Start officials and parents, and make arrangements for testing children in the schools in the fall. It is a tribute to the field interviewers' work that the field examiners encountered few problems during the testing phase of the study.

In summary, resistance to the field study was not great. Head Start officials and parents were highly cooperative, and only a few schools raised obstacles for the field workers. The general cooperation may have been the result of the federal government's endorsement of the study, which might have generated a feeling that the community *should* participate in the evaluation if it were receiving federal Head Start funding. Thus, some defensivness or apprehension on the part of local people may have been masked or suppressed. There was no reason to believe, however, that the data collection was adversely influenced.

Reactions to the Recommendations

The findings of the study were given national publicity quite prematurely. A first draft, which excluded some alternative statistical analyses, was circulated to the OEO project officer and the board of consultants for their comments before a final draft was made. Political pressures from within the Nixon administration forced the preliminary draft to be released. White (1970) gives a good account of the political situation. As a result, local Head Start and school people and interested parents learned of the study's findings from the news media instead of from the researchers, who had planned to send them a summary of the study (which was, of course, mailed to them later).

While the project staff received no direct communication from the areas involved in the study, newspaper reports from various parts of the country indicated the reaction of localities, which, as it happened, were not included in the study. For example, in the Cincinnati *Dispatch*, 23 April 1969, we read:

> The study's findings resulted Tuesday night in a meeting attended by about one hundred parents of preschool age children who jammed the Community Action Council rooms in Cincinnati. They joined forces to voice dissent against the study which downgraded the present Head Start program.

In the Blytheville, Arkansas, *Courier News*, 15 April 1969:

> Head Start locally has been judged by school administrators, teachers and various OEO officials to have considerable merit. First grade teachers speak highly of Head Start and say they can pick the Head Start children out of the group.

In the *Suffolk Sun*, Deer Park, New York, 15 April 1969:

> John Reynolds, acting director of Suffolk Economic Opportunity Council, says he hopes Head Start aid will continue. Suffolk has 575 children enrolled in various centers. While no follow-up studies on Head Start have been made since the program began, "We do evaluate the program, but generally in terms of the staff. Comments from the communities where centers are in operation have been generally favorable."

In the *Easton Express*, Easton, Pennsylvania, 15 April 1969:

> Wakefield R. Roberts, executive director of the Lehigh Valley Community Action Committee, feels the committee's Head Start program has generally been effective.

In *Newsday*, Garden City, New York, 16 April 1969:

> Francine Shectman, like other Head Start officials, said she was "deeply distressed" by the survey . . .

The survey was based on only a small percentage of centers and took into consideration only academic progress, she said . . .

Her Head Start graduates are "adjusting well" to public school, Mrs. Shectman said . . . "Teachers can pick out the ones who have had Head Start experience without our telling them," she said. "Maybe they're not all No. 1 in the class, but academe is not the only thing we deal with here. How do you measure the progress of a child who comes to us droopy and lethargic and enters school bright-eyed and ready to learn?"

And, in an editorial in the Battle Creek, Michigan, *Enquirer and News,* 16 April 1969:

Mrs. Thelma Robinson, director of the Calhoun Community Action Agency cites Head Start shortcomings, but finds hope in "the beginnings of a good parent participation program." Stephen Glaza, superintendent of the Calhoun County Intermediate School District, which operates a separate Head Start program, said: "We think our program has had a real positive effect on the children."

How are such local appraisals to be reconciled with the new federal report? They can't be entirely, because they are informal evaluations compared with the OEO-purchased study. But they are typical of the responses which President Nixon and Congress must consider as they decide where to go from here.

As is evident, the essentially negative findings of the study provoked local testimonials to the merits of the program. Like the parents interviewed in the study (of whom between eighty-five and ninety percent felt that their children had definitely benefitted from Head Start) local Head Start officials and school people generally felt that the children had gained in some way from the program. Most of the statements we read suggested that no formal evaluation or follow-up of children in the local programs had been done, and that the expressions of satisfaction with the program were based on other grounds.

Reaction from "experts" in child development was swift and predictably critical, predictable because the negative findings of the study threatened the cherished views of many in the "early intervention" camp. Their views were expressed in statements to the press, in letters and formal criticisms addressed to the OEO and other government agencies, and in papers in scholarly literature. These criticisms seemed to fall into three major areas: criticisms of our methodology and statistics, of our selection of the program outcomes to be evaluated, and of the scope of the evaluation. As most of the methodological and statistical criticisms were related to the fact that the study was retrospective, they will not be considered here. The interested reader is referred to Madow (1969), Smith and Bissell (1970), Campbell and Erlebacher (1970), and White (1970) for some of the criticisms. McDill, McDill and Sprehe (1969) review many of the criticisms that were made and conclude:

> To summarize, although the Westinghouse study has all the defects inherent in nonexperimental research, it is by far the most rigorous national assessment of Head Start which has been undertaken since the program's inception. In closing this discussion, we would like to pose a question: would this study have been subjected to such strong criticism from so many quarters had it shown an overall positive effect rather than essentially no effect? It is our opinion that some social researchers, educators, and program administrators have become so involved personally in social action programs that they are unable to accept the apparent failure of many of them as a challenge, and to modify them in the hope of obtaining better results in the future. Instead, many such people have a tendency to take a defensive stance and to express the fear that [the] federal government is going to "shut up shop." (p. 27)

One of the expressed limitations of the study was that it would investigate mainly the cognitive and affective aspects of the children's development because these aspects were the most important objectives of the Head Start program. Nevertheless, many critics felt that other aspects of Head Start should have been included in the evaluation, and that inferences that applied to the entire program should not have been made on the basis of the cognitive and affective results alone.

For example, Robert Finch, secretary of the Health, Education and Welfare Department, was quoted in the *New York Times*, 25 April 1969, as saying that the study should include "aspects of voluntary parental involvement and nutritional benefits." Smith and Bissell (1970) say:

> Although summer Head Start programs are well known to have beneficial effects on children's medical and nutritional status, there is little reason, in view of their short duration, to expect them to have significant impact on children's cognitive performance (p. 79).

and, in the same paper:

> As a result, we find it difficult to believe that "overall" policy decisions about increasing, decreasing, or removing funds from Head Start can be justified on the basis of a study that focused only on childrens' performance on a few cognitive and affective tests (p. 102).

In a program as widespread as Head Start, it is difficult indeed to reach a consensus about which outcomes should be evaluated. According to Mendelsohn (1970), the real test of Head Start's success would be the extent to which the family had been lifted out of poverty as a result of the Head Start experience, measured in terms of their income before and after their participation, and when compared to families in control groups.

The overall scope of the evaluation provoked the third major flood of misunderstanding and disagreement. The study was primarily to determine the effects of the program across the nation. Admittedly, the quality of local programs differed greatly, but it was felt that some estimate was needed of just how effective the programs were "on the average," that is, just how effective a mass implementation could be. Many critics felt that such an overall evaluation should not have even been attempted, and that Head Start should be judged only on the basis of what its highest quality programs could accomplish, or what programs could accomplish with specific types of children.

From the reactions quoted above, the reader can gain some appreciation of the resistance to the results and recommendations of the study. More specifically, certain government officials felt threatened by the results because they might lose their funds, certain experts in child development felt threatened by results that contradicted their beliefs and commitments, parents felt threatened because the results indicated little improvement in their children, and local Head Start administrators, personnel, and parents all felt threatened by the recommendation to phase out the summer Head Start programs.

APPLICATIONS OF TRANSACTIONAL EVALUATION

Most of the controversy surrounding the Westinghouse/Ohio evaluation of Head Start has long since died away. In retrospect, we might examine the question of whether the principles of transactional evaluation could have been applied to reduce some of the misunderstanding and conflict surrounding the study. Because the evaluation was initiated long after the program had begun, we cannot be concerned with the resistance in terms of program innovation, only with the resistance to the study itself and its results and recommendations.

The size of the study and the fact that it was carried out in 104 communities across the nation would make direct participation of all the people concerned with the evaluation a formidable if not impossible task. However, during the planning stages of the evaluation, it would have been possible to obtain from regional samples of Head Start officials and school administrators, their views on what should be considered in the evaluation and what implications the evaluation might have for their own positions. Later, when the data had been analyzed, the same group might have met to consider the implications of the findings.

Although the pressures of time made it impossible to recruit local personnel for the Westinghouse/Ohio study, a local research coordinator might have been able to deal more effectively with the resistance of local school staff to the study. More important, a local coordinator might have served as a link between the project headquarters staff and the local people. (Communication with local Head Start and school officials throughout the study should have been improved. Even though letters and telephone communications reached the top administrator in the local Head Start center or school system, field workers often found that other local people knew very little of the study.) Efforts to include local people in the evaluation would, of course, have been expensive, and the cost would have to have been weighed against the benefits to the evaluation and to the program.

On the national level, some effort was made to take the views of recognized experts into account through the use of consultants, consultants on the OEO's board and consultants employed by the project staff. However, the project staff tended to use consultants to help them to solve specific problems in carrying out the study rather than to deal with broader issues, and the OEO board of consultants was called in only sporadically during the investigation. Also, the process of gaining consultants' views on the results and recommendations of the study was cut short by its premature release. While not all of the consultants agreed with the evaluation, there was certainly no effort to select a group of experts with diverse views (antagonists as well as protagonists), or actively to include government officials, although to some extent, the OEO's evaluation division took on the latter function. The study might well have been improved by the opinions of a diverse group of consultants both in the planning stages of the study and, periodically, during its implementation. Thus some modifications of the study might have been introduced to satisfy some of the objections. Such a procedure would surely have been quite time-consuming and would have added substantially to the cost of the evaluation. It has been suggested that it would have been extremely difficult, if not impossible, to get such a group of experts to agree sufficiently ever to plan an evaluation study acceptable to all, or to agree on its implications when complete. Whether the benefits (a possible reduction of resistance to the study) would have been worth the increased cost is debatable. However, the approach was not tried.

Transactional Evaluation in Summative Studies

A summative evaluation may be made more effective and more acceptable if the following principles of transactional evaluation are taken into account:

1. The groups that might feel threatened or be adversely affected by the evaluation and thus resist it should be identified.

2. This resistance should be reduced by getting these groups, or representative samples of them, involved in the evaluation (this participation will include their assessing the reasons for their own resistance), beginning in the planning stages of the study and continuing through the actual evaluation and the consideration of results. There should be opportunity for modification of the evaluation procedures, based on the input of the various groups.

3. "Outside" evaluation experts should have some kind of veto power to insure that the study is objective and that it does not get stalled in interminable discussion, although the various interest groups should have their views heard during the evaluation process, rather than being restricted to expressing their outrage in the public media once the results have appeared.

If a summative study affects the decision of whether or not to continue funding a program, any evaluation will be threatening. It appears, however, that the contribution of transactional evaluation to the summative study would minimize the threat by recognizing it and accounting for the views of those involved.

REFERENCES

Campbell, D. T., and Erlebacher, A. "How Regression Artifacts in Quasi-Experimental Evaluations Can Mistakenly Make Compensatory Education Look Harmful." In *Disadvantaged Child,* 3 vols, edited by J. H. Hellmuth, pp. 185-210. New York: Brunner/Mazel, 1970.

Cicirelli, V. G. "Project Head Start, a National Evaluation: Brief of the Study." In *The Britannica Review of American Education,* 1, edited by D. G. Hays, pp. 235-243. Chicago: Encyclopaedia Britannica, 1969.

Evans, J. "Evaluating Social Action Programs." *Social Science Quarterly* (December 1969): 568-581.

Evans, J., and Schiller, J. "How Preoccupation with Possible Regression Artifacts Can Lead to a Faulty Strategy for the Evaluation of Social Action Programs: A Reply to Campbell and Erlebacher." In *Disadvantaged Child,* 3 vols, edited by J. H. Hellmuth, pp. 216-225. New York: Brunner/Mazel, 1970.

Madow, W. "Project Head Start, a National Evaluation: Methodological Critique." In *The Britannica Review of American Education,* 1, edited by D. G. Hays, pp. 245-260. Chicago: Encyclopaedia Britannica, 1969.

McDill, E. L., McDill, M. S., and Sprehe, J. T. *Strategies for Success in Compensatory Education.* Baltimore: Johns Hopkins, 1969.

Mendelsohn, R. "Is Head Start a Success or Failure?" In *Disadvantaged Child,* 3 vols, edited by J. H. Hellmuth, pp. 445-454. New York: Brunner/Mazel, 1970.

Smith, M. S., and Bissell, J. S. "Report Analysis: The Impact of Head Start." *Harvard Education Review* 40, no. 1 (February 1970): 51-104.

Westinghouse Learning Corporation, and Ohio University. *The Impact of Head Start: An Evaluation of the Effects of Head Start on Children's Cognitive and Affective Development.* 2 vols. Springfield, Va.: U.S. Department of Commerce, Clearinghouse for Federal Scientific and Technical Information, 1969.

White, S. H. "The National Impact Study of Head Start." In *Disadvantaged Child,* 3 vols, edited by J. H. Hellmuth, pp. 163-184. New York: Brunner/Mazel, 1970.

10

STRATEGIES
FOR EVALUATING
FOLLOW THROUGH

W. RAY RHINE

Follow Through is a comprehensive longitudinal education program of service, social action, research, and development. Poor children in kindergarten and the first three grades are offered instructional, medical, dental, nutritional, and psychological services. As a social action program, Follow Through encourages the development of new models of cooperation and decision making among the school, the family, and the community. The research and development component of Follow Through is an attempt to evaluate the effectiveness of several approaches to the improvement of educational opportunities for poor children.

Follow Through is a response to the consistent finding that the benefits of preschool education programs such as Head Start tend to disappear when children enroll in regular schools. The Follow Through instructional programs are experimental efforts to preserve and strengthen the advantages of preschool education (Maccoby and

Zellner 1970). The program is an escalation of the attempt to break the link between poverty and failure in school, but the results of the Follow Through explorations may significantly improve educational opportunities for all children.

Follow Through began, as a pilot program during the 1967/68 school year, with approximately five thousand pupils enrolled in forty community projects. The program had grown by the 1971/72 school year to include one hundred thousand pupils enrolled in 170 projects in fifty states, the District of Columbia and Puerto Rico. Most projects operate in the inner-city neighborhoods of large metropolitan areas, the rural south, Appalachia, and Indian reservations. Ethnic minority pupils comprise approximately two-thirds of the Follow Through population.

Funded under the Economic Opportunity Act (EOA) and Title I of the Elementary and Secondary Education Act (ESEA), Follow Through is administered by the Office of Education (OE) under the terms of a "Memorandum of Understanding" with the Office of Economic Opportunity (OEO). In 1964, the Economic Opportunity Act and its amendments provided for a broad range of programs designed "to mobilize the human and financial resources of the nation to combat poverty in the United States (Public Law 88-452, 1964)." In 1967, Congress amended the Economic Opportunity Act (Public Law 90-22, 1967, Section 222[a]) to establish

> a program to be known as Follow Through focused primarily on the children in kindergarten or elementary school who were previously enrolled in Head Start or similar programs and designed to provide comprehensive services and parent participation activities ... which the Director finds will aid in the continued development of children in their full potential.

Between December 1967 and February 1968, the Office of Education convened a series of meetings to develop and refine the pilot program. The consensus of these meetings was that Follow Through should combine both education and social action in a program of research and development implemented through the public schools. The most important educational objective was to study a variety of approaches to the education and development of young children through a strategy of "planned variation." The plan was to select several dissimilar approaches differing in educational philosophy, teaching techniques, and instructional goals. The social action objective was to change the interaction between the school and the community by increasing the parents' participation and influence in their children's education. Each participating community was to have a Policy Advisory Committee of the parents of Follow Through pupils and members of community groups interested in education. Section 222 (a) (2) of the amended Economic Opportunity Act provided for "direct participation of the parents ... in the development, conduct and overall program direction at the local level." The community action goals of Follow Through were further emphasized by the requirement that local health, welfare, and social service agencies funded by OEO be consulted in the development and operation of local programs (U.S. Office of Education 1969).

The Office of Education invited groups that had done significant work in educating young children to submit descriptions of programs that they proposed to implement in local school districts. Some groups responded enthusiastically to the "planned variation" strategy, but others were reluctant to participate in a "horse race" conducted to pick a winner in the field of early childhood education. There was also some concern about the actual control of the program at the local level. The Follow Through director assured the groups that the evaluation would benefit the development of their programs and that each project would have ample time for such development. He also indicated that the summative evaluation would be directed more toward an identification of the strengths and weaknesses of each approach rather than toward comparisons between programs. He pointed out that the "planned variation" strategy required that the sponsor maintain a high degree of control over his program to ensure that it was implemented consistently in each community.

When the prospective sponsors were convinced that the Office of Education would attempt to protect their interests, they agreed to participate in Follow Through. Several colleges, universities, regional education laboratories, and research and development centers submitted proposals. Thirteen sponsors were selected to begin programs in the 1968/69 school year (U.S. Office of Education 1969/70):
1. Bank Street College of Education; Elizabeth Gilkeson
   Bank Street College of Education Approach
2. University of Kansas, Department of Human Development; Donald Bushell, Jr.
   Behavior Analysis Approach
3. Eastern Michigan University; David Weikart
   Cognitively Oriented Curriculum Model
4. Education Development Center, Newton, Mass.; David Armington
   Education Development Center Approach

5. University of Florida, Institute for Development of Human Resources; Ira Gordon
   Florida Parent Education Model
6. University of Pittsburgh, Learning Research and Development Center; Lauren Resnick
   Individually Prescribed Instruction
7. New Jersey State Education Department; Lassar Gotkin
   Interdependent Learner Model
8. Southwest Educational Development Laboratory, Austin, Texas; Elizabeth Ott
   Language Development—Bilingual Education Approach
9. Far West Laboratory for Educational Research and Development, Berkeley, California; Glen Nimnicht
   Responsive Environment Approach
10. University of Illinois; Siegfried Engelmann and Wesley Becker
    Systematic Use of Behavioral Principles Program
11. George Peabody College; Rosemary Giesy
    The DARCEE Approach
12. University of Arizona, Early Childhood Education Laboratory; Ronald Henderson
    Tucson Early Education Model
13. University of Georgia, Research and Development Center in Educational Stimulation; Robert Aaron
    The University of Georgia Approach

The communities participating in Follow Through were nominated by state education agencies and the state technical assistance offices of the Office of Economic Opportunity. In a meeting arranged by the Office of Education, the sponsors described their program models to community representatives. After each community had selected a model, the sponsor negotiated an agreement with the Office of Education and the local board of education to implement his program. The sponsor and his staff developed a working relationship with the community, trained teachers, procured materials, and selected pupils. The Follow Through guidelines required that forty percent of the total participating pupils be residents of rural counties. The number of pupils for each region of the country was determined by the OEO "poverty index."

Because Follow Through is an expensive sociocultural experiment, the public is interested in its accomplishments. The total cost of implementing the program through the one-year pilot phase and the five-year development phase has been approximately $300 million. The cost of enrolling a single pupil in Follow Through from kindergarten through third grade is approximately $4,000, or $1,000 for each school year. When Follow Through reaches the dissemination phase in 1973, the approaches evaluated as successful are likely to be applied in considerably more communities.

The experimental character of the program and the interest in public accountability resulted in a substantial investment in program evaluation. The Associate Commissioner of Education, Lewis Butler, stated, July 1969, "We must take every precaution to insure that we are not open to criticism with respect to the management as well as the substance of the evaluation of this complex experimental program." He said that the Follow Through evaluation was the most costly single evaluation study ever sponsored by the Office of Education; in fact, the allocation of $2 million in fiscal 1970 was larger than the total amount allocated for evaluation of all Office of Education programs in fiscal 1969. In fiscal 1971 the allocation for evaluation and the final report increased to $6 million.

PLANNING THE EVALUATION

Evaluation was conducted on a relatively small scale during the first-year pilot phase in 1967/68. Achievement tests were mailed to local school districts, and teachers administered the tests. So much confusion occurred in the classrooms that several school districts refused to allow teachers to collect any more data. In some communities teachers' unions declared that teachers should not be requested to perform as testers. Several other problems were encountered in reducing and analyzing the data. The evaluation effort for the first year was judged a failure.

The decision to move Follow Through from a pilot program to a national longitudinal program required major changes in the approach to evaluation. The total evaluation plan for the 1968/69 school year consisted of four phases: (1) The Stanford Research Institute (SRI) was selected to conduct the longitudinal evaluation; (2) Bio-Dynamics, Inc., was chosen to evaluate health services, and the NTL Institute for Applied Behavioral Science agreed to study, in a few communities, the relationships between Follow Through projects and local school districts; (3) several sponsors were to evaluate their own programs; and (4) several school districts were to assess program effects against local objectives.

In the summer of 1968, the Follow Through director clarified the purpose of the longitudinal evaluation. He emphasized that Follow

Through would ultimately be judged on the sponsors' success in changing the behavior of poor children to improve their academic performance. His pupil change model assumed that the deprived socialization of poor children prevented them from benefitting from regular education programs. As a compensatory education program, Follow Through was to provide these children with the cognitive skills and values they required to reach white, middle-class performance standards. The five-year longitudinal evaluation was to consist of formative and summative stages (Scriven 1967; Bloom, Hastings, and Madaus 1971). The formative stage, scheduled to extend for four years, until the first cohort of kindergarten students completed third grade, was to assist sponsors to develop instructional techniques and to clarify objectives. Specifically, the formative evaluation was to collect data to describe the entry, or baseline, capabilities of pupils in Follow Through and comparison classrooms; to provide evidence to assess the academic progress of Follow Through and comparison pupils at each successive grade level; to obtain a set of sponsors' instructional objectives for each program; and to design data collection procedures that would distract the pupils as little as possible from learning. Summative evaluation in the fifth year was to assess the strengths and weaknesses of each sponsor's approach, and select those approaches best suited for wider use.

In the summer of 1968, the SRI staff began to formulate an evaluation framework by studying the Follow Through guidelines, interviewing sponsors, and analyzing program descriptions. The Follow Through guidelines were not very useful for identifying instructional goals or evaluation instruments. Written in the rhetoric of compromise, the guidelines resembled the platform of a political party. They indicated general educational goals that had received enthusiastic support from stakeholders who differed sharply on specific instructional objectives. Analysis of the sponsors' materials indicated that specific instructional objectives and evaluation criteria had been formulated for only a few programs. Most sponsors were reluctant to define evaluation criteria lest their freedom to clarify program objectives over the years be restricted. Several sponsors indicated that data from standardized academic aptitude and achievement tests would assist them develop their programs but doubted that such instruments would be satisfactory for the summative evaluation.

The SRI evaluation strategy was similar to that advocated by Cronbach (1963). He held that the summative evaluation criteria for education programs should include both the limited group of instructional objectives stated in a particular curriculum and the larger group of instructional objectives advocated in other similar education programs. A longitudinal evaluation that identified the universe of sponsors' instructional objectives had several advantages for both the formative and summative phases: stated instructional objectives could be compared with observed outcomes; unintended project effects, or incidental learning, could be evaluated to determine whether pupils possessed information and skills not specified by the sponsor; a sponsor could compare his objectives with those of other sponsors; and the evaluation framework could be expanded to embrace objectives added later.

The cooperative effort to determine the evaluation criteria began by the selection of a pool of standardized achievement test items that appeared consistent with the sponsors' objectives. Tests composed of items drawn from the pool would describe the Follow Through and comparison pupils on currently accepted evaluation criteria. Each sponsor was requested to rate each test item according to its suitability for measuring the outcomes of his approach. Items endorsed by one or more sponsors would be retained; items endorsed by no sponsors would be discarded. SRI invited sponsors to recommend additional items and procedures for evaluating their own programs as they clarified their objectives. In this manner each item in the evaluation pool would reflect a program objective stated by one or more sponsors.

Evaluation Design and Data Collection

In the 1968/69 school year Follow Through pupils were enrolled in 780 classrooms in 334 schools in ninety communities. Evaluation data were collected in a sample of 137 kindergarten and first grade classrooms and in sixty-six comparison classrooms that were not included in the Follow Through program. The sample included one district or school considered by each sponsor to be an exemplar of his approach and excluded those that sponsors considered unsuitable for evaluation. Follow Through communities that also had comparison schools and classrooms were preferred. Most sponsors were represented by two, three, or four school districts. Wherever possible, data were collected in two schools in each district and two classrooms in each school. The children's achievement and aptitude were measured. A basic survey of language and number skills was made in the fall of 1968 and again in the spring of 1969. A supplementary test, consisting of items recommended by the sponsors, was administered in the spring of 1969. The short form of the Stanford-Binet test was administered at midyear.

The basic survey covered the educational objectives that all sponsors were promoting. The instrument was constructed by including items from a number of tests: the Lee-Clark Reading Readiness Test, the Metropolitan Readiness Test, the Caldwell-Soule Preschool Inventory, and six tests (Premathematics, Prescience, Prepositions, Shape Names, Alphabet, and Numerals) developed, in the Early Childhood Inventory project, by the Institute for Developmental Studies, New York University. Item-sampling and pupil-sampling were employed to obtain a profile for each classroom without requiring excessive testing for any one child. Three samples, identified as the A, B, and C forms, were drawn from the aggregate pool of 334 items. The items in each sample were distributed in five test booklets. Pupils were randomly assigned to take the various tests. A team, consisting of the tester and two or three aides, administered the test booklets to groups of between five and seven pupils at a time. Testing sessions were conducted outside the classroom to minimize the disturbance. Approximately seventy-five local testers were trained.

The supplementary test consisted of items that sponsors recommended for evaluating their own programs. The items were classified by content and sorted into one group suitable for administration to pupils, or another group better suited for use either in a classroom observation scale or in interviews with parents and teachers. Items in the first group were discarded if they were too similar to items in the basic survey, if they required elaborate materials that could not be conveniently reproduced or transported, or if they could be administered only by professionally trained testers. After the remaining items were classified by sponsor and content, they were randomly allocated to the A, B, and C forms, or samples, with the items in each sample distributed in two test booklets. An advantage of the supplementary test was that it could be expanded to include program objectives not accounted for in the basic survey.

The short form of the Stanford-Binet test was administered to a subsample of 820 pupils selected from the sample that had been tested in the fall: one classroom was randomly selected from each school and six pupils were randomly selected from each classroom, two each from the A, B, and C groups of the original basic survey sample. The Binet was chosen because several sponsors had considered it to be a useful criterion for estimating the effectiveness of their programs. Spokesmen for the ethnic minorities have charged that the Binet is culturally biased and inappropriate for ethnic minority children, but its usefulness as a differential predictor of program effects was considered important. The Binet scores, used as covariates with scores on other measures, would be useful for classifying pupils in several analyses.

CRITICISM OF FOLLOW THROUGH

The Follow Through director frequently convened meetings to review and plan policy to insure that Follow Through was relevant and responsive to changing circumstances. Most of the meetings were conducted at the Office of Education in Washington, D.C., or at the SRI International Headquarters offices in Menlo Park, California. Participants in these meetings included program sponsors, representatives of ethnic minorities, behavioral science research consultants, and SRI staff. The consulting researchers included Eleanor Maccoby and Robert Hess from Stanford University, Jerome Kagan from Harvard University, Urie Bronfenbrenner from Cornell University, Halbert Robinson from the University of Washington, and Raymond Mack from Northwestern University.

The array of Follow Through goals created several groups of stakeholders, each with distinctive interests and objectives. Consequently, the discussions of the program and its evaluation often evoked strong feelings, criticism, and confrontations as the stakeholders competed for control and funding. They disagreed on many issues such as the definition of Follow Through goals, the criteria acceptable for evaluation, and the representation of their own interests in the selection of those criteria. Much of the criticism came from two sources. Representatives of ethnic minorities contended that the Follow Through director was not conducting the program according to the guidelines. Some sponsors and consultants complained that the evaluation emphasized the outcome measures of academic achievement excessively and failed to measure classroom environment and the noncognitive characteristics of the children.

Ethnic Minority Criticism and Recommendations

Representatives of ethnic minorities first expressed their concerns in the policy review and planning session convened in Atlanta in November 1968. A general criticism was that the program was insensitive to their communities, parents, and children. They contended that the absence of ethnic minority senior professionals on the director's staff, among the sponsors, and among the evaluation group was inconsistent and intolerable because two-thirds of the children in Follow Through were from ethnic minority groups. They disputed the director's statement that the educational needs of ethnic minority children could be met simply by improving their reading and arithmetic skills, and insisted that the needs be discussed within the broader context of social justice and the control of the institutions that affect their lives.

The program was also criticized for dispensing compensatory education to culturally deprived children when the guidelines had promised innovative approaches to the education of ethnic minority children. The cultural deprivation hypothesis and compensatory education were attacked as contemporary manifestations of the "melting pot" philosophy and the historic aim of American education to anglicize the ethnic minorities. Having inspected Follow Through projects, these spokesmen concluded that the sponsors had accepted the traditional view that the history and culture of ethnic minorities were inferior and to be excluded from the curriculum. They urged that Follow Through provide an alternative to compensatory education and insisted that the program recognize that ethnic minority children were culturally different, not culturally deprived. A philosophy of cultural democracy should replace the melting pot philosophy: ethnic minority children should be educated to live in a multicultural society rather than merely to fit into the dominant Anglo society.

The third criticism was that a pupil change model was not appropriate for evaluating Follow Through. The disappointing results of efforts to improve the academic performance of ethnic minority children were usually attributed to their inferior learning ability. The correct conclusion, it was held, was that American education had failed to meet the educational needs of these children, and the spokesmen feared that "failure" in Follow Through would provide fertile grounds for renewed charges of racial inferiority. They recommended that a social system change model replace the pupil change model to guide both the implementation and evaluation of Follow Through projects. The evaluation should specify and measure the institutional changes necessary to produce the changes in pupils that the community desired, such as an increase in the parents' participation in decisions on curriculum and staffing. The measurement of the pupils' performance should have a low priority, particularly if conventional instruments are to be used. Evaluation instruments such as the Stanford-Binet test, or other aptitude and achievement tests that have been standardized for middle-class white populations should not, they felt, be used to evaluate program outcomes. New instruments to reflect appropriate educational goals for ethnic minority pupils should be constructed.

The fourth criticism from the ethnic minority spokesmen was that, in many communities, the school officials ignored the assurance made in the guidelines that the parents would participate in the selection, implementation, and evaluation of the programs. The parent advisory committees seldom had a power to make decisions consistent with the guideline promise of "direct participation of the parents . . . in the development, conduct, and overall program direction at the local level." It was held that the "planned variation" strategy controlled by white sponsors represented an approach to human service characterized by the attitudes of noblesse oblige usually associated with the plantation. The spokesmen recommended that Follow Through sponsors be directly accountable to the communities they served. Direct funding would ensure that local communities had effective decision-making power over curriculum and staff. As employees of the community, rather than of the Office of Education, the sponsors would help the community to articulate its educational needs and to develop appropriate answers. The schools would respect and reinforce the cultural heritage and identity of the pupils; pupils would improve their academic performance.

Demands for direct funding and community control of local Follow Through projects posed a dilemma for the director. If the requests were denied, parents could refuse to allow their children to participate. But local control of the projects would invalidate the plan to test the effectiveness of a number of approaches to the education of young children. The strategy of "planned variation" required that a sponsor's approach be implemented consistently in several communities. The essential characteristics of the procedures were supposed to be the same, whether conducted in a small rural community or in the ghetto of a metropolitan area. Local control of each project would probably result in as many different approaches as there were communities.

Other Criticism and Recommendations

The sponsors and consultants generally agreed that it was important to offer individual classroom instruction for poor children, but they disagreed on how to implement the curriculum. The group advocating "social reinforcement" approaches contended that the critical educational needs of poor children required more effective methods of teaching basic language and number skills. They advocated that a highly structured curriculum be taught to each pupil at his own rate of learning, and a variety of verbal and token reinforcement systems be used to motivate the child to learn. A basic assumption of this approach was that the mastery of academic subjects would strengthen the children's self-concepts and self-esteem, giving them positive attitudes toward school attendance and learning. The social reinforcement group, believing that educational evaluation should diagnose learning difficulties and prescribe effective teaching methods, favored emphasizing academic achievement criteria in a longitudinal evaluation of Follow Through.

The other group of consultants and sponsors contended that poor children fail in school because they are alienated from the traditional techniques and goals of classroom learning. Influenced by cognitive field theory and humanist concerns, this group contended that basic skills cannot be taught effectively unless the children feel secure and confident in the classroom and develop a positive attitude toward learning. The group aimed to develop a new curriculum that stressed both the personal and academic development of poor children. They opposed a highly structured curriculum that provided the same sequence of learning experiences for each pupil; they favored an individual model of instruction that would attempt to capitalize on the particular interests and needs of each pupil and adapt the curriculum to him. They believed that this teaching approach was better suited to their intention of providing responsive learning environments where each pupil could select the learning experiences that interested him, learn from his peers, and learn by discovery. Accordingly, the evaluation plan must encompass methods for measuring differences in both learning environments and academic achievement. The evaluation for the humanist approach should also include measures of the children's personal and social development. Since positive changes in self-concept, self-esteem, and curiosity were likely to improve classroom learning, the group felt, appropriate instruments for measuring these changes should be included in the evaluation plan. They cited the guidelines that clearly stated that Follow Through programs should "serve not only the educational needs of poor children but [also] their physical, social, and psychological needs."

NEW DIRECTIONS IN FOLLOW THROUGH

To accommodate the pressures for change in Follow Through, the director authorized major modifications in both the implementation and evaluation of the program for the 1969/70 school year. Three important structural changes were made in the summer of 1969: several educators who were members of ethnic minorities were invited to become Follow Through sponsors; funding for the measurement of institutional change was increased, for the measurement of pupil change decreased; and the evaluation criteria were expanded to include measures of classroom environments and noncognitive characteristics of the children.

Ethnic Minority Sponsors

Several ethnic minority sponsors were invited to implement their educational programs in the fall of 1969. The sponsors were selected because their approaches embodied educational goals and procedures advocated by ethnic minority parents and their representatives (U.S. Office of Education 1970/71).

The Parent Implementation Approach.   Sponsored by AFRAM Associates, Inc., in New York City, the parent implementation approach encourages parents and other residents of the community to become more active and influential in making decisions on how the schools can best educate their children. The participation of parents is an integral part of the educational process, not merely supplemental. In the classroom parents, as teacher aides, could encourage the children in their learning and thereby strengthen their own influence on the educational process. Parents, paid and/or voluntary, could become foster teachers, community educators, and peer-learners with other parents. Through their own participation parents could learn how to contribute to the education of their children by helping the teachers to understand and respond to the children's needs and by helping the children with their homework. As participants, parents would have more information about the school and be better qualified to influence education decision making.

The Language Development/Bilingual Education Approach.   Sponsored by the Southwest Educational Development Laboratory in Austin, Texas, the language development/bilingual education approach aims to improve the quality of education for poor children whose native language is not English. The major goals are to enhance the child's image of himself as a successful learner and to prepare him better to participate in the English-speaking culture. The program teaches Spanish-speaking children mathematics, science, and social studies in their native language while they are learning English as a second language. A basic assumption is that a child will find it easier to learn a second language if he first learns content materials in his native language. The goal is to teach children to speak, read, and write equally competently in both Spanish and English. Curriculum materials are designed to relate to the child's background and experience; teachers and school staff study the child's cultural heritage. The program encourages parent and community involvement in education to create more effective communication between the home environment and the classroom.

The Home/School Partnership. A motivational approach, sponsored by Southern University in Baton Rouge, Louisiana, the home/school partnership enlists parents as partners with their children and the schools in the learning process. The intention is to strengthen instructional opportunities at home. Parents are encouraged to participate in cultural and extracurricular activities with their children. An important program objective is the improvement of the parents' academic and job skills by regularly scheduled adult education classes. The parent-aide program trains parents to be home teachers and to conduct interviews with other parents. Home teachers help parents to develop the teaching skills that will enable them to continue their children's education at home. Home teachers may also work as classroom aides. Parent interviewers visit homes to obtain information on the health and general welfare of the children, as well as the parents' views on the effectiveness of the instructional program.

The Cultural-Linguistic Approach. Sponsored by the Center for Inner-City Studies, Northeastern Illinois State College, the cultural-linguistic approach is an oral language program that presents a curriculum based on the child's own culture and language. The child's patterns of thought and his educational gains achieved in an English dialect, or in another language, are used to improve his reading, writing, and problem-solving skills in English. The sponsor trains the school staff to improve their understanding of and communication with ethnic minority children and parents. Parents are taught methods for reinforcing the child's classroom learning at home and techniques for organizing parent groups to work effectively with and for Follow Through.

Measurement of Institutional Change

The emphasis on measuring institutional change was a response to demands from the ethnic minorities for an alternative to the pupil change model for evaluation. The effectiveness of Follow Through in changing institutional relationships was investigated in community studies, interviews with parents, and questionnaires for teachers and classroom aides.

Community studies were made to investigate and evaluate the impact of Follow Through on the overall pattern of relationships among parents, teachers, administrators, pupils, the general community, and various community agencies. The case study approach was adopted to obtain a better understanding of what was really happening in several communities. The method was expected to stimulate hypotheses about the nature of the change that Follow Through induced in local communities. The studies also promised to provide historical, social, and demographic information so that particular changes might be interpreted with greater confidence. Primarily patterns of communication, information exchange, and the power relationships among schools, parents, and local boards of education were assessed. Some stakeholders viewed Follow Through as an innovative social subsystem introduced into the community to instigate change and redistribute power in the relationships between parents and local school boards, between parents and the school staff, between teachers and school administrators, and between pupils and teachers.

Interviews with parents served two purposes: they identified changes in attitude, belief, and behavior resulting from the Follow Through program, and they provided demographic information and descriptions of home circumstances so that pupil and parent groups might be more precisely categorized for the analyses of the change stimulated by the program. Developed jointly by the Office of Education, the Stanford Research Institute, the National Opinion Research Center, and their consultants, the interview questions were formulated to assess a broad range of knowledge, behavior, and attitude. Some questions explored the parents' knowledge of Follow Through, the frequency of their contacts with school programs and staff, and the extent of their participation in decisions made by the District Board of Education and the local school. Other questions assessed the parents' perceptions of their chances of influencing change in their own lives or in the schools, their aspirations for their children's education and careers, the learning opportunities that their homes provided for the children, and the degree to which parents encouraged the children to participate in the school's education program. During the 1969/70 school year, the National Opinion Research Center completed parent interviews with approximately fifteen thousand families in forty-nine communities.

Separate questionnaires for teachers and classroom aides were developed over a period of several months and administered in the spring of 1970. The teachers' questionnaire elicited information on professional education, teaching experience, and demographic characteristics. One group of questions requested the teacher to state educational goals for children, the preferred teaching techniques, and the availability and use of equipment and materials in the classroom. The questionnaire also explored the teacher's knowledge of Follow Through, participation in the program, and general evaluation of the program's influence on pupils. The instrument probed the teacher's perceptions and attitudes toward visiting pupils' homes and on parents' participating in classroom activities.

The questionnaire for classroom aides also obtained useful demographic and background information. The respondent was requested to state how the position was obtained and whether helpful in-service training activities were provided, and to evaluate the effectiveness of both the Follow Through program and the teacher's classroom behavior.

Measuring Classroom Environments

The expansion of the evaluation criteria to include measures of classroom environment and the noncognitive characteristics of the pupils took two forms: a structured classroom observation scale that was adapted to a wide variety of classroom facilities and patterns of interaction between pupil and teacher, and procedures for assessing the children's noncognitive growth and development. Both expansion efforts were cooperative ventures involving sponsors, consultants, and the staffs of the Stanford Research Institute and the Follow Through department of the Office of Education, and were incorporated in the longitudinal evaluation that is to continue for several years.

The structured classroom observation scale was to provide several types of data: information on the agreement between the instructional procedures that sponsors wanted teachers to use and the procedures that teachers actually used in the classroom, a description of the process of classroom instruction, and information on the effects of various instructional approaches on child behavior. Sponsors were divided into three groups according to their program descriptions. Sponsors in the first group offered the most highly structured programs, systematically using stimulus-response and reinforcement-learning paradigms, relying heavily on behavioral analysis, and concentrating on academic and preacademic skills. Sponsors in the second group placed greater emphasis on inquiry, curiosity, discovery, and learning to learn in the earliest school years. Humanist values such as strong, positive feelings of self-worth and respect and trust for others were considered important. Sponsors in the third group tended to be more eclectic, incorporating elements from a variety of educational theories and techniques.

The classroom observations focused on three general dimensions of implementation: the allocation of time to activities (academic work, play, arts and crafts, etc.); the organization of classroom learning groups (large groups, small groups, individual children working independently); and the number, kind, and focus of communication patterns in the classroom (the amount of time the teacher is talking, the amount of time the children are talking, the nature of teachers' responses to children's questions, and whether teachers and aides communicated with children individually, in small groups, or in large groups).

In the development of the observation scale a field study was conducted, in April and May 1970, in approximately sixty Follow Through and comparison classrooms in seven projects. Two projects were those of the first group of sponsors, two those of the second group, and three those of the third group. Before observations were begun each participating sponsor was asked to specify the profile he expected for his classrooms. Generally, these preliminary data indicated that the sponsors' expectations were consistent with the procedures implemented in the classroom.

Measuring Noncognitive Characteristics

Several procedures were used to identify the sponsors' noncognitive objectives and appropriate evaluation instruments. In the fall of 1969 SRI staff interviewed sponsors and examined their program descriptions to determine noncognitive objectives of the various programs. Under the auspices of the Social Science Research Council, Dr. Eleanor Maccoby and Dr. Miriam Zellner interviewed sponsors on their program assumptions and objectives. The program objectives elicited by the interviews clustered into these areas of measurement: attitudes toward school, task orientation skills, curiosity and exploration, autonomy, self-esteem, school fearfulness, and locus of control. The sponsors and consulting researchers on child development and early childhood education were invited to recommend noncognitive instruments. The SRI staff also examined the research literature to identify appropriate instruments. Several instruments were tested in the field, and a pilot study, conducted in the spring of 1970, tested 845 pupils in forty-five classrooms in eight communities, each located in a different state. Four instruments (*Ethnic Pictures, Response to Social Influence, Task Performance Skills,* and *Classroom Behavior Inventory*) were individually administered to twelve randomly selected pupils (six boys and six girls) in each classroom in kindergarten and the first three grades. Four instruments (*Test Anxiety Scale, Intellectual Achievement Responsibility Scale, In My Classroom,* and the *Picture Motivation Scale*) were administered to the entire class at grades two and three.

DATA COLLECTION AND ANALYSIS

The Follow Through longitudinal evaluation collected an enormous amount and variety of data during the first four years. The range of achievement tests was expanded to include kindergarten and the first three grades by refining the original basic survey and adding items from several standardized achievement tests. The number of pupils included in the basic evaluation sample increased from 17,500 in 1968 to fifty-five thousand in 1972. Substantial amounts of data were generated from the thousands of interviews and questionnaires administered to parents, teachers, and classroom aides, and from the program implementation review. Large quantities of data were produced by the three developmental projects: community case studies, classroom observation, and noncognitive measures for pupils. Approximately two thousand people have been employed in developing, printing, and shipping test materials and in collecting, coding, processing, analyzing, and storing the data.

Field Work Organization

A field work staff of over a thousand collected data in 1972. Regional representatives appointed for most of the sites in the basic evaluation sample supervised the recruiting and training of the testing teams and performed other coordinating and liaison functions. These representatives typically held doctorate degrees in education or psychology and positions as associate professors at local universities. The testing teams consisted of a supervising tester, assistant testers, and aides. The supervising testers, usually local college or university faculty or graduate students, maintained quality control by training the testers and aides to administer the tests and by supervising the actual data collection.

The problems of coordinating the relationships among the evaluators, local school districts, and sponsors required further changes in and elaboration of the field work. Approximately twenty field supervisors were employed to increase the efficiency of the data collection and to help prepare and revise testing materials. They visited project sites regularly and maintained personal liaison with local Follow Through projects and sponsors to ensure that the data collection proceeded as planned. Another group, designated Joint Fellows because their salaries were shared by the Stanford Research Institute and the sponsors, was to ensure liaison and cooperation within the entire Follow Through project, to help reduce overlapping and duplication in the measurement activities of the sponsors and the SRI staff, and to contribute to the development of measures that reflected the sponsors' instructional objectives.

Quasi-Experimental Character of the Evaluation

The operational requirements of the Follow Through program limited the choice of evaluation design (Sorensen 1969). Pupils, teachers, classrooms, schools, and projects were not assigned randomly: the school districts participating in Follow Through were selected according to criteria determined by the Office of Education; often individual schools were assigned Follow Through programs by district administrators; and local communities selected sponsored programs that complimented local circumstances. As a result, the evaluation could not be based on a before-and-after design that assumed the random assignment of subjects to experimental and control groups. Follow Through is a series of quasi experiments in several natural settings (Campbell and Stanley 1963). Data collection procedures were planned and scheduled, but little or no control was possible over the specification and scheduling of experimental treatments.

One of the most critical consequences of the quasi-experimental character for the national evaluation was that, essentially, each project had to be treated as a separate experiment. Thus, each of the projects included in the basic evaluation sample required a similar comparison group that was not participating in the program. In the natural setting of the Follow Through evaluation, the term "comparison group" is more accurate than the term "control group." For several reasons, it was difficult to identify acceptable equivalent groups of pupils for comparison. Social action programs for poor children cannot employ random methods of assignment lest eligible children be denied participation. In urban schools that have Follow Through classrooms the economic levels of families vary significantly, and classes that are not participating in Follow Through may still be influenced by the "ripple effect" from the Follow Through classrooms. In smaller schools and rural areas often most or all of the eligible pupils were participating, so it was necessary to go outside the school district for comparison groups. Thus, the chances of differences in economic status and ethnic, cultural, and educational background were increased.

The difficulties in matching Follow Through children and families with comparison children and families made necessary the collection of extensive descriptive information. These descriptive data facilitated certain analytic adjustments that compensated somewhat for the problems of matching that are inevitable consequences of quasi-experimental designs in natural settings. For example, face-to-face interviews were conducted with nearly fifteen thousand parents in 1969/70 to obtain information about the home and family background of children both in and out of the program, so that changes attributable to participation in the Follow Through program could be identified and better understood.

Because of the expense of data collection the numbers of districts and pupils in the basic evaluation sample should have been small. But because Follow Through pupils were not assigned randomly to the experiment, the number of cases was large. The attrition of subjects that inevitably occurs in a longitudinal study lasting several years imposed an even greater need for a large number of cases initially. It is expected that at least forty or fifty percent of the pupils will have left the Follow Through program before they complete third grade, primarily because their parents will have moved away. Not all children participating in the Follow Through program meet the OEO eligibility definition of poverty and these children must therefore be excluded from the analyses of evaluation data.

Storage and Analyses of Data

The evaluation data have been coded and stored in a computerized data bank. The data are organized by a number of computer programs: the editing program checks the input data for validity and identifies the subject, the updating program adds new cards to the existing bank and maintains an index of information in the bank, and retrieval programs allow users to obtain information from the bank without writing special-purpose programs. The data bank accumulates information on numerous variables for all pupils included in the study. Card image tapes have been prepared to accumulate all the data. The 1968/69 data bank contained over sixty-five thousand card images, the 1969/70 bank over five hundred thousand. The two banks have been merged into a single bank that will incorporate all data collected through the completion of the project. The entire bank included over a million card images by the end of the third year of the project.

Independent, mediating, dependent, or criterion variables were identified in the selection and construction of the instruments. Statistical methods were used to identify those variables that reflected significant program effects and those variables that appeared to be associated with change. The units of analysis were the child, the classroom, the individual project, the sponsors, and the Follow Through program as a whole. To reduce the large number of variables to manageable proportions, they have been consolidated both logically and statistically. Arguments for the consolidation or elimination of some variables were generated from behavioral science theory. Other variables were discarded if they appeared to have little or no impact on the dependent variables. Composite scores were constructed from subjects' responses to a number of questions. Similar variables were grouped into one single variable; for example, family income, education, and occupation were combined to yield a single socioeconomic index for multivariate analyses of covariance.

The number of units of analysis and the number of participants and variables have generated a great quantity and variety of data. Consequently, the number of tabulations, computations, and specific analyses performed over the five years will be large. The three main types of analyses used to identify changes and relationships in the data are cross-tabulations of independent variables on which dependent variables are the cell entries, multivariate analyses of variance and covariance, and multivariate analyses of relationships among variables. Supplementary analytic techniques such as factor, cluster, and discriminant function analysis, and correlation and regression analysis, have been employed as necessary in grouping variables or identifying the effects of different combinations of independent variables. The statistical methods used to interpret the effects of Follow Through had to account for the quasi-experimental character of the program. In a quasi experiment it is more difficult to reach statistical conclusions in which one has confidence than it is in an experiment with appropriate randomization. The analyses must be performed *as if* certain underlying probabilistic hypotheses were valid. The probability statements were computed *as if* the children had been allocated randomly to Follow Through and comparison classrooms. Such probability statements serve only as indicators to demonstrate the nature of the results qualitatively rather than quantitatively.

One of the most persistant and embarrassing dilemmas in the

evaluation has been whether or not to provide information feedback to Follow Through and comparison schools. This topic has been discussed frequently since the beginning of the project, but no clear policy has been agreed upon. Local school districts exerted increasing pressure for the release of information, and some schools withdrew from the program to protest the lack of feedback. The Follow Through director consistently justified restricting information on the grounds that premature and inappropriate comparisons between Follow Through and comparison classrooms, or among Follow Through approaches, constituted a hazard that could endanger the future of the project. There was also concern that data might be improperly interpreted to the disadvantage of some participating teachers and administrators. Some school districts chose to conduct their own evaluation to obtain information necessary for local decisions on the expenditure of education funds.

CONCLUSION

Follow Through is using behavioral and social science data and researchers to seek solutions for urgent social problems. The evaluation of Follow Through reflects a significant change in the strategy for implementing national social programs. The marginal success of such programs as Head Start has convinced the planners that they must have substantial evidence to indicate that programs will be successful before they request more funds. The current policy is to conduct pretesting of sociocultural experiments before they are applied on a large scale. For Follow Through, this policy has meant an attempt to develop a rigorous model for evaluating a booster program for poor children in kindergarten and the first three grades.

Follow Through began with a simple, optimistic view of the prospects for improving educational opportunities for poor children. If enthusiasm and high expectations were alone sufficient to guarantee success, the outcome of Follow Through would have been assured from the beginning. However, experience has shown that improved education for poor children must be developed in the context of multiple constituencies and competing power groups. The logistic and methodological problems encountered in conducting the evaluation have been enormous. But the greatest challenge has been to formulate an effective, representative, decision-making process for accommodating the differences between, and sometimes within, competing stakeholder groups. In social experimentation the recurring problems, confrontations, and stress cannot be resolved by simply eliminating one or more stakeholder groups from participation.

The task of improving educational opportunities for poor children cannot be accomplished in isolation from the social, ethnic, and group tensions that exist in the larger society. The Follow Through director had the major responsibility for resolving differences, but the struggles often surfaced and were thrashed out within the context of the evaluation effort. Thus differences were converted into dramatic heated discussions on methodological and design issues. Without the arena of the evaluation in which differences could be expressed and debated, a project such as Follow Through probably could not have been conducted. Many of the divisive issues and concerns are so personal and inflamatory that they cannot be dealt with openly and directly. The expression of issues as methodological problems makes practical compromises more likely (Weiss 1970). A basic issue has been whether the programs at the local level would be controlled by the sponsors or by the ethnic minority parents and their spokesmen. The trend in Follow Through has been to diminish emphasis on model testing and to increase emphasis on community participation and control. Accordingly the evaluation moved away from a pupil change model and toward a social systems change model. The result has been comparatively less attention to measuring pupil change and more attention to measuring institutional changes that increase the community's decision-making power in the operation of the school. One sponsor recently stated that "model testing in Follow Through is a dead issue." The point of his remark was that effective education programs must be developed within the community and not imported from outside.

REFERENCES

Bloom, B. S., Hastings, J. T., and Madaus, G. F. *Handbook on Formative and Summative Evaluation.* New York: McGraw-Hill, 1971.

Campbell, D. T. and Stanley, J. C. "Experimental and Quasi-Experimental Designs for Research on Teaching." In *Handbook of Research on Teaching,* edited by N. L. Gage. Chicago: Rand McNally, 1963.

Cronbach, L. J. "Course Improvement Through Evaluation." *Teachers' College Record* 64, no. 8 (1963): 672-683.

Economic Opportunity Act, Public Law 88-452 (1964).

Economic Opportunity Act, Public Law 90-22 (1967).

Maccoby, E. E., and Zellner, M. *Experiments in Primary Education: Aspects of Project Follow Through.* New York: Harcourt Brace Jovanovich, 1970.

Scriven, M. "The Methodology of Evaluation." *AERA Monograph Series on Curriculum Evaluation,* no 1. 1967.

Sorensen, P. H. "Problems in the Evaluation of Follow Through Projects." Paper read at the annual meeting of the American Educational Research Association, February 1969, at Los Angeles.

U.S. Office of Education. *Follow Through Program Guidelines.* February 1969.

U.S. Office of Education. *Follow Through Program Approaches.* 1969/70.

U.S. Office of Education. *Follow Through Program Approaches.* 1970/71.

Weiss, C. H. "The Politicization of Evaluation Research. *Journal of Social Issues* 26, no. 4 (1970): 57-68.

11

DOING IT IS
SOMETHING ELSE:
EXCERPTS FROM AN
EVALUATOR'S JOURNAL

EDWARD F. KELLY

DENNIS D. GOOLER

One focus of transactional evaluation is on practice; it is concerned chiefly with the day-to-day occurrences of the course, program, or institution being evaluated. Transactions occur between various elements of a course, program, or institution; transactions occur between the evaluation specialist and the program personnel.

Fourteen incidents that occurred in an attempt to use evaluation in the development of a curriculum are described by one of the authors who was conducting the evaluation. The comments that follow each incident were made by the other author who did not take part in the project. The incidents are described as the evaluator remembered them. No claim is made for the accuracy of the perception in terms of how other people saw the same events, but we hope the incidents illustrate the breadth of the transactional dilemma. Not merely a prescription, the commentary that follows each incident raises more questions than it answers, in an attempt to seek some understanding of what was observed.

LANGUAGE

There have been days of orientation—days of getting the feel of the place and the people—but today there was work to do. One project has produced a set of objectives and is ready to start the development of criteria. It would have been easy enough to let the objectives stand as they were drawn up, but so heavy an emphasis on the recall of facts and principles seemed to warrant a justification. Why was there so much emphasis on the lower level of the taxonomy? The answer seemed to be connected with the difficulty of defining behavior so that we might observe it. The content people have formulated low level objectives (Bloom) because they did not know how to express higher level objectives. Possibly, an early emphasis, by the development people, on operationalization in the development process has caused them to avoid making statements that they could not define in some observable terms.

An effort toward operationalizing outcomes gets people pretty concerned with verbs. Bloom's taxonomy has been helpful here. But it takes so long to get people to understand a new language. The development has to proceed very slowly in order to prevent people wasting hours on tasks that ultimately will have to be redone. Everyone wanted to know why they hadn't been told earlier; everyone wanted to know why they weren't taught how to consider objectives for analysis, and synthesis, and evaluation.

The problem of language is inescapable. To evaluate something, in this case the adequacy of a set of objectives, requires the use of a common language, one of the most difficult parts of evaluation. Most evaluators are trained in the peculiar language of assessment, a language not often found in others' repertoires. But can the evaluator insist on a clarification of objectives, *his* clarification? Can he evaluate if the objectives are *not* as clear as he would like them to be? What does it do to the relationship between the evaluator and the client if the latter must come to terms with his objectives on the evaluator's grounds?

Potentially, there is a major role indicated for the evaluator by this incident: the evaluator often has an opportunity to be an instructor. In this case, the evaluator found himself instructing people on how to state objectives at a "higher level." In transactions between the evaluator and the client this instructional role is not without power. Perhaps this idea is related to the question of the worth of goals. The evaluator certainly seems to comment at least on the adequacy of goals when he points out that only low-level goals were stated. That the evaluator can be an instructor further underscores the potential of formative evaluation. Had a conversation about the level of goal setting occurred at the conclusion of the project, the entire project might have focused exclusively on the originally stated objectives, and undoubtedly would have pleased no one.

The first mention of time—clients should not be required to waste time developing things that will later need to be redone—could perhaps indicate that both the developer and evaluator know what ultimately must be done, but they feel the client must become aware of the objective on his own. Does this remark say anything about the time needed to accomplish such an awareness?

> Students in an introductory course are to be tested for their competence at prerequisite skills. The instructor has been convinced that it makes sense to test some of the assumptions he has been making about the background and abilities of his students. We discussed a diagnostic test that will enable him to prescribe remedial teaching if it is necessary. We considered the content validity of the test and the difficulty of building a good diagnostic test that is not based on a careful analysis of the skills and concepts that are to be the content of the course.
>
> He is displeased with the instruments that are commercially available. They do not get at the specific skills that he wants to know about. I explain how he can use a test grid to plan and watch the content of his test items, and he sets about developing items that will help us estimate the students' competence. There will be very little time to develop the instrument.

The evaluator mentions time again. It is one thing for him to describe the ideal, what really should be done; it may be quite another to do it, for "there will be very little time to develop the instrument." Questions of validity and utility must take into account the reality of time. No wonder so much frustration is generated in transactions between the evaluator and the client! The ticking of the clock resounds in the ears of those who think they know what ought to be.

Someone, probably the evaluator, has convinced the instructor of the value of knowing something about his students, so reasonably, he asks about the relationships among antecedents, transactions, and outcomes. Herein lies the question of both logical and empirical contingencies: given these conditions, and desiring these outcomes, do these activities look as though they will be appropriate? So if the evaluator argues that this is an important sort of question to raise, must he not also offer the capacity for getting answers to that question? Do we know what kind of information he wants? What does it mean to place someone accurately? Does any such placement affect the course an individual's life will take? Interesting. The instructor will probably shoulder the praise or the blame, a probability that says something about his confidence in both the evaluator and his evaluation.

> Suddenly everyone wants to measure student attitudes. In every project, we're being asked about attitudinal dimensions. What are students expecting from this course, from this college? What are their attitudes toward the course; toward the content of the course; toward the instructor? What are the specific materials and methods we propose to use? Will the students be more positive after the course? Will they have changed as a result of instruction?
>
> It would be easy to oversell the thing. There are many questions that we cannot answer. Attribution is always a problem. In instructional development it is not usually possible to make the generalizations that some people desire. I explain the limitations and constraints of development as it occurs naturally. There are many questions that we don't have the time or the resources to pursue. The popular view, it seems, is that one considers attitudes only as an outcome variable, something to be considered only as a result. It's hard to convince people that there may be good grounds for describing the affective dimensions of the transactions of the course or project.

Suppose the evaluation turns up evidence to suggest that student attitudes toward the course are *not* positive, that students do *not* consider their expectations realized. What then of the transactions between evaluator and client? What then of transactions between instructor and students? In a formative sense, attitudinal indicators are devised to provide a barometer of feeling, to suggest that something may need to be changed. But none of us takes too well to defeat, or even to criticism. If criticized, or even defeated, the evaluator must squarely confront the emotions of his client and that may not always be easy. It is most likely that we will want to know something about attitudes as an outcome variable. We don't want students leaving a course feeling disappointed in it. Attitudes appear to have something to do with how we involve ourselves in the *process* of learning. But, having convinced the client of the need to examine the affective dimensions of the transactions in the course or project, can the evaluator deliver an accurate explanation of the affective dimension? Having raised the client's expectations of an evaluation, the evaluator will find his credibility determined by his ability to meet these expectations consistently.

Here we find more hints about the instructive purpose of evaluation. In terms of attitudes, how shall the evaluator condense social psychological insight into attitudes, so that he himself, the client, the students, and others who are interested can understand what they will and will not get from any attempt to examine attitudes?

TIME

It's getting harder to avoid playing the role of expert. I'm not sure about it but feel that to expect the content expert or project manager to be able to tell the evaluator what he wants to decide, when he wants to decide it, and what he will need to make the decision, is rather unrealistic an approach. I haven't found many people who are able or willing to answer such questions. They tend to say, "You're the expert in these matters. What do you think we should look at?" I'm usually troubled by that. More and more, it doesn't appear to make much difference what you look at, as long as you look. In the end, the decisions about effectiveness may be based on other criteria altogether.

There's a lot to be expert about. Sometimes, for example, much of the day-to-day operation of the formative evaluator could be handled by whoever produces the measurements and statistics. I think that we had better give the evaluator more training in interpersonal relations, group dynamics, and value theory if he is to be successful in the development system. He had certainly better learn more about how to fish for unintended outcomes.

Sometimes honesty, hesitancy, and legitimate

doubts will be construed as incompetence, and lead to a loss of credibility. Credibility is part of the process of development.

The articulation of a problem requires a delicate balance between the ability to probe the thoughts and feelings of an instructor or program director for what he perceives to be a need or problem, and the ability to plant a need in that person and subsequently enable him to express it. The evaluator will, almost always, be an interventionist. He will be regarded as an expert. So often he is considered an expert in all categories of problems or endeavors: if he is good at X, he must also be good at Y and Z. The evaluator must decide whether the situation will permit him to be expert beyond his expertise.

What do you buy when you buy an evaluator? Shall the buyer indeed beware? One may be buying a diagnostician, but does one also get a chemist, a psychologist, an art historian? One may be buying an advisor, but does one also get a political activist, a professional lobbyist, a man with a cause? One may be buying an expert in the measurement of what happens, but does one also get a judge of the value of what happens, or of what was desired? One may be buying a prober of inconsistencies, an analyst of transactions, an instrument of communication, but does one also get a highlighter of failures, a dispeller of hopes, a champion of unflinching rationality? And what from this range would the client choose?

In all the development projects, we're asking students to tell us what they would like to do and what they would prefer to avoid. We're asking about the types of instruction they prefer, about the content they think most relevant to the course and to their goals in the course. Students have expectations, which sometimes seem to be so grandiose that one wonders whether they aren't somewhat unrealistic. But we gather them. I don't think that we can yet translate them clearly into indications that will enable us to change or redesign the courses. Many people have expectations about what a freshman course in composition should be about—people other than the students who have enrolled in it. Usually there isn't enough time to ask all those other people what they think. Usually we will have to make do with the expectations of the students and the faculty and trust that the rest won't come back one day to haunt us.

Collecting information about expectations is one thing; getting them translated into practice is quite another. "Seventy-nine percent of the sample expects the course to be extremely interesting." What does that mean in practice? By itself, very little I suppose. Taken as a description of a group of people beginning the course, the information may have a place. It's probably important to build accurate descriptions, so that we will know more about the project, the course, the student. Whether all the data will provide a logical contingency to transactions, for example, may not matter in the least, so long as people think that they have some understanding of the phenomenon.

This entry seems to highlight a pervasive problem: we all tend to agree on the worth of some principles, for example, that we should "pay attention to expectations," but having actually collected data on expectations, we are not sure what to do with them. What do we do differently if we know what people expect? Suppose seventy-nine percent of the sample indicated that the course would probably be *uninteresting*. Then what?

Maybe the evaluator is right when he maintains that people need to believe they have some understanding of the phenomena. And maybe they believe that a set of figures indicating what different people expect of the course contributes to their understanding? If so, such figures may be necessary. It may be true that what is perceived, is. What does this axiom say about evaluation? Is evaluation a process of manipulating perceptions? Somehow, expectations seem very important. But expectations that people have when starting a course change rapidly, almost with the first breath of the instructor. Is the significant relationship that between the expectations at the beginning of the course and the achievement at the end, or that between the expectations in the early part of the course, when they have been modified to some extent, and the achievement at the end? Maybe we should measure expectations two weeks after the course has begun?

The semantic differential may help us monitor some of the attitudinal outcomes that appear to be of interest in all the projects. We can have commonality in the scales and cluster the concepts in similar domains. The data will help us know more about whether the semantic differential factors vary across content areas, since we will have data from five different areas. Probably such data are more interesting to me and some researcher than useful to those who will have to recycle development systems after the data have been analyzed. Yet the semantic differentials will give a general indication of attitudes and, when combined with the adjective rating scales and the statements of expectations, may provide a general basis for discussion of the affective aspect of the projects. One way or the other, we're going to need considerable advice on the best way to analyze and interpret the data.

It is possible that semantic differential results *cannot* be translated?

What do you have when you have gross estimates of something called affect?

Where will the evaluator get his advice?

CREDIBILITY

Two hours spent with a college's curriculum council discussing the evaluation of teacher performance are enough to raise all the issues and to offer a few warnings. The shortage of money and the administration's attempts to satisfy some of the demands for increased accountability are making a more intense evaluation of collegiate instruction necessary. I'm not sure that the system will wait until there are validated instruments for faculty assessment. Nor do I know whether faculties will be able to withstand, or rationalize, the necessity for much longer. I am afraid, though, that they may run off with something that is too narrow to be of much use.

I will prepare a collection of instruments, which will be representative of what has been used in other colleges and universities, for the committee's consideration. No single instrument will answer their needs. There will have to be a package, a portfolio of information on faculty instruction that will have to be comprehensive enough to cover the complexity of the function called teaching.

The intricate complexity of instruction, development, and evaluation is nowhere more evident than in the type of situation described above. Education must be done in the swirl of the potentially conflicting personal fortunes of the teacher, the learner, and the multiple consumers of the product of the educational system. Hit one knee, and you can never be sure which of a thousand others will jerk. It is inevitable that the assessment of the performance of individual teachers will be suggested. Is it not strange how nervous we get when trying to assess the performance of teachers, but how regularly and without qualms we presume to measure the performance of the students?

> In one project we will assign students to a remedial course in writing, if the pretest shows that they are below standard in any of four aspects of writing. We have found a published, standardized instrument that we think will fit the bill.
>
> Discussions about the limited correlation that exists between a student's knowledge of formal grammar and the quality of his composition have not altered the disposition of the content experts on the question of the emphasis that should be given to formal grammar. There appears to be a belief that, even if knowledge of formal grammar is not directly translatable into good writing, such knowledge is still a necessary, if not sufficient, condition for good composition. We will have to see how effective the test is in predicting a student's ability to write.
>
> I have not been able to persuade people by references to the research that has been done on a problem. Their sentiments and priorities are not easily changed by an appeal to the evidence or warranted assertions. Poor Dewey.

Well, maybe we are looking at the wrong relationship. Grammar may be related to something else, not competency in writing.

Evidence is so easily qualified. A number of things might have gone wrong in research studies, there might be a number of reasons why the evidence need not be believed. The evaluator worries about validity—what does validity mean in terms of what will be accepted as valid evidence? In most instances, the client is free to accept or reject the findings and explanations of the evaluator. How is the evaluator to deal with this freedom? What is to prevent the client from displaying what is supportive, and burying what is not?

> Everything takes longer than it should have taken. The data will not be very useful unless they have been processed and translated into a readable form by the time they are to be used. It takes a long time to learn one's way through the programs on the computer. That alone could be a full-time job for someone.
>
> I'm afraid that we will have far more information than we shall ever be able to process thoroughly

before the decisions on implementation and recycling are to be made. Perhaps we have collected some irrelevant information; perhaps not.

Too late with too little. It seems that so much of the evaluative information can be used only in retrospective explanations or descriptions. There is some question about whether this serves a purpose in on-line decision making. Doesn't the client have to look with reservation on the probability of the evaluator doing something utilitarian? What this must ultimately lead to is a reassessment of the proportion of project resources to be allocated to evaluation. Should its utility be the most important criterion for judging the worth of an evaluation? If so, how does the evaluator handle the problem of not being able to complete his evaluation satisfactorily in the time allotted? The same problem arises in the next entry.

TOLERATION

The projects have been using a tremendous quantity of instructional materials. Textbooks, programmed units, slides, tape and slide combinations have all been used. We will have to monitor the use of materials closely if we are to have any basis for change when results do not meet standards. All materials will be monitored in a brief questionnaire that will be completed by the students after they have completed the specific learning component. We hope that the questions we have asked will provide data useful to the developers when they attempt to make revisions.

The demands of the development process seem to force us to be increasingly concerned about the difference between rigor and relevance. Sometimes the exigencies of time do not allow us to be as rigorous as some would like.

We generally assume that rigor is right. Why do we feel more comfortable if we have been more rigorous? Because our explanations are then more accurate, our outcomes more predictable, our diagnosis surer? Does it all boil down to *control*?

Anecdotal data are powerful beyond belief. They lead people to reach conclusions that are sometimes based on the power of a student's metaphor rather than on any carefully reasoned judgment. It is not enough to know what to collect and how to collect it. We have to learn more about how to control the results of what we collect, and how to ensure that the results are not misinterpreted or overgeneralized. The situation described above forces me to question almost daily the ranges of tolerance within which I will countenance decisions.

The administrators of at least one educational center have argued that their mission is to develop in educators the capacity for reasoned judgment. The interpretation of data must have something to do with that capacity. Transactions between evaluator and client occur primarily about data. The evaluator is usually hampered by the necessity to disclose and interpret data before he is ready because the client is being pressed to make decisions. The client is no less hampered: he must make the decisions, not when he would, but when he must.

The evaluator must indeed consider the range of tolerable data disclosure. He probably learns by trial and error. But the client too, must establish some parameters of data use. He must come to understand something about the adequacy of samples, about weighting, and about consequences. He, too, learns by trial and error, but maybe also by learning about data interpretation and appropriateness from the evaluator. The evaluator cannot shirk from *that* responsibility. This is a transaction of major importance.

> Data come out before results. Within the formative evaluation, content people, developers, and others frequently have the opportunity to review the responses to instruments, to examine the responses to open-ended questions, and to see the initial results before a complete tally is made or before the data have been analyzed. The outcomes of such an uncontrolled data disclosure may be best described as the premature interpretation of evidence. Transactional data in the formative evaluation, difficult as it is to collect, is equally difficult to control.
>
> Process evaluation, in addition to grappling with the practicalities of proper focus and method, may also have to contend with the premature disclosure of circumstantial indicators.

Transactional data? Consider the following:

> The planners of one project are hesitant about transactional data. They are not concerned with monitoring the relationships between teacher and student, or

> with monitoring the cognitive and affective dimensions of those relationships. The applicability of transactional data must be discussed, their rationale and possible usefulness demonstrated before they will be admitted as important components of the formative evaluation.
>
> Possibly as the result of some strong outcomes orientation, it certainly seems that the debate over the utility of observation and category systems that purport to have some correlation to learning in the classroom may be a bit premature. In some cases, instructors feel there is little need for such information.

There are a good many questions to be asked about the idea of transactional data. But there is an interesting corollary question: what is the genesis of the "strong outcomes orientation?" Did the development team (implicitly or explicitly) build that orientation? Is an outcomes orientation, as strong as is suggested, simply a part of the fabric of all educators?

At what point *does* it make sense to ask clients to consider data about transactions? And in what way can the evaluator demonstrate the rationale and possible usefulness of transactional data?

> What does it take to translate the findings of a field test into a decision to implement an entire program? It appears that the answer does not lie in the "hard" data that are generated. Quite the contrary, since such data seem to have little to do with the decision. In the final analysis, whether or not most of the decision makers will have judged the project successful may contribute far more to the decision than the suggestions of the evaluator, or for that matter, than the data. Possibly this is as it should be. One might hope that one of the prime purposes of the transactional evaluation would be to raise alternatives, and if anything, to make the decision process more cautious, if not more rational, than it had been in the past.

What is still not clear is how information about transactions contributes to rational decisions. Do we derive some hunches about possible, alternative ways of getting things done by considering data on what is actually happening? What in the nature of transactional information gives us such hunches?

There is always some winning and some losing when decisions are made on the basis of process data. Such data do not inherently mean that wiser decisions will be made, even if the data are accurately understood. Claims might be made that transactional data reduces guesswork, but such claims are probably no more than assumptions. How would we decide whether transactional data yielded better decisions? Pick your definition of *better*. With few exceptions, decisions are probably not right or wrong in themselves, but become foolish or wise depending on what happens after the decision is made.

SOME FINAL THOUGHTS

What happens *during* an evaluation is frequently just as important as what happens *after* it. The various ranges of tolerance that describe the operational parameters within which evaluator and client will work operate from moment to moment. In one sense, the organizational thread of the narrative of the journal is represented by the attempts to suggest where some of the various critical tolerances may be found.

One aspect of transactional evaluation, the relationships that exist among the evaluator, the developer, and the client, for example, seem to be determined to some extent by the range of problems and the possible sets of criteria that are implicit in the evaluation. The two primary criteria appear to be language and time. The first is apparent in the discussion of the objectives, and in problems of conducting the evaluation and of communication. The second is a thread that appears to connect practice to ideals, theory to practice. In a sense, the complaint that we are "wasting time" implies that there is at least some hope that we can use it better and can find out how that better use can be translated into practice. A third criterion might be credibility. In several of the entries, it seems that both the evaluator and the client are concerned with remaining or becoming credible. In addition, standards for rigor and relevance appear related to credibility just as are time limits and competence. The question of uncomplimentary information—what it is, how it should be reported or destroyed—seems to vary depending on the evaluator's desire to remain supportive and reasonably unthreatening within particular levels of tolerance. Ranges of tolerance will differ from client to client and from one evaluation system to another, so the client must, in practice, recall the caveat of the marketplace. When the evaluation is formative—a fishing trip into the realm of possibility and feasibility—it seems that the criterion of credibility is fairly important.

Language, time, and credibility are three criteria that can be used to judge evaluation transactions. The incidents recorded suggest that there are other criteria. What is totally unclear from this account is the range of tolerance—standards or scales of acceptance—within which the evaluator will feel comfortable with an activity or a decision. A determination of their ranges of tolerance might well help evaluators and clients describe what they consider to be acceptable transactions.

12

TRANSACTIONAL EVALUATION IN PROGRAM DEVELOPMENT

WAYNE J. DOYLE

The Ford Training and Placement Program (the Ford program) is intended to train professionals to work in schools and their communities, and to equip the professionals with effective curricula, materials, methods, and support service to improve the education standards in urban schools. The evaluation of the program was intended to find the answer to the question: What difference does the Ford approach to training and placing professionals make in the lives of the ultimate client—the youngster in the classroom?

The usual method of describing an evaluation is to present the plan and cite examples of action programs to demonstrate a particular point. Another method is to present a general evaluation model and follow up with a brief example. Both these methods may be viewed as more scholarly ways of describing an evaluation, but it is my opinion that they are not necessarily more useful to those who are actually involved in the evaluation. By presenting an overview of the program being evaluated, discussing the barriers we encountered in eliciting information from participants and our strategies for dealing with them, presenting a model for transactional evaluation in the program, and describing the evaluation design employed presently to assess the program's impact on the ultimate client, I hope to demonstrate the utility of an illustrative treatment of evaluation. By treating rational and operation models at the same time, I hope to enhance an understanding and appreciation of the myriad problems one usually encounters in implementing an evaluation plan.

THE PROGRAM

In the fall of 1967 J. W. Getzels, in an article published in *School Review,* discussed the training and employment of staff for inner-city schools, and provided the conceptual framework for a new approach. The conception of the school as a social system suggests that each school provides unique roles. The role of the teacher in Woodlawn differs from that of the teacher in New Trier, and so training should differ according to the place in which the individual will be working. Roles in schools function, not in isolation, but in complementary relationships to other roles, so school staff should be trained together. If they are trained together for specific localities, they will understand one another, and if they teach together they should increase the effectiveness and efficiency of the school. If the school is to function properly, those who train, those who employ, and those who are served by the staff must be able to communicate with one another. The university, the school and the community must all interact with one another. The notion of forming and placing cadres of teachers who have been trained together and constitute various role sets should mean that the special training they have received will be used effectively.

The Goals

The fundamental task of the Ford program is to train professional educators in the school-community and equip them with effective curricula, materials, methods, and support services to improve the education in urban schools. They are not expected to introduce dramatic changes into the larger school social system until the individual group members of the cadres have become competent at their individual tasks, have developed and matured as a group, have learned a great deal about the larger system, and know something of the strategies for effecting change.

The initial goal of the program is to develop competence. If an individual is to take his place as a professional in the school and the community, he must be able to cope with the day-to-day operations of the classroom or the school. His competence will include at least:

A knowledge of himself

A knowledge of the learning process and the development of skills to help others to learn

An increased comprehension of black culture

Knowledge about the learner as a social and as an academic animal

Knowledge about the classroom, and the school, as social systems

Knowledge about the community and the environment that surrounds the school

Knowledge of the process of change

Knowledge of his subject matter

Skills in the development of curricula and related materials

Knowledge of how to be an effective group member

Knowledge of how to identify and define problems

Problem-analysis skills

Decision-making skills.

The second goal of the program is to facilitate the induction of newly trained professionals into the school community. The first few months on the job are extremely crucial for an aspiring professional. Information, support and assistance are needed if he is to survive the demands of his new role. He must have:

A clear understanding of his own role in the school and in the cadre

A clear understanding of the other roles in the cadre and in the school

Support and assistance from the Ford program as he assumes his role

A knowledge of the human and material resources available to him in his roles as an individual and as a member of a group

Knowledge of the resources available to him in the university

Acceptance as a peer who is regarded as a potential source of ideas

Interaction with cadre members and other school personnel to reduce the feeling of isolation

Interaction with the community.

The third goal is to promote close relations between the school and the community, relationships which, regardless of the specific situation, will require:

Knowledge about the values and mores of the community

Two-way communications with the community

Knowledge of the resources available in the community and their use

Awareness of the expectations the community holds for education

Knowledge of community problems

The participation of the community in the function of the school.

The fourth goal of the program is the development of appropriate programs for the specific classes of cadre members. It is assumed that these social benefits will result from cross-role training, from the support and assistance that the cadre arrangement encourages, and from the added resources of the university. The major responsibility for developing new and appropriate curricula rests with the educators in the schools.

The fifth goal of the program is for the cadre, or an extended cadre including other faculty members in the school, to identify problems that affect the school and the community, and act on them within its professional competence. Nothing can be done about this goal until the cadre has put its own house in order and the individual members are accepted in the system. Innovation in the school social system is clearly the responsibility of the staff. The responsibility of the university is to train the staff to identify, define, analyze, and describe alternative solutions to problems. The resources of the university are still available to cadres that are already permanently employed, but to a lesser extent than when they were interns.

The final goal is to develop an aura of shared responsibility, among cadres, other staff members, and the community, for the educational program of the school. Shared responsibility, which should lead, not only to a sounder program, but also to a more enthusiastic and effective implementation, will require, at least:

That the staff be employed over fairly long periods of time

That there be increased communication in the school

That collegial relations among the professionals in the system be encouraged

That the faculty be encouraged to make decisions on matters important to them

That the notion of accountability be promoted

That the school and the community support each other

That ideas be processed according to their merit rather than their source

That factors in the system that tend to reduce morale be identified and controlled

That the functions of all roles in the system be articulated and coordinated to accomplish tasks

That the community's opinions on matters that are relevant to it be obtained.

Implementation

The Ford program represents a collaboration between inner-city schools in Chicago and the University of Chicago to train and place professional personnel in schools and communities. The Department of Education and the Graduate School of Education at the University of Chicago, with the cooperation of the Chicago Board of Education, presented a plan to the Ford Foundation. The program, envisioned as a six-year program, was begun in January 1968, and implemented in the schools in the 1968/69 academic year. Professional personnel are specifically trained and placed in inner-city schools—that is, in schools serving communities that are both poor and poorly educated. The population of such schools in Chicago is predominantly black.

The organization of the Ford program is based on a committee system. The four permanent committees, to which are added ad hoc committees when needed, determine the broad policies. The Ford staff operates, coordinates, and implements the committees' policies. The program is a complex one. Teachers and other personnel are trained in the university in six different programs designed to prepare teachers for elementary schools, teachers for secondary schools, social-psychology specialists, adult educators, reading specialists, and school social workers. Training lasts three years, an initial training year, an internship year spent as a member of a cadre, and a year of bona fide employment in the Chicago public school in which the trainee spent his internship.

First Year Training. During the first year individuals are trained in their own special graduate programs designed and implemented by separate graduate schools in the university. Prospective teachers may indicate their interest in the Ford program before or during this first year, and some of the training may focus on problems of inner-city schools. Practice teaching and other field work also take place during the first year.

Second Year Training. The second year marks the beginning of coordinated training for service in a specific inner-city school. In the Ford program, people trained in specific graduate programs come together, learn to understand one another, and find out what each person can contribute. During this internship year the trainees, while based at the university, spend approximately half their time in the schools. This year includes preservice training, in-service training, and clinical experience, and cross-role training and performance. Cooperating schools are selected and the cadre for each school is determined before the summer program of training begins.

The Summer Program. The first formal meeting of new cadres begins in the summer before the cadres spend their intern year in the schools. The summer program is unique because it attempts to coordinate learning activities for experienced and inexperienced teachers, administrators, specialist trainees, and Ford program staff members. It introduces new teachers to the specific school in which they will serve their internship, broadens their general knowledge of the learning problems of black children, offers opportunities to develop additional skills in classroom teaching, initiates the cross-role concept through cadre activities, and promotes opportunities to plan curricula.

The Cadre in the School. Some in-service training is offered during the internship year. The cadre facilitates cross-role understanding and performance, provides mutual support among its members, develops group resources, and makes use of additional human and material resources available through the university. The group continues to mature and to develop relationships, among all members, that tend to promote their confidence and trust in one another. The competence of individuals and the group is particularly emphasized during the first part of the internship year. Other faculty members from the schools are invited to participate in the cadre's activities.

Typically, a cadre will include five interns with Master of Arts in Teaching (MAT) or Master of Science in Teaching (MST) degrees, and three or four specialists. The Master of Arts in Teaching interns work in secondary schools, teaching a variety of subjects. The Master of Science in Teaching interns work in the elementary schools, teaching a variety of grades. The specialist interns come from the university's adult education program, the social-psychology specialist program, the social work program and the reading program. Some members of the cadre are full-time teachers in the schools. Their subject matter or grade level usually matches the interns'. The administration of the school is represented in the cadre by the principal and his assistant. There is at least one community representative in each cadre. The university is represented by a process consultant, a liaison person, and a researcher.

Less formal in-service training continues during the academic year. The cadre meets once a week to discuss problems and plan courses of action. Once each month the groups meet other cadres at the university.

Proposals for projects on which the cadre wishes to work are usually submitted to the Ford program for funding during the latter part of the internship year. The proposals define some school problem and present a detailed plan for dealing with it during the following summer or academic year.

Third Year Training.   The third year, referred to as the placement year, requires full-time service for the interns and a continuation of the cadre's activities. The human resources of the university and limited material resources are still available to the interns during this year.

EVALUATION

In the last two decades many programs have been designed to alleviate educational ills. Several of them have been considered inadequate because inappropriate criteria were used to make judgments about their effectiveness. More often than not little consideration was given as to whether an intended treatment had occurred or whether, logically, the treatment should have resulted in a change of the criterion variables under scrutiny. Other programs have been claimed as unconditional successes, often without any empirical support. Their proponents have developed such positive rhetoric in describing the programs that only the most discerning do not feel guilty because they failed to think of the solution themselves.

Background
Evaluation during the first operational year (1968/69) of the Ford Training and Placement Program was in the hands of a committee. No provision was made to decrease the other responsibilities of the committee members so that they might devote the time and energy required to evaluate the program. Considerable time was spent discussing research and evaluation; very little time remained for the development of a plan to implement the evaluation—not an atypical situation for a research committee in a university to find itself in.

In the second year of the program (1969/70), a full-time director of research and evaluation, and four part-time research assistants were employed. A proposal for research into and evaluation of the program was drawn up by the new director in June 1969, before he became involved in the program in September. The plan was similar to typical evaluational designs that require a description of what the program is delivering and an examination of changes expected in the perceptions and behavior of the program's clients. The two basic suppositions of the design later proved to be faulty. The plan assumed that the intention of the program was as clear as the conceptual framework on which it was based. It also assumed that participants in the program were as anxious to provide information as the evaluators were to get it. Both assumptions strongly influenced the direction that the research and evaluation took.

Resistance to Evaluation

The attempt to research and evaluate the Ford program met with much resistance. A hard line was adopted by a number of participants in the program. The need for research and evaluation in social action programs has a "commonplace obviousness" about it (to borrow Westbury's term [1970]). Scriven (1967) has pointed out that one can be against evaluation only if one can show that it is improper to seek an answer to questions about the merits of education, which would involve one's showing that there are no legitimate roles in which such questions can be raised.

The Reasons.   The reasons for resistance had to be explained in other ways. The nature of this resistance was examined in interviews with program participants in late 1969. The interviews revealed that the traditional method of conducting research and evaluation was viewed as inadequate by a large number of the participants. As they saw it, the researcher comes in, introduces himself, gathers the data, promises feedback on the findings when the data are analyzed, and then the subjects never see or hear from him again. Eventually they may be able to read about themselves in some book or article, but so often the researcher writes in such a way that only other researchers want to read the study. It became apparent that research and evaluation must be made the business of all the participants in the program.

The trustworthiness of the people conducting the research was important. Was the researcher really looking for an answer to the question he had posed? Respondents often fear that the information they give may be misused. The researcher, it seems, is not committed to offering information of any real value to the practitioner. His motives are often suspect and in many cases these suspicions are well grounded. Researchers have become stereotyped as a result of the "hit and run" tactics of many of them. The white researcher is often suspect in the black community. It may seem that his understanding of the problems of the black person is inadequate. His very presence is viewed with alarm that, often, is justified: too many white researchers have "used" the black community as a source of information for their own purposes. It takes some time to establish that the researcher's motives are acceptable. Some people are unwilling to give information because they feel that they are being viewed as objects. Often a deep resentment develops against research and evaluation if people feel they are being manipulated.

A fairly large number of participants in the program felt that they had no stake in the research and evaluation, and that the findings would make little or no difference to them as practitioners. Even when they did consider that the information asked of them was relevant to their work, they often felt that, because the decision makers would not be influenced by the findings, research and evaluation enjoyed a low priority.

The University of Chicago, regarded as an elitist, research-oriented institution, and the Ford program, being part of that university, were both highly suspect. Additionally, at that point, the Ford Training and Placement Program was striving to establish itself as a viable alternative to traditional teacher training programs for urban education. Our research and evaluation studies were clearly visible, accessible targets.

Not many of the program participants expected to do research and evaluation work and, in the first two years of the training program, the inclusion of such activities had not been mentioned. Several people indicated that they would not have become identified with the program if they had known about the research and evaluation component. The various methods of data collection occasioned different degrees of resistance, and we came up against an almost total resistance to the more classical methods of education psychology and the quantitative orientation of contemporary sociology.

If I may speculate for a moment, I shall digress on still another problem we faced in implementing research and evaluation, and that is the high degree of anxiety that evaluation provokes. Although we are making judgments about people every day, evaluation, systematic or not, is usually met with considerable resistance. Educators, extremely reluctant to evaluate themselves, have succeeded in disguising their successes as well as their failures. Educators can no longer afford to keep themselves immune from research and evaluation if the profession is to survive and grow. They must learn to discuss their successes and failures among themselves before they can communicate them effectively outside the profession where much of the pressure for accountability, unfortunately, has come, from many sources: funding agencies, businesses, turning their technological discoveries loose on the schools, individuals, anxious to make a name for themselves, who find the schools an easy target, and parents, who are demanding more accountability from the schools than they have in the past, but are still willing to let the schools conduct the evaluation.

The Solutions

What did we do to combat the massive resistance we encountered? The first step was to determine the nature of the resistance, which told us something of the attitudes toward research and evaluation, information we used as a guide to action.

The second step was to make absolutely certain that prospective participants were aware that the Ford program was part of a research-oriented institution and that they would be expected to conduct research. They were informed, verbally and in writing, in the contact phase, in the negotiation phase and, again, during the summer training phase. The role of research and evaluation in an experimental program must be viewed as a reciprocal process.

Frequently throughout the program research people explained what they needed by way of research and evaluation, and so did cadre members. We considered the question of responsibility for developing knowledge in a social action program. Evaluation has been viewed as a process that occurs continuously but at many levels. We had to plan to examine issues more rigorously than is usually possible in day-to-day situations, and our planning had to be cooperative. The responsibility for sharing results is tied very closely to the notion of sharing responsibility in gathering information. We made an intensive effort to furnish feedback. Written feedback information was provided and, on several occasions, individuals sought out research people to discuss findings personally.

Additionally, we made an effort to build social capital for the research and evaluation department among the participants in the program. The resources of the department have been made accessible to them. We have spent a great deal of time over the past two years discussing various problems with individuals. Still more important for the development and sustenance of social capital is the quality of the people who represent the department. Their competence and commitment is a prerequisite for any activity in which we become engaged. Trust cannot be built on words; confidence in people emerges when their behavior warrants it.

Is there presently any resistance to research and evaluation in the Ford program? The answer must be yes. We have not eliminated resistance, but we have reduced it significantly. The evaluation plan for the last operational year (1971/72), which assesses the program's impact on the ultimate client, the student, reflects that resistance has diminished appreciably.

Developing an Evaluation.   The second false supposition was related to the developmental stage of the program. The research and evaluation plan assumed that it would be appropriate to examine the program's impact upon the intermediate clients (the functionaries in the program) in 1969/70, and the impact upon the ultimate clients (the students) in 1970/71. The real situation quickly suggested otherwise. The program's goals had not been spelled out, and we needed to establish a sequential arrangement of goals to reduce their incompatibility with one another and to enable us to devise effective mechanisms for their implementation. A study in the first year (1968/69) by one of the original committee members (Bridges 1968), revealed considerable disenchantment among functionaries who had been in the program for one year. It became increasingly clear that research and evaluation must play an integral role in program development. Originally we had planned both process and product evaluation simultaneously. We revised that plan in the fall and winter of 1969/70 to include *transactional evaluation*—a term, which should be credited to Robert M. Rippey, that includes not only process and product evaluation, but also the perceptions and interactions of participants in the system or systems. At the time, however, we did not employ the term to describe our approach. We adopted the stance that Stuffelbeam described (1971): we maintained that the purpose of evaluation is not to prove, but to improve.

The Revised Evaluation Model.   Although the original plan had included process evaluation, in that information would be fed to both program developers and participants, process evaluation now became the major thrust. In fact, the interviews with the participants, to determine the nature of resistance to research and evaluation, and our careful appraisal of the developmental stage of the program, represented the beginning of a movement toward transactional evaluation.

General Evaluation Model for Training Programs

There is one basic question that all evaluation models for training programs must ask. Does the program produce the intended skill, perception and behavior in the immediate client? All other evaluation issues are either concerns to be incorporated into the research design used for investigating the principal question, or are questions that depend on the circumstances for their answers and, in the Kepner and Tregoe (1965) sense, are desirable but not essential. A general evaluation model for training programs, which incorporates the above notion, is presented in figure 5.

In some training programs information to be used in the selection of clients is essential and is situationally determined. In others, it is not, and therefore resources should not be allocated to research the issue. If the training program is expected to change the skill, perception and behavior of the clients, the levels of skill, perception and behavior before program exposure must be assessed. This necessity emerges from the evaluation design.

The intention of the training program will be stated in its goals and objectives. The statements must be clear and precise if the evaluation is to determine the extent to which the program is producing the intended skills, perceptions and behavior in the client. If the intent of the program is not clear, more resources will need to be allocated to the clarification of this issue. The research and evaluation design must assess the consistency of the program's objectives, its plan, and its activities. The program plan (the intended treatment) must first be scrutinized as the operational equivalent of intent and as the operational independent variables which are intended to induce change in the criterion variable. Next, the evaluator must check to see that the treatment is being delivered to the subjects as planned. All of these essentials are dictated by the design; however, the situation will influence the allocation of resources in this phase of process evaluation.

The treatment should produce some change in the skill, perception and behavior of the immediate client. The change may be assessed at appropriate intervals during the program, or at the end, by examining the differences observed before and after. When the achievement intended has been clearly spelled out, the evaluator can examine the differences between what is and what was expected. An extremely important point needs to be made at this juncture: if the intention is vaguely expressed, if the program plan bears no logical

FIGURE 5

General Evaluation Model for Training Programs

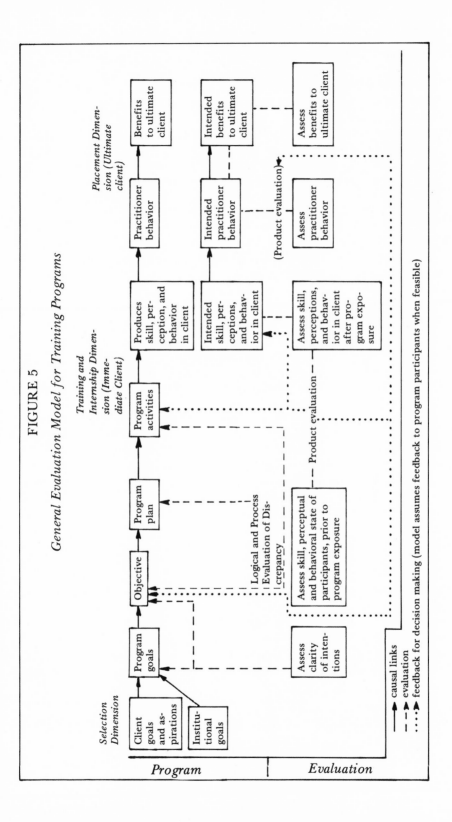

connection to the program's intentions, if the prescribed treatment is not delivered to the immediate clients, it will be premature to look for change in the criterion variables. If we do assume that positive and significant changes have occurred in the criterion variables between the two assessments, to what shall we attribute the change when all of the conditions mentioned above prevail? The most one can say at this point is, "It looks as if we have something good here; let's find out what it is that we are doing so that we can tell others to do the same." Although a decision to identify the treatment would be preferred over a decision to disseminate the program immediately, at best, it represents an inefficient use of resources. If we assume that no positive, significant change has been found under the same conditions, what would we do? We might abandon the project; we might start over; we might double the effort so that, while we are still riding madly in all directions, we will be riding harder, and faster, and travelling much farther. We might find that the easiest alternative to live with is to discredit the evaluation.

What can the evaluator do to avoid such reactions? Product evaluation can be delayed until a transactional process evaluation has provided the information that permits program developers to take remedial action. What happens when the developers do not wish to use research and evaluation information when making decisions? Both Cohen (1970) and Mitchell (1970) have discussed the problem. For the present it suffices to say that, when the evaluator resorts to political action, he risks losing his objectivity. The effect of political action can be lessened by having outside evaluators assess the ultimate program impact. There are usually people on the program staff, besides the top decision makers, who have social power and influence, and may be willing to carry the ball.

Most evaluation plans do not follow their clients into the world of practice. The same is true of training programs for teachers. An assessment of the behavior of the trainee and the benefits to the ultimate client is viewed as desirable in the general training model but seldom carried out. The prevailing view is that such assessments would provide valuable information if it could be gathered expeditiously.

The Operational Model

The operational model illustrated in figure 6 deals primarily with the requirements of evaluation that stem from the necessity to assess the impact of the program. Our program of research and evaluation met two major problems in the fall of 1969: program participants

FIGURE 6

Ford Training and Placement Program and Evaluation Model

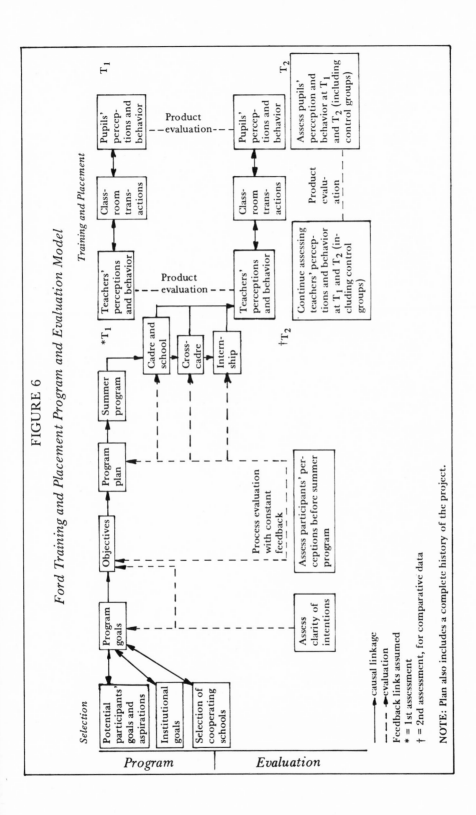

NOTE: Plan also includes a complete history of the project.

resisted the whole notion of research and evaluation, and the intent of the program was not clearly specified.

Before the program's impact on either the immediate or the ultimate clients could be assessed, we had first to determine at what level the program was operating. Problems with the program's intentions, its plan, and its activities had to be identified. We found it impossible to suggest alternatives that would eradicate the sources of the problems, and, of course, the program could not stand still while we were working. However, the program did seem to stall in the 1969/70 academic year. Information about requirements for research and evaluation was gained through interviews with participants and brainstorming sessions with the full program staff and participating faculty members at the University of Chicago. Concerns for research and evaluation emerged and telling questions were formulated. A paper, entitled "The Function of Research and Evaluation in the Ford Training and Placement Program," written and distributed to all functionaries in the program, in the late fall of 1969, described the situation at the time:

> The program is in a nascent or rudimentary stage with the major problems in the process of being identified. Conceptual goals are being examined and the operationalization of conceptualizations are necessarily in a state of fluidity. The program is problem-oriented and must necessarily be kept flexible. This condition militates against control, a prerequisite of *basic* research. Research interest at this stage is necessarily problem-oriented, and may be referred to as *applied* research. This research entails the study of a particular class of phenomenon on the grounds that knowledge about the phenomenon will help solve significant problems. It is expected that, in the Ford program, movement between applied and basic research may be made with some degree of facility as it becomes prudent to do so.
>
> Research and evaluation in the Ford program will be presently focused on developing knowledge which addresses itself to:
> 1. The identification and selection of professional personnel for the program
> 2. The training of professional personnel for service in urban education
> 3. The placement of professional personnel as a group in urban schools
> 4. A case study of each cross-roles cadre as a social system

5. Follow-up in the placement year
6. A history of the project.

The identification and selection of professionals for urban schools involves both university-based and school-based personnel. A model will be developed to facilitate the selection of professionals for urban education. Another model will be developed to facilitate the selection of school-based staff who will become fully functioning members of the group. The most important inputs in this program are the people in the cross-roles cadre. Surely there are some commonalities that suggest effectiveness in working with urban youngsters.

The training experiences before and upon entering urban education constitute another extremely important input. What strengths should be developed in urban schools? What aspects of the present training program are not especially helpful? What experiences should be substituted or added? These questions can best be answered when the program planners use broad information sources.

A great deal of attention needs to be given to the information about placing cross-roles cadres in cooperating schools. We should have information about the community, the school, the faculty and the principal. Most of this information must be impressionistic. However, we can gather considerable information that will provide valuable guidelines for future selection of cooperating schools.

A case study of the cross-roles cadre as a social system will be made. A nonparticipating observer will sit with the cadre in the summer training program before the internship year and will then go in to the cooperating school with the cadre during the academic year. Each cadre will be considered as a unique social system, and attention will be given to its own particular mode of operation.

A few of the questions to be examined are:
1. How does the cadre go about identifying its own problems and those of the school?
2. What issues concern the cadre most?
3. What model for decision making does the cadre employ?
4. Does the cadre provide support for its members?
5. How are the cadre members received by other faculty members?
6. How functional are the roles within the cadre?

A follow-up will occur in the placement year. Information about issues such as the following will be gathered:

1. What happens to cadres as units?
2. What happens to individual cadre members?
3. What are the attitudes of placement year participants toward cadre experiences?
4. What component of the program needs to be changed and in what way?
5. Were there any benefits in being cadre members and what were they?
6. Were there disadvantages in being a cadre member and what were they?

An historical account of the project, being developed, includes, not only a chronology of events, but also an interpretation of the more salient developments within the context of the society in which the program operates.

After the intent of the project has been achieved, it will then be in order to look directly at the teaching of Ford program trainees and examine its impact on students.

The information obtained by the researchers was processed and fed back to program participants, program staff, and decision makers at the University of Chicago, both informally and through reports, during the spring of 1971. The information, its implications, and the recommendations of the research and evaluation department played a significant role in the adoption of a model more responsive to the needs of educators in the inner city.

Reports on the specific findings or changes that resulted in the program are available on request from the Ford Training and Placement Program, Graduate School of Education, University of Chicago. The salient areas in which research and evaluation findings influenced changes in the program may be summarized:

1. The Need to Clarify the Program's Intentions:
Goal statements were revised and put into sequence
Goal statements were elaborated
The developmental nature of the program was stressed
An orientation toward problems, as opposed to an orientation toward solutions, was stressed
The functions of the program, first, as a training and placement agent, and second, as a producer of change, were stressed

2. The Need for New, Inclusive Authority Relationships among Program Participants:

The trainers, the trainees and the users—all who are involved in the training and assimilation process—have learning needs

Expertise derives from a multiplicity of sources

Inclusive relationships must be developed and maintained among the aspiring professional, the academic community, and the community in which the school is situated.

For a newly qualified teacher to become a functional part of the faculty, there should be communication, support, and sharing among all the people in the school social system.

3. The Need for a New Training Model for Urban Educators:

Training inputs became more consonant with the cross-roles model

A self-directed teaching/learning model replaced the typical university model for training programs in both the summer training program and in the monthly cross-cadre meetings during the academic year.

4. Cadre Development:

We stressed:

The need for a balance between process and content

The need to process ideas on the basis of merit, rather than source

The need to incorporate nonteaching roles into full cadre memberships

The need to build social capital with peers before suggesting dramatic changes

The need to recognize the cadre as both stimulus and threat to a school social system

The need to recognize the view often held by the rest of the school faculty that the cadre is an elitist group. The cadre's purpose and function must be explained to the rest of the faculty, and the cadre group must be extended to include other faculty if it is to establish functional authority

The necessity for leadership in the cadre to evolve and evolve again as the tasks vary

The need for trust between cadre members and the other faculty, if the cadre is to be functional

The necessity that cadre autonomy not consume the need for cooperative relationships with other components

The necessity for cadre members to understand what is expected of them as a group, as well as what they can expect of one another

5. *Impact on the School Social System:*

The placing of a single cadre in a school usually does not have a sizable impact on the social system of the school

The research and evaluation department was instrumental in the decision to reallocate resources. The notion of extending the cadre experience to a new group in a single school to provide maximal impact was tried in the 1971/72 academic year.

Information from the research and evaluation studies has been quite helpful in revising and refining the program's selection models for schools and participants, the role of the Ford program staff, our methods of conducting research and evaluation, and our use of university resources; in determining the consequences of decisions; in defining relationships among the University, the Board of Education, the Ford program staff, and the schools and communities in which they are situated; and in clarifying the perceptions of school faculty, who are not members of cadres, and the perceptions of placement-year cadre members. The academic year of 1971/72 brought a shift from process evaluation, most of it transactional, to product evaluation.

Research and Evaluation: 1971/72

The 1971/72 academic year was the last operational year for the program, and the time was ripe for product or summative evaluation. Evaluation of training experiences, the attrition study, and the historical aspect of research and evaluation were continued. The case study method of examining cadre life was replaced by periodic tappings of the group members' perceptions of participation, leadership, communication of ideas and feelings, nonverbal communication, authenticity, acceptance and freedom of persons, climate of relationships, and productivity (Anderson 1965).

Study of Communication Structure. It had been anticipated in the original plan of 1969 that communication patterns in the schools would constitute an important criterion variable. If the cadre model did facilitate socialization of new interns and thus reduce their isolation, and if greater support and sharing do in fact occur and thus promote collegiality among professionals, such effects should be reflected in the quantity and quality of interaction in the system. A study conducted in 1972 compared communication bonds in schools that participated in the Ford program with those in schools that did not, by using a sociometric device to gather appropriate information.

Teacher-Student Beliefs and Behavior. What we really had to evaluate was the difference that the Ford approach to training and placing professionals made in the lives of the ultimate client—the youngster in the classroom. We had to develop an evaluation design that, when implemented, would tell us what we needed to know. We do know a great deal about how professionals are supposed to behave toward one another. They are expected to interact more freely, communicate more openly and clearly, support one another, and share their resources—in short, to work together as a team to accomplish tasks more effectively. However, it is a different matter to identify intended behavioral regularities in classrooms. The phenomenon is not peculiar to this particular experimental training program. Most traditional teacher training programs are not clear about what they expect of either their immediate or ultimate clients. The evaluator has several ways of dealing with the problem. He can take the position that the allocation of resources to examine the question cannot be justified until the intended ultimate impact is clear. (This is not a productive alternative if the program is in its final stage.) He can take the line of least resistance and examine gains in achievement. (If the program is not designed directly and immediately to affect student achievement quantitatively, this alternative cannot be defended.) He can select classroom variables that he believes to be indicators of quality education, and examine changes in them. (This approach often works at cross-purposes with program developers and leads to unhealthy conflict.) Or he can derive criterion variables by deduction. The treatment that the immediate clients receive will reflect classroom behavior in the internship or practitioner stages. (This is the alternative that was taken by the research and evaluation staff in the Ford program.)

Our evaluation of the program was essentially to find out how educators learn together and relate to one another to accomplish tasks more effectively. If the premise is accepted, it appears logical to arrange training experiences designed to facilitate relationships. If the training inputs are successful, the beliefs and behavior of intermediates should be affected. The teacher's knowledge about himself, about the role of the teacher, about the student as a social and academic animal, about the community, the school, and the class as social systems, knowledge about the learning process, his skill as a teacher, his skill in developing and analyzing curricula and related materials, his skill in identifying problems, in analysis and synthesis, his work on his own special projects, his learning how to be an effective group member, and his group's manner of relating to one another, should all be reflected in his classroom behavior. Students normally take their cues from their teacher's attitudes and behavior. The teacher is the formal leader in the classroom, the chief initiator and reactor, and his actions should be reflected in the students' actions and reactions in the classroom. The way in which teachers and students behave in classrooms should have some effect on how students view classrooms and how they view themselves. Studies have consistently established that students' attitudes toward the class and their concept of their own academic performance are related positively to cognitive growth. The cognitive growth of the students in the Ford program was not assessed for two reasons: the program was not specifically designed to promote cognitive growth directly, and our research (Reynolds 1971) indicated that, in this particular program, the students' achievement levels decreased with the adoption of new curricula at the end of the intial year, and increased in the second and third years, an indication that some time is required to deliver the program to the students.

It was first necessary to identify the specific effects of the Ford program on the teachers. We decided that, if the program is to be considered effective, Ford teachers, by the end of the academic year, should differ from those teachers who have not been exposed to the same training experience in their beliefs about education. They should perceive greater value in classroom research, be more receptive to curricular change, not place as much importance on subject matter, be more oriented toward personal adjustment of students, stress the importance of the student's viewpoint, place less importance on maintaining classrooms according to established rules and procedures, and place a greater emphasis on integrating content with the broader aspects of the students' world, so that the children are aware, not only of the facts of what they learn, but also of the meaning.

From the students' point of view, the teaching practices should be different. The students in Ford classrooms should judge the work to be more exciting. Ford teachers should use praise more often to reinforce students positively; they should encourage students more often to express feelings about the teaching. The teachers should encourage students to express ideas that are different from their own, they should talk less than other teachers, should encourage students to think for themselves more often, should permit students to lead discussions, should assign individual and group projects more often, use small groups for special projects, and, in examinations, should not test facts and memories exclusively. The students in Ford classrooms should consider that their teachers have less rigid expectations of them and are more creative and open.

Nonparticipating observers, gauging verbal behavior only, should have noticed differing classroom practices; they should have been able to notice that: Ford teachers talk less than other teachers, use praise to reinforce students positively, seek fewer responses that call for factual information from students, seek more responses that call for critical thinking.

Students in the program should differ from their counterparts who are not in the program: they should be giving factual or specific information less often, and offering the results of their critical thinking more often; they should express more positive sentiment toward their classes and higher estimates of their own academic performance (for that specific class).

We did not believe that all of the teachers exposed to Ford experiences would change, if their psychological makeup inhibited change. The kind and amount of information that we could gather would be limited. It was a matter of selecting a few control variables that would provide the best explanation for any lack of change.

The Assessment Process

The evaluation plan includes teachers and students who are participating in the Ford program and others who are not. The Ford group includes teachers in the schools and interns in several subjects. The control group is made up of teachers in the same schools, who teach various subjects. Secondary and elementary classrooms are considered as separate, distinct populations. There are fifty secondary and twelve elementary classrooms in the sample.

Initial perceptual assessments are made before the teachers join the Ford program. Perceptual and behavioral assessments of both teachers and students were made in the fall after school has been in session for about six weeks. Other comparison data are taken again toward the end of the academic year. The information is obtained in two ways: by administering instruments to both teachers and students and by observing and coding verbal interactions in classrooms. The instrumentation for teachers provides data on their psychological makeup, their beliefs about education, their receptivity to curricular change, their beliefs about the value of classroom research, and their perceptions of their own classroom behavior. The instrumentation for students includes estimates of their teachers' behavior, their attitudes toward the class (class attendance is also used to measure student sentiment), and their perceptions of their own academic standard. Observations of verbal interaction are made in approximately half of the classrooms. The CERLI Verbal Behavior Classification System is used to record and classify verbal statements made in the classroom. The statements are coded according to their process (seeking, informing, accepting, rejecting) and their content (cognitive-memory, productive critical thinking, management).

The data are processed and analyzed, and individual profiles are developed. The information, along with appropriate norms, is fed back to Ford teachers and to half of the control group teachers. The same procedure will be used for comparison data, except that all the teachers will receive feedback. Results will be analyzed by examining differences between the data collected on the two occasions. Results will also be examined for differences between Ford teachers and control group teachers who received feedback, between Ford teachers and control group teachers who did not receive feedback, and between the two control groups of teachers. The analyses should give us information about the effect of the training program. The results also will be examined to test and refine the selection process. When one accepts the premise that high class sentiment and high academic self-concept in students are indicators of good teaching, one is obliged to establish the link between these variables and the social conditions that are expected to differ between Ford and control group classrooms. The data we collected at first are being used to investigate such linkages; the data we collected later will serve as a check against the findings of the original collection.

SUMMARY

Several salient points have emerged from our illustration and are worth summarizing:

Resistance to research and evaluation can be reduced appreciably, if the causes for the resistance are known. If action to reduce resistance is to be effective, it must be designed to eradicate the causes.

Product evaluation activity may be inappropriate if the program is in a nascent or rudimentary stage.

Product evaluation that assesses the impact on the ultimate client should be delayed until the program treatment can be refined.

Process and product evaluation may be inadequate for the program. Transactional evaluation includes both and adds another important dimension, that of the interaction of evaluative acts and subsequent information with human systems.

Judgments about the state of the program are needed at various stages in its development, not just at the end.

Evaluative information can perform an integral function in program development.

Evaluation activity should be complementary to program activity (in this the author agrees with Provus [1969]).

Even when the intent is not stated, it is possible for the evaluator to deduce the intended direct and indirect impact of program treatment.

The question of what ultimate benefits derive from a training program must be answered eventually.

Most of the essential elements to be evaluated emerge mainly from either the situation or the design to measure impact.

REFERENCES

Anderson, P. *Church Meetings that Matter.* Philadelphia: United Church Press, 1965.

Bridges, Edwin M. "A Report to the Executive Committee, Ford Training and Placement Program, 31 January 1969." Mimeographed.

Cohen, D. K. "Politics and Research: Evaluation of Social Action Programs in Education." *Review of Educational Research* 40, no. 2 (April 1970): 213-238.

Getzels, J. W. "Education for the Inner City: A Practical Proposal by an Impractical Theorist." *The School Review* 75, no. 3 (Autumn 1967): 283-299.

Kepner, C. H., and Tregoe, B. B. *The Rational Manager.* New York: McGraw-Hill, 1965.

Provus, M. "Evaluation of Ongoing Programs in the Public School System." In *Educational Evaluation: New Roles, New Means.* Sixty-eighth Yearbook of the National Society for the Study of Education. Chicago: University of Chicago Press, 1969.

Reynolds, J. A. "Organizational Change and Goal Attainment." Paper read at AERA Convention, 1971, in New York.

Scriven, M. "The Methodology of Evaluation." In *Perspectives of Curriculum Evaluation.* American Educational Research Association Monograph Series on Curriculum Education. Chicago: Rand McNally, 1967.

Stuffelbeam, D. I., Foley, W. J., Gephart, W. J., Guba, E. G., Hammond, R. I., Merriman, H. O., and Provus, M. *Educational Evaluation and Decision Making.* Itasca, Ill.: Peacock, 1971.

Westbury, I. "Curriculum Evaluation." *Review of Educational Research* 40, no. 2 (April 1970): 239-260.

III TRANSACTIONAL EVALUATION IN THEORY
The Philosophy

13

THE PSYCHOLOGY OF CHANGE WITHIN AN INSTITUTION

HUBERT S. COFFEY

WILLIAM P. GOLDEN, JR.

While there is little in the psychological literature formally classified under the heading "psychology of change," many of the differentiated fields are concerned with the conditions and processes of change. These include such fields as classical learning theory, social psychology, group dynamics, and clinical psychology, particularly as the latter is oriented to therapy. We are especially indebted to the approach developed by Krech (1949), Lewin (1935), and Parsons (1951). We realize that our approach represents a particular theoretical bias, and, although there is no theory that embraces consistently every aspect of change, we believe we have selected the one that has the most usefulness to the practitioner at this time.

We think of ourselves in terms of what we *need*, what we are *interested in*, what we *want to do*. When we think of our "basic needs," we call to mind such universals as "hunger," "thirst," "sleep," and "sex." We know, too, that the natural drives that accompany these needs lead the organism to change its relationship to the environment so that its needs can be satisfied. Likewise, we know that our *interests* also have the character of driving us to act in a way that accomplishes satisfaction even though they may not seem as "basic" as our needs. When we describe the relation of our need to the objects of our interests and explain the behavior by which we undertake to obtain satisfaction, we use the term "motivation."

CHARACTERISTICS OF BEHAVIOR

Motivation may be thought of in reference to a concept of "tension." Tension describes the state of a system which is in a process of change, and the change is in the direction of equilibrium in relation to the state of neighboring systems. Thinking of experiences or situations as "tensional" means that the environment and the person are regarded as related and interdependent systems. The concept of tension is, then, more inclusive than that of need or drive. It means not only that such "basic" needs as hunger are motivational but also that the perception of any aspect of the environment may create a tendency for change in relation to it; it may be equally "motivational."

We would all agree that a political ideology which promises subsistence to a starving Chinese peasant is likely to motivate him to accept this ideology. But we would insist that the desire of an American schoolboy to achieve acceptance in the peer group is also an example of motivation. Both motives, one of basic physiological survival, the other of social acceptance, induce tensions that are resolved by the creation of a new relationship between the individual and his environment.

Differentiation and Change

As we think in everyday language about needs (tension), we also think in terms of what we have learned, what we know, how we perceive, how we see something differently from the way we have seen it before. These changes we may conceptualize by the term *differentiation*. What is unknown is actually equivalent to having no differentiated psychological structure for us, as being unstructured. As we learn about something, our perception and our knowledge of it become more differentiated, more structured. Thus, a stranger in a city learns more about the city as the unstructured whole becomes differentiated into parts and subregions. He may do this by the actual experience of walking and motoring about the city, or by becoming familiar with maps of the city, or by conversation with "old timers." The differentiation may be one which is exclusively geographical or it may be one which includes sociological or social psychological knowledge.

We can, following Lewin, think of differentiation in relation to the two major aspects of the process: the differentiation that goes on *within the person,* and the differentiation that goes on *within the environment.* In some sense this is an unreal distinction, yet perhaps a necessary one if we are to emphasize that what is differentiated is learned and will, under normal conditions, endure. When the organism changes, there is a difference in its future behavior in respect to expectations and desires. We can think of this kind of learning, those changes, as differentiations *within* the person. But just as these changes within the person are brought about in connection with changes in the environment, so also do they determine how the environment itself is perceived and experienced. The small child's concept of a "table" may readily be as something upon which desirable articles are placed beyond his reach. Later when his experience with "table" includes sitting at a small table, his concept of table is enlarged and his expectations concerning his own behavior are changed. His concept of "table" is then said to be more differentiated than before, and this differentiation has behavior consequences. This implies a change in the way the child sees things and responds to his environment.

Akin to the particular use of the concept of differentiation is the more general concept of cognitive structure. We have seen that cognitive structure may be produced by increased differentiation resulting from the subdividing of regions into smaller units. But "sometimes a change in cognitive structure occurs without increase or decrease in the degree of differentiation" (Lewin 1942). In some situations a change in cognitive structure is brought about by one's seeing a connection between areas which previously were not seen as related. Much problem solving and "insight" represent this type of change in cognitive structure. Thus, to use an oversimplified example from therapy, the patient may be well aware of two aspects of himself, his self-depreciation and his strong need for unrealistic perfection. Through his therapy he may see a connection between his own perception of himself as unworthy and his belief that all his goals are unattainable.

Not all change is initiated by the effects of newer concepts on cognitive structure; in some instances the observed effect is related to the tension system. Thus, we may think of change in the person's own needs or interests, or a change which is induced by forces in the environment. The latter may involve compelling the individual to do an unpleasant action by the imposition of force, or through the counterbalancing of one set of needs or interests by establishing another more powerful set. For instance, a school system may require that its teachers take certain courses if they are to be eligible for promotion. The goal of promotion may be stronger than the dislike of having to spend time and money on something which, at the time of choice, may be seen as intrinsically worthless, so the teacher may choose to enroll in the course. The imposition of force by the setting of requirements does not in itself, however, decree that the activity will continue to be disliked.

In some cases where direct force is imposed, particularly in those cases where the disliked activity leads to a reward, there may be an actual change in interest or valence with a consequent change in cognitive structure. Thus, although there may be initial resistance to embarking upon the required activity, the teacher may find that the activity is one he likes. Most teachers are familiar with the change in attitude toward reading that the child experiences once he is able to master the effective techniques. The steps involved in becoming a speedy reader, for example, may meet with great resistance to learning and a negative attitude toward reading; yet, once these skills have been mastered, the child may become an avid reader. However, where force is imposed without any change in cognitive structure or without development of intrinsic interest or motivation, the desired effects are not likely to survive after pressure has been relaxed.

The impetus to do something, to learn, or to carry out a new activity, may be associated with the meaning which the activity acquires and the goals which are established. A change in interest or the awareness of a new need may give a particular activity a new meaning and, hence, a new goal and a new value. New interests, changed needs, and newly established goals are associated with new ways in which things are seen. Frequently the sources of changes in perception are related to one of the following conditions: there is a crisis that indicates that new methods of approach are necessary if the problematic situation is to be resolved (for example, new methods of approach may be required by some change in the cognitive structure of the particular situation); or there is a sensitization to new ideologies or goals with consequent shifts in the levels of aspiration, so that what may have been perceived at one time as satisfactory, is now, in the frame of reference of a new set of values, regarded as inadequate. Under these conditions the new values set new goals, and the new goals are associated with the creation of new tensions or new needs. Thus, an adolescent boy found himself an accepted member of his group when he became adept in playing a guitar as an accompaniment to group singing. His motivation to learn the skill was related to his awareness that he could not compete with others on the basis of physical prowess because of his small size but would be accepted through the development of this skill. Another illustration might be an adolescent girl who influenced her "gang" to accept peers of different racial backgrounds after her own significant experience in an interracial camp.

The needs of an individual are to a very high degree determined by social factors. Thus, the fact that one belongs to a group, or many different groups, may induce needs which lead to change. The needs of the person are also affected by the ideology and conduct of those groups to which he would like to belong or from which he would like to be set apart. Needs may be induced by the force of another person or a group, particularly where the force is related to social status and prestige, or where the person is seen as an instrumentality for achieving a goal or as the agent for preventing the movement of others. In many ways similar to the needs induced by the force of another person are the needs or tensions the individual experiences as a result of belonging to a group or adhering to its goals. The similarity between the two is apparent if we think of the power of one person as emanating from his importance to the other person, particularly in the case of one with whom he shares goals or ideologies.

Relative Connection and Isolation

It is a matter of common observation that some attitudes of a person or some of the objects in his environment have greater significance to him than do others. When aspects of his environment —what he perceives, what he apprehends—have deeper significance, we usually think of this significance as having more emotionally toned meanings to the person. Thus, the symbols of family, nation, religious group, or even political ideology are likely to evoke a more potent emotional response from him. Sometimes we say he has "deeper" feelings about these things—that they have greater meaning for him. If we employ a Lewinian concept, we can say these things are more *central* to him. They are less easily expressed, more private, more intimate, more personal. Just as some things are more central, so other attitudes on his part or objects in his environment have less emotional significance to him. We say these latter aspects of the person are more *peripheral.* Thus, we can differentiate regions of the person, just as we can differentiate regions in the environment.

Concepts of tension and differentiation have a basic relationship to any consideration of change, for they involve what might be thought of as both the emotional and the cognitive aspects of the relationship of the person to his world, particularly to his world of other persons. In any relationship, both aspects—the *cathectic,* by which we mean the feeling and emotional aspects, and the *cognitive,* by which we mean the differentiated way of seeing and knowing the world—become integrated. Change in the individual takes place in connection with both of these characteristics. When we use the term *cathectic,* we mean the emotional investment which the person makes in an object or in a goal. Its importance in change lies in its motivational significance. Rarely does change come about without the person's developing dissatisfaction with things as they are, without his developing a new level of aspiration for himself. But dissatisfaction or a new level of aspiration may be very threatening unless the person sees how he can change, unless it is possible for him to understand the regions through which he must travel, psychologically, in order to reach the goal. Thus, he must see himself in relation to his world in a different way. We think of this differentiated construct as *cognitive.*

At times we see these aspects compartmentalized. An inspirational talk to teachers may have the salutary effect of bringing about dissatisfactions or raising the level of aspiration to new heights. It may, however, have a deleterious effect in the long run if there seems to be no way in which the aspiration can be realized; for without some implementation of the inspiration, the exhortation to change may eventuate in despair or in the total rejection of the briefly envisioned goal. When only the cognitive aspects are stressed without any attempt to arouse emotional involvement, the differentiated way of perceiving may be just another set of techniques unrelated to any felt need or deeply perceived value. The individual must want what he has not wanted before, must recognize the barriers that are to be overcome if he is to reach the new goal, and must be able to perceive the pathways to the goal.

While it is true that most persons have aspirations that would indicate dissatisfaction with their present behavior, some of their values and beliefs seem mutually antagonistic or antithetical. Thus, a person may have considerable resistance toward this goal. Becoming a better teacher may mean, for instance, that he must realize that he is not perfect, as he now thinks he is, or achieving his goal may involve changing his relationship to his principal, who seems to like him as he is now. He may be torn between his own desire to function more effectively and his desire not to impair the esteem that he feels he now enjoys in the eyes of his principal. We have all seen the internal struggle of children who try to resolve the conflict between living up to the expectations both of their peers *and* their parents.

Individual Change Process—Psychotherapy

The psychotherapist involved in the process of producing change in the behavior of another person is essentially concerned with dealing with the struggle between different subsystems of the central regions which are in a state of tension. Thus, the objectives of psychotherapy are essentially to help the person make new differentiations, discover new meanings, see relationships anew, and correct distortions in his perception of existing relationships. Acquiring a new motor skill by learning to drive an automobile and developing more reality-oriented relationships to other persons (learning to express the way one feels) are both instances of learning. But they differ, and in the process of reeducation this difference is very great in several respects: in the centrality of the tensions that the patient has, in their effect upon his perception of reality, in the relation between the individual's level of aspiration and his realistic conception of himself, and in the conflict between those subregions which are related to values he wants to achieve.

Experiences in psychotherapy have placed great emphasis upon the primacy of the phenomenological world of the patient—that is, the world as *he* sees it. What has meaning, what has value, what he honors or dishonors, what invites him to approach or frightens him into withdrawal—these are based upon the way he sees the world in which he lives, his cognitive structure. One of the prime sources of his discomfort or ineffectiveness is the extent to which his cognitive structure departs from what we might call "social reality." Thus, his level of aspiration may clearly be incongruent with what is realistic. His requirements for himself may be beyond that which can be expected for the human being. He may repress all of the impulses that normally are expressed in aggression. He may regard other persons with suspicion as threatening and destructive agents, when there is no reason to perceive them as such. He may be caught between his need to see himself ministered to by others while defying their authority, and a need to see himself independent beyond any boundaries of social living. In all of these typical instances the patient sees his world and himself in a way others cannot share.

What is the true basis of reality is a philosophical question, the ramifications of which we cannot pursue here. Unlike the scientifically constructed physical world, social reality depends upon the overlapping character of many phenomenological fields, and the criterion here of social reality is what Sullivan (1953) calls "consensual validation." The patient is likely to depart quite clearly from that which is consensually validated, even though within our culture considerable range of perception is permitted. Thus, neurotic patients have been shown by studies to have a significantly different perception of themselves from what is seen by others. A patient may see himself as benign, generous, loving, and giving, but others in a therapy group, for example, may see him as hostile, aggressive, and dominating. What the true characteristic of the patient is we are more likely to find in the consensus of other patients, providing there is not a collective distortion of the person. This consensus or agreement of others about a person is called "consensual validation." Providing we have no more objective measure of the reality than this agreement, we must rely upon this as the standard. Much of what we know about social standards and social perception belongs to this level of agreement.

Clinicians seem to agree that the perception of the patient is likely to be distorted because of rather central areas of tension. The clinician usually relates the way the person sees his environment to certain areas of disturbance within the "deeper layers" of the person. Probably the meaning of "deeper layers" can be equated with the concept of more minute, more central, differentiated areas of the person. Most clinicians trace disturbances to historical causes, such as difficulties with parents, sibling rivalry, or anal fixations. We would not deny the importance of the history of the individual and the effect of childhood relationships or traumatic experiences. But of greater relevance here is that, rather than dealing with these events as incidents in the life of the patient, we are encountering the consequences of these events in the impact they have made in developing certain stable valuations and perceptions.

Much of what is known about the psychotherapeutic situation has implications for effecting change. The relationship between trainer and trainee must be a permissive one, that is, it must permit the trainee to express his feelings, to indicate his needs, to communicate his tensions. It must deal with the tensions and the cognitive structure as he presents them, not in the way in which the trainer might idealistically hope that he would see them. The trainer must be willing and able to tolerate and respect resistance. The trainer must serve in many ways as the representative of reality, as the person against whom the perceptions of the trainee can be tested, and as the person who can transmit to the trainee effective methods of determining the nature of reality.

We have evidence that change takes place most significantly in a relationship which is *participative* and *collaborative*. What is transmitted to the trainee is most significantly communicated through *two-way communication*. It is a relationship that is *essentially cooperative* even though there may be a distinct division of labor. For change to be significant in its effects, it must involve the central regions of the person, the *deep-lying values* and *attitudes about the self*. For this to occur, the change must be oriented to *felt needs* and *greater sensitization*, and must include *opportunities to engage in the process of interaction* that express these feelings and translate them into concrete action steps.

STABILITY AND CHANGE IN SOCIAL SYSTEMS

Thus far we have focused our attention exclusively on the person and on the conditions that bring about change. We have thought of the person in relation to tension systems, differentiation, and isolation, but we have tried to view him as having direct and continuous communication with his environment and as having a dynamic relationship with it. Perhaps the most influential aspects of his environment are those forces that emanate from the social system of which he is a part. These forces are particularly influential in determining individual behavior because they represent the world of human relationships.

Boundary-Maintaining Characteristics
We can think of social phenomena as they exist apart from the person by using many of the same concepts that we have used in thinking about the person and the environment. We can think of the social system as a boundary-maintaining structure existing in relatively constant patterns, which we may think of as "moving pattern-constancies." We use the concept of "moving pattern-constancies" because the social system is always in a process of adaptation. The tempo of this moving equilibrium may vary considerably in time and place. Thus, on the one hand, in a preliterate society isolated from

the effects of other cultures, the tempo of change may be very slow, and such institutions as puberty rites, for example, may continue relatively unchanged from one century to another. On the other hand, our own social system is in a constant state of change largely because of the demands that our technical advances place upon social institutions. A survey of changes in attitudes, folkways, and mores brought about by the automobile would give us an excellent picture of the constant process of social adaptation to a technological innovation. And even as this is said, the example is a little quaint, for already our attention is focused on the jet-propelled and supersonic airplane.

Social systems tend to receive the impact of disruptions which go on in the physical environment. Thus, where there are significant disruptions, such as a change in economic base resulting from the disappearance of a natural resource or the invention of a new instrumentality, the social system undergoes considerable alterations. These may range from transformation of the previous patterns toward more adaptive ones to even the dissolution of the system itself and the creation of an entirely new arrangement. This is not to say, however, that social institutions are themselves "sensitive" to changes in environmental forces, and that we can expect systematic and adaptive modifications as a matter of course. The phenomenon of internal stability frequently desensitizes the social system to the environmental demands. In some cases such internal stability may actually amount to rigidity and, in these cases, the intransigence of the system itself may jeopardize survival of the inhabitants, as is notable in the extreme case of Labrador fishing villages, where the "rituals" of a particular type of fishing persisted long after they were economically effective. More typical, however, in institutional complexes, is the outmoding in one part of the system by developments in another. Semiautonomous attitudes within one part may be incompatible with technological advances in another. We think of this as "cultural lag."

We can emphasize in another way the connection of the individual and the social system when we examine the way in which the person is seen as intimately related to the preservation of the system itself, as contributing to its boundary-maintaining characteristics. The phenomena of learning and socialization, the values to which the individual is exposed and, in spite of the apparent wide divergences in our own culture, the finite repertoire of possible behaviors, all of these are in a general sense perpetuated to support and insure the continuation of the social system. For example, in preliterate societies, child-rearing practices are designed to produce the socially desired character structure. The social system would seem in an implicit way to specify those purposes and objectives that, through the processes of socialization and learning on the part of the individual, tend to maintain the system and develop individuals that fit it. It goes without saying that the simpler the social system, the more easily is this congruence of individual and social pattern achieved.

Individual and Institutional Role Integration

There are several ways in which we may view individual behavior as it appears in an institutional setting. One of the most useful of these methods involves the concept of "role." Thus the "teacher" can be thought of in terms of the role that is prescribed for teachers in the general sense of the social system and in the particular institutional subpart, "the school." Actually, the institution can be said to consist of a "complex of institutional role integrates." The institution of the school consists of a prescribed set of roles that inform the teacher what his behavior ought to be. Within any institution there is some latitude in the way the role is assimilated; likewise, there are defined limits to the amount of deviance that will be permitted. In addition to general role prescriptions for "school people," there are differentiations made between the roles of classroom teachers and administrators. In fact, the belief and value systems of these two groups frequently differ substantially and in such a way as to result in conflict.

Roles Are Interactional: Involve Relationships

The essential aspect of the concept of role is that it is interactional and complementary. The role of the person is interactional in the sense that it always involves relations to some object other than the self, or the person. Usually, if not always, this interaction is with another person, hence the role can be said to be *interpersonal.* However, this does not mean that what is interpersonal is necessarily "face to face." It may be interpersonal because it involves a series of expectations on the part of one individual with respect to others. These expectations define how the individual should act. It is just this element of expectations that, although it involves an image of interactions, may operate as an attitude, or disposition to act, without involving others directly in a face-to-face fashion. Thus, in the role of the teacher there are certain expectancies that the teacher has concerning his behavior with students and also certain behavior that he expects from students. This role is not limited to specific educational tasks as such but includes a great deal that has to do with his total position or status as a person.

Roles Are Complementary

A second characteristic of roles is that they are complementary. By this we mean that the expectations of one person are related to the expectations of another. More properly speaking, we can think of this relationship as one that involves the *expectations* of the one and the *sanctions* of the other. Expectations are often supported and reinforced by sanctions. What the child feels is expected of him by the parent or the teacher may often be just what is sanctioned by the parent or the teacher. It is not inevitable in a social relationship. A person may discover that his expectations, what he perceives his role to be, are quite different from what is expected or, more properly, sanctioned by others.

The role is likely to involve a feeling of approval or disapproval. From the standpoint of the social system, it involves the dimensions of conformity and deviance. Self-approval does not always mean conformity with the sanctions of the other. Frequently the person may realize his expectations through deviance from the sanctions of the other. Thus, the "bohemian" would be embarrassed by the sanction of approval from the "philistine." Of course these two contrasts do not exhaust the catalogue of possible deviance-conformity relations. While two persons might involve mutually complementary expectations and sanctions, this mutuality may be in deviance from the total social system, or some aspect of it. The deviance expectation, through which the person may seek and, indeed, receive disapproval from the others, is somewhat related to his feeling of approval in some other expectation-sanction relationship. Dissent from one value aspect of the social system means conformity with some other aspect.

The complex of role expectations and sanctions is not typically confined to a single act or a particular relationship. Rather, the person may very well *internalize* within his role a whole motivational disposition to conform to or deviate from the institutional pattern. This may become, through internalization, a part of the central regions of the person, a part of a more or less enduring relationship to the institutional complex. Thus, the person in a particular situation behaves in a manner consistent with his usual behavior in many interpersonal relationships. He is usually concerned that he not only perform in a manner sanctioned by the other but that his behavior in general is sanctioned, that he is, indeed, a sanctioned person.

Institutions and Individual's Motivation

Institutional systems must incorporate, to a greater or lesser extent, the major motivational interests of the participants. Freud has described the major problems of the person as centering around the issues of *work and love*. Both aspects of the person's relationship to society demand institutional forms that provide appropriate roles in which these needs can be fulfilled. For instance, the problem of work is likely to demand the acceptance of certain role expectations, and these vary widely in a complex society where many different types of work relations exist. Similarly, in love relationships the society institutionalizes the roles of husband, wife, parent, brother, and sister and, because the control of sexuality is so important for the survival of society, these roles usually permit less deviance than those which are occupationally oriented.

Cultures vary greatly in the particular institutional prescriptions that define the role behavior with respect to these central social concerns. Through socialization and indoctrination, the essential affective factors in training to be a social participant, the role expectations involved in behavior concerned with work and love, are communicated and internalized. While much of what is internalized has application to the social system as a whole (sex differentiated roles, for instance), an institution within the social system, such as the *particular* occupation, develops a set of standards and beliefs that characterize it and determine to some extent the relations that its *particular* participants have with other segments of the social system. The medical profession is an excellent example of this. It goes without saying that these value standards may be codified into law or made explicit in a public body of ethical standards including permissions and taboos. On the implicit level, however, the role makes certain demands in behavior and attitudes which are role-syntonic, that is, they become an intrinsic characteristic of the person. Often the stereotypes associated with an occupation are caricatures of the actual extent to which the person internalizes his occupational role and becomes in a total way the "physician" or the "teacher."

CHARACTERISTICS OF INSTITUTIONAL GROUPS: STATUS QUO

Although social institutions are a complex of role integrations that arise historically over a considerable period of time, they tend to develop a formal, rationalized structure. The degree of organization required may well be a result of the scope and comprehensiveness of the function that a particular institution has in relation to the total structure of society. Thus, while we may think of the school as an institution that performs a function delegated to it by the larger society, the difference between the "little red schoolhouse" and the complex metropolitan school system directly reflects the greater complexity of the urban community. In addition to the highly developed institutional characteristics, the urban school reflects the increasing range of responsibilities that are thought of as "educational" and are being delegated to the school by the larger social system.

In a modern social structure, the offices of a specific organization are integrated in a manner designed to carry out the purpose of that organization. These offices usually form a hierarchy, and each office or each level of offices within the hierarchy has an established social status around which are organized certain obligations and privileges. Thus, the obligations of the principal are different from those of teachers, as are his privileges. Similarly, the obligations and the privileges of the supervisor are likely to be different from those of the persons supervised. These offices, with their corresponding obligations and privileges defined by specific rules, prescribe the competence and responsibility that their officers must have. Thus, the office of the principal demands certain competencies not required of the teacher. This is true in reverse, also. Authority involved in decision-making responsibility and power (manifest in the degree of influence) is included in the office itself as a part of the institutional structure.

Clearly defined social distance between occupants of different official levels denotes the corresponding difference in obligations and privileges. These status differences signify the distribution of power and authority within the social structure of the particular institution and serve to objectify official contacts by prescribing their modes. Moreover, explicitness in prescription of modes of relationship minimizes the friction that usually arises from ambiguity in relationship. The specific institutional roles, with their supporting expectancies, may facilitate interaction on a formal and public level. Thus, each officer is protected from the impulsiveness or arbitrariness of the others by the constraint of mutually recognized procedures and regulations.

Ends and Means in Social Structure

The distinctive attributes of hierarchic organization in social institutions are clearly illustrated by the urban school system. The hierarchy of offices of superintendent, principal, supervisor, and teacher, together with the official sentiment that surrounds the prescription of "going through channels," is in itself a regulation that recognizes the authority of existing hierarchical status. Though usually justified, such a regulation may be a jealous guarding of power, with clarity of communication an excuse for its existence. The formalized social structure, or a particular institution thereof, is characterized by at least two essential elements. One is the culturally defined goals, purposes, and interests that indicate what is held "worth striving for," objectives that are legitimate for all members of the society and comprising sentiments and values more or less accepted by most persons. The other element is the culturally accepted modes of achieving these goals, which are defined by what is considered allowable in the sense that they are permitted by the sentiments or values of the society, not necessarily because they are efficient.

Cultural goals and institutionalized means for achieving them are not always in a close correspondence. Merton (1949) has pointed out that emphasis on cultural goals may be accompanied by little stress on the means of achieving such goals. Thus, the educational goal of "educating the whole child" may represent an aspiration with little attention paid to the institutional means of achieving it. Under such conditions, aspirations are likely to be idealistic or sloganistic. An alternative to the overstress on ends, as compared to the anemia of means, is what is substantially its opposite. Thus, a school system may develop highly institutionalized procedures and, at the same time, become forgetful of the goals. Institutionalized means may become self-contained practices while institutional conduct becomes a virtual ritual, with conformity with procedures elevated to a central value.

Equilibrium in Production Institutions

Both these variants from a truly productive relationship between institutional goals and institutional practices are barriers to the development of change. For we must think of productive institutional structure as maintaining an effective equilibrium between these two aspects of social structure, thus bringing satisfactions to individuals through accepting institutional goals and attaining them by institutionalized procedures.

The problem of institutional change follows directly, we think, from this analysis. Any institution is built around a set of purposes and values. Moreover, the institution develops means by which these purposes are carried out. The function of the particular institution, however, is influenced heavily by what is going on within the total social system. Thus, if the economic structure of the society changes, this is bound to have an influence upon the institutional subparts and will demand some revaluation of goals and some reassessment of means. *The central problem of institutional change is the develop-ment of those conditions in which institutional goals and means can be reassessed for the purpose not only of adapting to change going on within the social system but also of assuming responsibility for exerting influence on the various alternatives of change that may be open to the society.*

Many of the problems of the modern school system can be seen in this frame of reference. Certainly the goals of the school as perceived by various segments of the community are in controversy. These conflicts are likely to be a reflection of conflicts about the goals and purposes of the larger society. Moreover, to defend one set of institutionalized means against another is to force one's self to accept one set of purposes in preference to another. That these are highly charged with emotion means that the goals are based upon value premises in which the choice is bound to have threats to existing vested interests. The school administrator is in the unenviable posi-tion of having to espouse one value and reject another, each of which may be supported by powerful segments of the community. He is likely to escape into the comfort of instrumental ritualism. Thus, "the school's business is to teach" symbolizes the new focus on administrative means. But the avoidance of partisanship by this means is an illusion; escape only contributes to the status quo.

Stereotyped Roles

As we analyze the characteristics of hierarchical organizations, their positive attainments and functions in emphasizing efficiency, we need also to consider some of the internal stresses and strains. In particular it has seemed to us that the efficiency of organization, which contributes to the functional achievement of an educational institution, may actually work against the realization of educational goals. In the general sense, hierarchical organization may develop what Veblen (1904) has called "trained incapacity," the technical skill which serves the particular end, but which, while successfully applied in the past, may be inappropriate under changed conditions. The well-trained administrator, to use a slightly expanded version of Veblen's intention, may be able to make keen discriminations in certain areas that involve his particular administrative skill (specific occupational role), but his very attention to these matters means that he develops blind spots in areas involving other perspectives. Frequently his "reliability, precision, and efficiency" become highly valued because external forces prescribe that this is what his administrative role should be. His acceptance of these sanctions often is related to his need for security and the wish to be protected from more controversial goal values.

In such situations there can develop a virtual displacement of sentiments from goals to means that in turn fosters the vast overvaluation of means, with little questioning of ends. Concern with adherence to regulations and the propriety of procedures becomes an end in itself that is coupled with "timidity, conservatism, and technicism," and, above all, conformity. Although many aspects of the bureaucratic role could be mentioned, one of the most essential is that any attempt to personalize relationships is likely to be looked upon as graft, favoritism, "apple-polishing"—certainly as improper. Although we recognize the extent to which personal relationships in an organizational structure may indeed promote individual exploitation of that particular system, creative advances toward productive change have their genesis in the quality of interpersonal relationships within the system.

Institutional Roles and Group Cohesion

The school organization frequently poses the conflict between what are administrative values, such as efficiency of records, orderliness, and technical excellence, and what are goal values, including concern for the growth and development of the individual child and the progress of mature group relationships. The latter values may necessitate the tolerance of conditions inimical to the efficiency of a bureaucratic system. The adventure and experimentalism of a progressive approach to educational goals may be hampered by the social distance that a bureaucratic organization prescribes as the proper relationship between different status levels. Although the conflict may exist as we see it with certain deprivations to the teacher who feels a victim of the impersonal organization, we should recognize certain important secondary gains to him as possibly one reason for his not rebelling against it. A well-organized structure develops an impressive solidarity that can resist intrusion from the segments of the community outside. Actually the teacher may be protected from criticism or complaints of those holding alien educational values, such as parents or noneducational groups, by the impressive *esprit de corps* and in-group cohesion that, in other situations, may be frustrating. For where there is a virtual monopoly of enterprise, such as in the school, protest from the outside is likely to be met with ideological uniformity, and in-group identification can occur speedily under the situation of attack from the outside, even though there be internal disagreement about the very values that are under threat.

In addition to the protection that such group cohesion gives to the erstwhile dissenting teacher, the organization, where it becomes thoroughly defensive, can resist changes that, under reasonable conditions of receptivity, might have been sparked by the "intruder." Organizations can develop highly specialized ways of seeming to be receptive; thus, the defense may be disarming to the intruder when it is essentially "nondirective," even though the status quo is resolutely maintained.

CHARACTERISTICS OF INSTITUTIONAL GROUPS

Social scientists tend to publish more about the characteristics of a given society than they do about the processes of change that go on within the group. The process of change is difficult to study under any circumstance, and particularly so when it is thought of in connection with the impingement of environmental conditions upon a given social system or studied with respect to the influence that one relatively autonomous part of a culture may have upon another.

Turning to the institution of science itself, we see a general cultural attitude toward knowledge and toward the social structure in which change is accepted and fostered. The acceptance of the validity of the scientific method, while widespread within our culture, is at times uneven. The approach of the scientific method to economics, to medicine, to welfare, and to education is welcomed by some but may be feared by others. Knowledge is bound to be inimical to some values and, by its nature, brings about thrusts toward change, perhaps followed by some disruption. As John Dewey pointed out (1938), every thinker places some part of a stable world in peril. Yet the climate of opinion that so universally supports research and the pursuit of truth, usually regardless of its consequences, is not isolated from a prevailing attitude toward the encouragement of progress and the existence of deeply rooted cultural attitudes associated with rationality and experimentalism. Research of a scientific character, either basic or applied, has become a necessary part of most social enterprises, even gaining respectability in quarters traditionally hostile to scientific advance.

It seems that one can hardly view these developments without being impressed by the extent to which they imply that social change and the direction of social processes are the legitimate and necessary activity of any segment of the community. Perhaps there has been a scarcely perceptible shift in the way in which we conceive of social change. Formerly, we associated social change with cosmic historical forces, and the problem of the social scientist was to identify, describe, and interpret these forces. Today the methodology of science is being applied more frequently to the solution of specific problems and the analysis of specific situations. Empirical methods of data collection, clarification of relevant hypotheses and variables, an attitude of objectivity, and other institutionalized precepts of science are increasingly taken as moral commitments which tend to characterize the process of intelligent analysis. The aim of such analysis is almost uniformly directed toward improvement in the functions of the institution or organization, and the values that may be observed would seem to imply the recognition of planned social change.

Change Within Institutions

Now all of this would have little interest for us were it not for the fact that it describes the social and cultural media through which individual change most typically takes place. Despite its popularity, psychotherapy is not the typical situation for individual change in our society. Much more common are the situations *within organizations and institutions* where individual change takes place. This change may take place in either of two ways: by studied arrangements as a part of organizational planning where the procedure is formal in character, or by the induction of the individual into a new group, the change being brought about under informal pressures.

When change results from organizational planning, the person is made aware of a preconceived plan directed toward him, although it may function primarily on an information-giving level, as in orientation programs. In the second instance, there is no formal program directed toward change, but it is quite clear from studies of informal groups within more formal organizations that membership in the new groups affects the values and attitudes of the new member as well as providing him with information. In any case, even though formal attempts at directing change in the individual may be undertaken, the greater potency of the informal organization for producing change can be verified.

The person's emotional relationship to the organization, his sense of belonging, his emotional attitude toward the objects that symbolize it are much more likely to be determined by the informal, or psyche-group, processes than by the formal, for his membership in the informal organization immediately mobilizes his feelings, his loyalties, his values for acceptance, and his need for belongingness. The extent to which the formal organization also pulls upon these motivational attributes—tension regions or quasi needs—depends primarily upon the closeness in communication between formal processes and formal directives and the degree to which needs that tend to be satisfied by the informal organization can be satisfied through task-oriented pursuits relevant to the purposes of the formal organization.

Effectiveness of Informal Organization

There is no guarantee at all that the purposes of the informal organization will mesh with those of the formal. In fact, there is considerable evidence to show that the two groups may operate in undercover conflict, the one providing covert resistance to the other. Change of the individual is most effective, however, when his membership in the informal group overlaps membership in the larger organization. This is to say, the identification that he has with the subpart is closely connected with and in no significant way antagonistic to his identification with the larger organization. The factors that influence the amount and direction of change in the *member of the group* can be seen as related to the extent to which the group in which he has most significant membership *is itself an agent of change.*

GROUP MEMBERSHIP AND INDIVIDUAL CHANGE

As we have indicated, much of the concern about individual change has been expressed in connection with the individual's membership in a group. To evaluate all of the studies that have been reported about the effects of this membership would go beyond our scope. Our purpose will be to emphasize various research findings and to indicate the particular theoretical positions as they seem to apply to the problems of individual change.

We find useful the basic assumption that the problem-solving activities of groups are similar to those of the individual. A group goal is reached by overcoming barriers in the process of movement toward it. As is true for goals sought by individuals, group goals are dependent upon the character of the environment, the possibilities that exist, the difficulties to be encountered, and the limitations that are imposed by environmental demands. Thus, for example, we have seen that for any particular group, the characteristics of the organizational hierarchy itself influence the ability of the group to reach its goal.

Internal Processes of Groups

Internal processes within the group help determine its ability to move toward the goal. This we can think of as a dimension of emotionality that characterizes the group in its problem-solving activities. Thelen (1954), following Bion (1948a, b), has studied empirically this aspect of group functioning and has been able to quantify Bion's clinical concepts of dependence, fight-flight, and pairing, as contrasted to "work." We can think of the concept of work as being primarily goal oriented, but the aspects of emotionality may be characteristic group tensions which either produce barriers to reaching goals or doing work or may, if organized in the direction of work, function as strong motivating forces. Groups that are dependent seek nourishment and protection by a strong member or leader; the group may mobilize forces against something, either to fight it or run away from it (fight-flight), or the group may see itself as existing to establish intimate pair relationships (pairing).

There is little doubt that the internal fabric of the group—its tensions, its ideology, and its "personality"—influences individual motivation and individual change. A work group may be characterized by a high degree of dependency, with all members sharing the same passivity, fearing the risks of incurring leader disfavor and at the same time experiencing restlessness and even intragroup rivalries because no member can realize his effective individual potential. In another situation, the internal rivalries may become so divisive as to exhaust the energies of the group in interclique hostilities in which alternate patterns of domination and submission drive the individual into either hyperaggression or passivity, whichever is most congenial to him temperamentally. Yet the very forces that produce destructiveness in groups are forces that may produce constructive behavior under effective leadership. Dependency, for instance, has on its positive side loyalty and identification with the group goal; conflict has in its positive dimension involvement in group activity and the development of creative alternatives. We can look at emotionality as a motivation-tension dimension of the group; it is effective if the resources for action can be directed effectively toward a goal.

Leadership, Decision Making, and Standards

We are interested in the internal processes of groups because the group's internal structure is closely related to the effectiveness of both the group and the individual in the group. This structure can be thought of as related to several dimensions that, while universal within groups, vary from group to group in degree and in the manner in which they exist. The first characteristic is *type of leadership*. The well-known studies of the social climates of groups (Lippitt and White 1943) indicate clearly that differences in atmospheres associated with autocratic, democratic, and anarchic leadership lead to differences in behavior of the members. It is sufficient to point out that where leadership engaged the participation of the group members in setting goals and planning work, as was done in the democratic group, the amount of cooperative endeavor and the heightened enthusiasm for the group was much greater than in the anarchic or autocratic groups.

The second characteristic affecting the group would seem to center about the *group's freedom and ability to make decisions*. The classic work here is that of Lewin and associates (1951) in the field of decisions regarding food habits. Lewin showed that in a situation in which group discussion was followed by a group decision regarding a course of action, the members were more likely to persist in carrying out the activities than in a situation in which the discussion did not result in a group decision. This observation is even more significant in view of the fact that the group decision was carried out, for the most part, by individuals after they had terminated face-to-face relationships with the group.

Closely related to decision making is the *development of group standards*, a third group characteristic. A group's members develop expectations or standards that apply to the behavior, attitudes, and beliefs of all members of the group. Standards are more strongly enforced by the group the more relevant they are to the group goals and activities. This seems to be true not only when the group develops standards with respect to a common goal but also when the group emphasizes the meeting of individual needs. Here the group develops standards for "confiding." Through this process, the conflict between dealing with deeply personal problems and being un-willing to be seen by others in a self-deprecating light can be worked through. The working through of resistance in this type of group develops the freedom to view his own position without subjecting himself to punishment and ostracism. This is an important factor in cooperative activities because failure to identify is deeply feared until a group norm of permissiveness is developed and internalized.

Group Support of Change

The establishment of group norms in the direction of change is not inevitable. However, where change is itself a goal of the group, norms that include change can be established and function to support change in behavior or attitude of the individual within the group. The fact that a group may explore, open up channels for change, and support newly acquired behavior and attitudes is of the greatest importance. For, to the extent that the group support of change in the individual helps members see the need for change, and helps them take the necessary steps in the direction of acquiring new attitudes and behaviors—to that extent the group can be said to have developed a *new culture* that, in itself, supports and encourages individual change. It should be noted that the individual's relation to any social system of which he is a member is such that change can scarcely take place if it jeopardizes his membership in the group or detracts from his sense of belonging. However, when change becomes a function of his membership and is a part of his group identifica-tion, then change itself becomes a valued property of the group.

While we have thought of these three characteristics of groups—*leadership, decision making,* and *group norms,* as of especial impor-tance in affecting individual behavior and have treated them sepa-rately, we are aware of their dynamic interrelatedness. The type of leadership in the group affects the freedom of the group to make decisions. Whether the group can make its own decisions with respect to goals, manner of operation, use of resources, planning for action, and evaluation of process depends upon whether the group can itself be permitted to assume these functions. Although the assumption of these responsibilities does not guarantee "efficiency," it is likely to enhance the group's cohesiveness and to develop the conditions under which the group exerts greater influence on its members.

Cohesiveness and Change

The principle of cohesiveness can be seen as one of cardinal importance in Cartwright's summary (1951) of the ways in which research findings have shown groups to be of influence upon individual change. He points out that those people who are apt to be changed and those who are to exert influence toward change on the part of others must have a strong sense of belonging to the same group. Further studies have reinforced this point by showing that discussion groups operating with participatory leadership have demonstrated greater influence toward change than these operating with supervisory leadership. The chances for change seem to be increased by the manifestation of a strong "we" feeling in the group. It is probably not amiss to point out that whenever educational aims have been directed toward development and inculcation of attitudes (character) as in the English university system, much more attention is placed upon the tutorial method (strong teacher-student relationship) than in those educational systems with a strong emphasis on information giving.

Cartwright also points out that the more attractive the group is to its members, the greater is the influence it can exert. Attractiveness of the group is related to the degree to which it satisfies members' needs. The satisfaction of members' needs, in turn, is related to the identification of needs and the building of group experience in such a way as to satisfy these needs. Thus, a group that is formed to satisfy the particular needs of its members, and in which these needs have a central focus, is likely to form a cohesive base. However, we should be aware of the fact that the needs of members are not static; they emerge and change in the process of the members' becoming more aware of and more sensitive to the values of group activity.

Cohesive Group May Be More Fluid

It is important that the productive relationship between need satisfaction and group cohesion be maintained. To this end, the group members must participate in the leadership functions, the processes of goal formulation, the planning of appropriate steps to goal realization, and the evaluation of these aspects of leadership experience. Under these conditions the attractiveness of group work is not synonymous with euphoric emotionality but with a realistic relationship between the group function of establishing procedures calculated to satisfy the selective needs of the membership. Thus, the forces of attraction and cohesion enable individual members of the group to respond with greater readiness to the ideas and suggestions of others.

Cohesion is also associated with another aspect of group activity conducive to change, namely, greater fluidity. When a group develops considerable cohesion, members may function much more freely in a "trial and error" fashion. Verbal expression, attitudes manifested, or values exposed under conditions of greater cohesion may be exhibited without fear of retribution or personal criticism. Whatever attitude or value is expressed in the group, there need be no unfavorable consequences. In other words, with group cohesiveness members may send out many "trial balloons," knowing that this will lead neither to their isolation not to any deprivation. To feel that admission of failure will have enduring effects in the eyes of others is to place a premium on defensiveness and concealment of one's failures. If, in the atmosphere of the group behavior, there is a realization that whatever is communicated is "not for keeps," then failures as well as successes can be brought into the open. In this sense, greater cohesion and greater fluidity may be associated with some degree of "irreality."

This is one reason why individual change may frequently first be induced under conditions removed from the real situation of everyday work. Some persons feel that the induction of change can *best* be accomplished under social and physical conditions as much removed as possible from the specific working environment. The concept of the "cultural island" carries with it the implication of the ecological and geographical conditions for greater freedom and fluidity.

The group functions to facilitate change in the individual in the following ways: by helping him meet his needs in an atmosphere in which he participates in establishing the goals and is supported by other members who are also engaged in such need-meeting activities; by encouraging his participation and involvement in a step-by-step evaluation of the process so that the group continues to be effective in helping him meet emerging need-goal relationships; by producing a situation where he can try out new behavior and express new attitudes without being threatened by the "consequences" of such behavior; by bringing to bear on the problems of his interest new resources of information and discovery, so that his behavior may have the benefit of mutual criticism and assistance.

Institutional Structure and Individual Change

Whether the change within an individual—his changed perception of the situation, his development of new goals and levels of aspiration—can be effective in any enduring way depends crucially upon the ability of the organization to facilitate and maintain individual change. In many cases where the individual or group has been stimulated to develop new patterns of behavior in response to new perceptions of what is a desirable mode of functioning, the new patterns may actually be discouraged by the other parts of the organizational hierarchy. In order for change on the part of the individual to be effectively established, he must have the opportunity of putting it into operation within the organizational structure.

One of the most interesting experimental studies of this relationship was made in connection with the training of supervisors in industry (Pelz 1951). It was found that the extent to which a supervisor is successful in attempting to help employees reach their goals depends upon whether the supervisor himself is perceived as having influence in the total organizational setting. If the supervisor is recognized as an influential official of the company, the more the supervisor aids goal achievement, the better satisfied the employees will be and the higher will be the correlation between supervisory behavior and employee attitudes. But when a supervisor is perceived as being "uninfluential," stronger attempts on his part to help employees cannot be expected to raise the level of employee satisfaction. Actually, employee satisfaction may even fall.

Group Leader Must Have Influence
The difference between an "influential" and an "uninfluential" supervisor in this study is of particular interest to us. The influential supervisor appeared to have a relatively high influence over the social environment in which his employees were functioning, by having a voice in departmental decisions made by his own superior, by having considerable autonomy in running his own work group, as well as by having higher general status as indicated by his salary. What is of most general importance, however, is that the influential supervisor has impact upon the organization as a whole and influence in levels above that of his face-to-face work group. It is reasonable to conclude that whatever decisions were made within his own work group were understood by the group to have been communicated by the supervisor through organizational channels and to have a good chance of acceptance. The supervisor as an effective gatekeeper of communication with the higher authorities was, therefore, able to help the group realize that its efforts were productive.

What is true of industrial organizations and supervisory groups can be applied to other hierarchical organizations as well—in particular, to the school. The gap between the inspired ideology and the possibilities for action may be in the chain of command—the supervision, the principal's office, or the "head office." What becomes a level of aspiration for improved work or what is seen in a different

PSYCHOLOGY OF CHANGE / 249

light through greater sensitization may actually avail nothing. For, to put ideals and ideas into practice, the cooperation of other levels of the organization must be assured.

Major Principles of Institutional Change

It would seem that for change in the individual or the group to be effective, it is essential that all levels of the organization be brought into the cooperative endeavor. Space does not allow us to go into detail about many of the specific ways in which the total organizational structure can be involved in the processes that lead to change. We should like to emphasize, however, that since any institution is a dynamic system, change within the whole system can be thought of as the degree to which all parts of the system are receptive to change. There are two major principles with respect to institutional change that should be constantly observed:

1. Communication within the organization must be two-way. It is essential that needs be communicated to supervisors and also that training activities for meeting needs be appropriately announced. Likewise, policies from above should be communicated down the line with as much participation as possible. Often the difference between organizations in the degree to which participation in policy making is present is actually the difference between institutions that are primarily custodial as compared to those that are truly educational. The challenge that is felt in a structure continuously responsive to changing needs is likely to be translated into a dynamic functioning that is truly educational in every sense; training under these conditions becomes a part of the institutional blood stream.

2. Role differences among organizational levels tend to create barriers to problem solving within a group and resistance to change within the individual. The principal has a different set of external pressures placed on him from the teacher, just as the supervisor in the factory has a different set of pressures from the worker. Many times the role character of the higher-level administration official makes it difficult for him to tell groups down the line what these pressures are. They seem to him static, fixed, and impenetrable. Yet when these demands and pressures are shared as aspects of the problem-solving situation, they can become channels for facilitating change rather than for instituting barriers.

Planning for Change: Resistance and Assistance

Social change would be easily accomplished were there not within every social system potent resistance to change. Just as there are forces that demand change, there are counterforces that work against any change. No stable arrangement is easily changed, and particularly is this true in a complex scheme of interpersonal relations where vested interests in authority and power become highly stabilized. Change in an institution or complex organization that has provided for no orderly means of change is bound to be disrupting. The communication system within an organization is seldom equal to the demands of the new arrangements, for rarely can all employees understand the change, and the informal organization becomes rife with rumors that only serve to increase resistance and engender hostility. Furthermore, the integrity of an institution is based upon its ability to withstand some of the forces that endeavor to change its character. If there were no resistance to change, there would be no stability or integrity.

When organizations face the possibility of change there is an aspect of resistance that is subjective and personal and that all members may share. We have a loyalty to the ways in which we have been seeing things and doing things, and we may have no internal commitment to what is new and essentially strange. Besides, we may be faced with demands that involve courses of action that are strange and essentially unknown to us. Further, the change may entail a new description of our roles within the organization, and we may be called upon to exchange our vested interest in a role that was comfortable and serene for one that, in its novelty, is anxiety provoking.

Resistance to change is manifested in many ways. Frequently there is a denial that any problems exist, whereas, before change was suggested, there were many. There may be surface collaboration with the process of change by paying lip-service without real implementation, or by postponement of the implementation. Sometimes resistance may be shown in excessive dependency where the individual shifts all responsibility for implementation to someone else. Not only do we find the individual resisting a state of affairs, and particularly a change in a state of affairs, but also it is a group phenomenon. Often the forms of resistance parallel, on the group level, the ways in which it appeared in individual cases. Sometimes there is a group dependency on the person in authority while covert resistance is manifest in undercover hostility.

Resistance itself usually is a symptom of the lack of recognition on the part of leadership that whatever changes come about develop most productively through collaboration and participation. Where the change is the result of an analysis of need, careful consideration of objectives, and intelligent scrutiny of the means by which the objectives are to be accomplished—and these steps are participated in by persons whom the change affects—the process of change is likely to be met with less resistance.

It is part of the great tradition of Western culture that it has built within the system a means for the critical evaluation of human needs and goals and the means employed in search of their fulfilment. This is the function of education, scholarship, and science. Such an evaluative function would have no real meaning were it not designed to achieve objectives, were it not to lead to change within the society itself. The wisdom with which this function prevails will depend on the freedom and openness of communication, undistorted by wishful thinking or the doctrinaire. Likewise, orderly change can be achieved when evaluation and problem solving are incorporated within the organization itself, allowing for the creativity that comes from freedom of expression and the responsible involvement that comes from full participation.

SUMMARY

The particularly significant concepts of the psychology of change in relation to programs of in-service education may be summarized:

Individual Motivation to Change.   The individual is motivated to change when there is a disequilibrium between the tension systems of the individual and the surrounding social field. The dynamics of the process of change are seen in the attempts to restore equilibrium within the individual or to change the tensional quality of the surrounding social field.

Process of Change.   The process of change within the individual comes about through increased differentiation both within the person and within the environment. This relationship develops a cognitive structure, within the person, through which he perceives the world in which he lives. All differentiations result in changes within the person, so that, by changes in cognitive structure, the world becomes more structured and more meaningful. Such changes in cognitive structure affect changes in needs, tensions, attitudes, and expectations.

Human Needs.   In addition to needs growing out of physiological processes, many human needs are determined by the groups to which one belongs or the status to which one aspires. Behavior that is characteristically human is most often in response to tensions arising in the field of social relationships.

Peripheral and Central Aspects. In describing the process of change within the individual, we find it useful to distinguish between those aspects of the person that are *peripheral* and those that are *central.* The peripheral regions, because of their proximity to the action level of the person, are more instrumental in their ability to carry out action. The central regions are more private, intimate, and personal, and their accessibility to the environment is less. Although they are less accessible to action, once there is a communication through connection of these regions, that is, through the peripheral to the surrounding social field, motivation is likely to be stronger and its effects more enduring. The central regions of the person can be described as being more "tensional" in character, since they involve deeply held values and beliefs. Strong feelings are the source of both sustained action and deep resistance. Psychotherapy gives us an example of the extent to which cognitive structure may be accompanied by strong affective or cathectic reactions of the person. It also illustrates the extent to which cognitive and cathectic aspects are involved in the process of change.

Maladjustments. Psychotherapy frequently treats persons who are maladjusted because of cognitive distortions. These distortions frequently are the result of not having a truly communicative relationship between the inner or central regions and the social field in which action takes place. The meaning of acceptance and permissiveness in the atmosphere of psychotherapy is that they permit tension to be released so that perception can be changed in congruence with reality.

Psychotherapeutic Change. The process of psychotherapeutic change comes about under conditions where the perceived needs of the patient are made the focus of attention, where the threats to his own perceptions are reduced, and where the relationship of therapist and patient are mutually collaborative. These are aspects of change situations which can be generalized to any situation.

Institutions. In considering problems of change within an institutional setting, we need to consider the characteristics of institutions themselves. Institutions are social systems which are boundary-maintaining and tend to exist in what has been called "moving-pattern constancies." The tempo of the moving equilibrium varies considerably in time and place. Social systems reflect the impact of environmental disruptions, just as they are reflected in the learning and values of the individuals that they mold to support them.

Role Behavior. Individual behavior within a social system is determined by the role that is prescribed by that system. Roles contribute to the functioning of the system by creating, within the individual, highly internalized expectancies as to how he should behave and how others will behave. Role behavior becomes highly fixed within the institution and is disrupted only under rather extreme conditions. This reciprocation in the maintenance of the status quo makes change difficult, both with reference to individual motivation and to social pressures.

Social Structure. Institutions usually develop a formal social structure as a method of performing their work. The structure is characterized by a hierarchy of offices which have distinctive responsibilities and privileges. These are exemplified in a status system that is based on differential prestige and a prescribed set of roles and procedures. Along with the formal structure are the informal functions, which have much less structure, are characterized by more spontaneous flow of interpersonal relationships, and are often effective in either aiding the formal structure in reaching goals or working as a very antagonistic core and in a private way against the public goals of the institution. An institution is likely to function more effectively and with greater satisfaction for its employees if the needs that are expressed in the informal social relationships are dealt with in the formal structure.

Change in Institutions. The processes of change can be productive within an institution only if conditions permit reassessment of goals and the means to their achievement. The function of science is, in part, directed toward the assessment of the processes that are critical in the attainment of goals. To function in a responsive manner to the changing needs it is designed to serve, any institution must provide within its structure the facilities for objective evaluation and creative thinking.

Barriers to Change. The most significant barrier to institutional change is the resistance that persons express when such change seems threatening to roles in which they have developed considerable security. The process of institutional change is facilitated by a number of conditions: when the leadership is democratic and the group members have freedom to participate in the decision-making process; when there have been norms established that make "social change" an expected aspect of institutional growth; when change can be brought about without jeopardizing the individual's membership in the group; when the group concerned has a strong sense of belonging, when it is attractive to its members, and when it is concerned with satisfying members' needs; when the group members actively participate in the leadership functions, help formulate the goals, plan the steps toward goal realization, and participate in the evaluation of these aspects of leadership; when the level of cohesion permits members of the group to express themselves freely and to test new roles by trying out new behavior and attitudes without being threatened by "real consequences."

Support for Change.   Any change within a given group must be supported by the organizational structure lest it become the storm center of ideological conflict within the institution. Therefore, communication must flow from one hierarchical level to another, and proposal for change must be sanctioned within the social structure. Resistance to change is to be expected at any level. Unless there is resistance, it is doubtful whether institutional change can endure or individual change can go very deep. Change is less threatening and, indeed, may be more validly tested if, in the beginning, while involving all levels within the institution, it can be placed upon an experimental basis to be evaluated as a part of an action-research program.

REFERENCES

Bion, W. R. "Experiences in Groups: I." *Human Relations* 1, no. 3 (1948): 314-320.
Bion, W. R. "Experiences in Groups: II." *Human Relations* 1, no. 4 (1948): 487-496.
Cartwright, D. "Achieving Change in People: Some Applications of Group Dynamics Theory." *Human Relations* 4, no. 4 (1951): 381-392.
Dewey, J. *Experience and Education.* New York: Crowell Collier and Macmillan, 1963.
Krech, D. "Notes Toward a Psychological Theory." *Journal of Personality* 18, no. 1 (September 1949): 66-87.
Lewin, K. *A Dynamic Theory of Personality.* New York: McGraw-Hill, 1935.

Lewin, K. "Field Theory and Learning." In *The Psychology of Learning*, pp. 215-242. Forty-first Yearbook of the National Society for the Study of Education, Part 2. Chicago: Distributed by the University of Chicago Press, 1942.

Lewin, K. *Field Theory in Social Science*. New York: Harper and Bros., 1951

Lippitt, R., and White, R. "The Social Climate of Children's Groups." In *Child Behavior and Development*. New York: McGraw-Hill, 1943.

Merton, R. *Social Theory and Social Structure*. Glencoe, Ill.: The Free Press, 1949.

Parsons, T. *The Social System*. Glencoe, Ill.: The Free Press, 1951.

Pelz, D. C. "Leadership Within an Hierarchical Organization." *Journal of Social Issues* 7, no. 3 (1951): 49-55.

Sullivan, H. S. *The Interpersonal Theory of Psychiatry*. New York: W. W. Norton, 1953.

Thelen, H. *Methods for Studying Work and Emotionality in Group Operation*. Chicago: Human Dynamics Laboratory, University of Chicago, 1954.

Veblen, T. *The Theory of the Business Enterprise*. New York: Kelley, 1904.

14

THE RELEVANCE OF
EVALUATION

ERNEST R. HOUSE

How many days, fresh from his data, the evaluator presents his work, only to be received with transparent disappointment or mock enthusiasm. The conditions from which his findings arise do not produce data to which his client can respond. For example, in a recent survey of evaluation case studies, Carter (1971) concluded that

> The examples cited so far have illustrated what happened when research findings were inconsistent with the beliefs and values of the clients whose programs were being evaluated. The net result in each case was the perpetuation of the client's ideology, self-image, and concept of social reality.

There is a natural antipathy between change and evaluation, often unrecognized by the evaluator and client alike. Changing something requires a faith, a belief in the new program beyond any data. To the client, evaluation means a confirmation of what he knows to be true. To the evaluator, evaluation is seeking after truth. Evaluating something means being skeptical, suspending belief. But the evaluator has a faith of his own—that the client will change as a result of the evaluation. The question then arises "What effect does an evaluation have?" and is asked particularly, rather belatedly, by a dejected evaluator who has seen the client shrug his shoulder as his only reaction to a carefully labored evaluation report.

The Meaning of Evaluation

Neither clients nor evaluators respond to bits of data with open minds. Each client, whether an individual or an organization, has an image of himself that structures his perception and his response. Only as the data relate to his own image do they mean anything to the client. Boulding (1956) was the first to explore the scope of what he called the "image," which he defines as the individual's entire subjective knowledge. This cognitive and affective map of the world contains one's facts and values, and provides the only means by which one can interpret the world at all. This model of the world is all we can ever know and our behavior depends on it. Boulding tests the power of this broad concept across a variety of domains, but the part of the image that we wish to pursue in this chapter is that value-drenched piece of the total knowledge structure that gives an individual his direction. For example, until fairly recently, an image that American boys held in common was that of "Horatio Alger." The principle that hard work leads to great success was embodied in a tale, a myth for which the individual could supply faces and dialogue. Vague and ill-defined as an image, this principle was nonetheless a powerful influence on individual behavior over a lifetime. The rest of the subjective knowledge structure was fitted into it. According to Boulding, the image begins to develop in childhood, strongly influenced by personal experience and even more strongly influenced by preexistent cultural images, and develops well into adolescence. Such images are extremely resistant to change. In a sense, the images are organic—they grow from within according to internal organizing principles. Since all information is filtered through the value system that is entwined with the image, there are no "facts"—only messages that are allowed to filter through. The image is impermeable to change.

The part of the total image that evaluators deal with is limited to the program being studied. Although considerably smaller than the total world view, this part of the image is by no means insignificant, since it carries implicit comments about the success of an individual's work, which is intimately related to his self-identity. For example, an "open classroom" program can be little more than an image in the minds of the developers, some vision that they are pursuing of what an ideal classroom would be like. An evaluation of the actual program is certain to show deficiencies when compared with the image, deficiencies that are not likely to be easily accepted by the developers. Depending on the data, the evaluation may challenge the ideological beliefs on which the program is based and depending on the success of the program, threaten the career of the developer, whose image will certainly include a notion of how he is going to benefit if the program succeeds. The same internal growth principles and impermeability to change characterize the image.

So the use of the term image here is more restricted than Boulding's. The image is an ikon, a manifestation of values, often visual, toward which the individual moves; sometimes it is an image in the literal sense. Within the total knowledge structure, the image represents the nucleus to which other parts are related, or the genetic material from which the phenotype will grow—a conception consistent with Rokeach's "terminal" and "instrumental" values (1969). The terminal value is a belief in some desirable end state that "transcendentally guides actions and judgments across specific objects and situations, and beyond immediate goals to more ultimate end states of existence." The instrumental value is a belief that a prescribed action will lead to a desired end state. All of one's attitudes and beliefs are organized around a small number of values.

Types of Belief

What the image consists of may be suggested by Rokeach's work with belief systems. Rokeach has analyzed subjective knowledge into five types of belief analogous to Boulding's image, each ranked in terms of its centrality to the total belief system. The more central the value to the system, the more difficult it is to change. The most peripheral beliefs (and the easiest to change) are the inconsequential beliefs, such as matters of taste. One may hold a particular brand of toothpaste in high regard, but a change of brands will affect little of the rest of the belief system. The next most peripheral beliefs are the derivative beliefs, which are derived from some type of authority. For example, belief in birth control may be related to religious affiliation. Derivative beliefs often form an ideology based on an identification with a particular reference group, and are subject to controversy and argument. Somewhat more difficult to change are the authority beliefs, that is, the beliefs in certain reference groups themselves, for example, a belief in science. But, although authority beliefs are highly resistent to change, they are controvertible. Most central to the belief system are the incontrovertible beliefs, which Rokeach divides into two. Primitive non-consensus beliefs, and primitive social consensus beliefs. The former are learned from direct experience and may be expressed in statements such as "I think I am stupid, no matter what others think." Only techniques such as psychoanalysis are able to change these beliefs. The latter are the most central of all, and are psychologically incontrovertible. They too are learned from direct experience and everyone else believes them. They involve a constancy of person and object, and may be expressed in statements such as "This is a table." Any questioning of these beliefs disrupts self-constancy and self-identity, and challenges sanity itself: they are beyond persuasion. That part of the image with which evaluation is concerned is obviously not the primitive belief structure but rather the authority, derived, and inconsequential beliefs.

Whatever the internal structure of the image, the meaning of a message is precisely the change it produces in the image. According to Boulding, there are a limited number of ways in which messages can affect the image. The data may not affect the image at all, as happens frequently in evaluation when the evaluators present information in which the clients are not interested, when, for example, evaluators present achievement scores to clients who are trying to accomplish affective goals. Although the data make sense to the evaluators, they are not relevant to the client's frame of reference, for he sees himself doing something totally different, and so the data pass through his image leaving him little but ill feeling. The data may confirm the image a client has of himself. For example, Harvard University may document that it is producing high-achieving graduates, but although the evaluation may serve a useful purpose in justifying the university to its constituencies, it will not result in any changes in the client's behavior. It merely makes obvious, formally, what the client already knew, informally. This kind of evaluation is perhaps the most common in government programs. The third effect is to sharpen the focus, or make more apparent, implicit facets of the client's self-image. For example, assistance in formulating his goals often gives the client a new insight into his own operation, and may induce him to change. The fourth effect that data may produce is a change in the image itself—a rare event. This type of change is the evaluator's counterpart to psychoanalysis and is perhaps as difficult to achieve. A person may see his program quite differently as a result of the evaluation, a revolutionary change that will then proceed to act on his new image indefinitely in the future. A program director may be convinced by an evaluation that improved self-concept has decreased achievement scores. Unfortunately, evaluators usually provide the first kinds of evaluation data and expect the last type of change.

The image of course is quite resistant to change. Information that will change it is almost certainly negative information, which is also likely to be rejected. Favorable messages are much more easily received, but are likely to add to the knowledge structure rather than to reorganize it. Rokeach has suggested that belief systems maintain themselves by rejecting any messages that are inconsistent with the individual's self-esteem and his conception of logic or reality. Hence, we may expect the client's beliefs about his program not to be easily changed. Of evaluation findings, Carter (1971) suggests that the greater the perceived threat to the client's positive self-concept, the greater his resistance to negative research findings; the greater the difference between the client's concept of the social reality being studied and the research findings, the greater his resistance to the results; and the greater the importance to the client of the function being evaluated, the greater the perceived threat to his positive self-image, and the greater his resistance to negative findings. So it is safe to say that the image is not easily changed by evaluation results.

The Evaluator's Role

The image of the evaluator himself is another constraint on the evaluation data. Apart from the idiosyncratic values and the personality of the evaluator (which really are not negligible), the training of the evaluator often works against his producing relevant data. Most evaluators are trained in psychology and, as in any science, the field is defined by a rigid paradigm. The purpose of the science is to exploit that paradigm (Kuhn 1962); science attempts to force nature, which is complex and undisciplined, into the inflexible box that the paradigm supplies. By concentrating intelligent minds on the minuscule part of the universe defined by the magnifying glass of the paradigm, a part of the natural world is discovered in a depth not otherwise attainable.

The significance of this for evaluation is that the science allows only those questions to be asked for which the paradigm can supply an answer. The problems of the real world cannot be reduced to the dimensions of the paradigm. In fact, training in a discipline is learning to ask questions that the paradigm will answer, rather than asking real questions that it cannot. For example, the inquisitive novice in statistics believes he will find answers to questions such as "Which program is best?". But statistics cannot answer such questions. Properly trained, the experienced student learns to ask a new set of questions that statistics can answer, such as "What is the chance of this score occurring in this type of distribution?". In effect, paradigms insulate the sciences from the overwhelming complexities of reality, thus allowing them to appear to progress rapidly by concentrating only on problems that they can solve and ignoring the ones they cannot. Kuhn (1962) suggests that perhaps we call scientific only those fields that have sufficiently divorced themselves from reality to be able to "show progress." The paradigm does for science what the image does for the individual, and what ideology does for organizations: it simplifies reality enough to allow us to operate. The sensitive mind of man, it seems, cannot take reality "cold turkey."

The social sciences have several relatively weak paradigms competing with one another. The dominant one in psychology, for instance, defined for all time by the pigeon and the white rat, is behaviorism. These paradigms provide the individual practitioners with important parts of their image of the world and, as such, serve them well in their trade. When the psychologist turns to evaluation, however, he is in serious trouble. To watch the use of abstract insulated paradigms to explain concrete social phenomena (for example, to watch a behaviorist explaining classroom behavior in terms of stimulus and response) is a sobering, sometimes ludicrous, experience. The complexities of reality overwhelm the paradigm's simplicity. Yet the evaluator knows only the paradigms he has been taught and can produce only the data they will yield. Like the teacher, he has a limited repertoire, and can do only what he can do, even when he knows something is wrong. Needless to say, much of the evaluator's data will be irrelevant to the teacher or program manager, since they will have constructed their own simplified images. There are several ways of attacking the problem. One way is to train evaluators in several disciplines and paradigms. A multidisciplinary evaluation will resemble reality somewhat more closely than will one produced by a specialist. A multidisciplinary approach may develop if evaluation becomes a field in its own right. The scientific disciplines cannot be abandoned because those are the knowledges and methods that we have. A second way in which to make evaluation relevant to the real world is to define problems in terms of the client's image. In the academic tradition, the collection of data is highly valued, but its dissemination is not (except that dissemination produces journal articles that lead to promotion). Like economists, evaluators have been concerned almost solely with production, not distribution—and perhaps for the same reasons. The distribution of either wealth or information immediately affects power relationships: under the right market conditions, both are convertible into power. It is easier for the producer's conscience if he can assume that there is a fine flow of both wealth and information, although obviously there is neither. After all, one is paid for the production of certain types of information.

Evaluation to Effect Change

What part then, does evaluation play in effecting change? Under current conditions the answer must be "not much." Given their rewards, it is not surprising that evaluators like to dump their evaluation load and hotfoot it back to the campus to find out the latest reliability scores. The safest and most natural role for the evaluator is that of the "technician." He reels off data derived from the paradigms in which he has been trained, tips his hat and is gone. Even though no change is likely to occur, this is a legitimate role for the evaluator: clients have a right to have their images confirmed occasionally. Evaluation is not synonymous with change and the evaluation that reaffirms current practice has its uses. A worse situation occurs when the data neither confirm nor deny; they are simply irrelevant. In such cases, the client's stereotype of the fuzzy, otherworldly researcher is reinforced, as is the evaluator's stereotype of the irrational program director who is too crass to rise above self-interest. For both, evaluation leaves a bitter taste. But the technician's role is not very satisfying. For evaluation to be "relevant" in the sense I have used it here, it must be understandable in the client's terms; for evaluation to be "meaningful" in Boulding's sense, it must change the image of the client. Hence, the data must be articulated in the client's terms or translated into terms to which he will respond.

A proven way to make evaluation findings relevant is to build a deepening relationship with the client. In time the client becomes convinced that the evaluator does indeed understand his problems, has his best interests at heart and truly wants to help the program, and the evaluator understands the client's problems and can ascertain what indeed is most relevant to the client. In such a relationship the client is more willing to accept the evaluation results even when they are negative. The client himself has a significant impact on the evaluation.

Such a relationship requires much time in which to develop, time in which the evaluator has the opportunity to convince his client to accept findings that he is resisting. The evaluator does this by collecting redundant data on key issues, by repeating his findings, by using personal persuasion. Often it is simply a matter of time before the client does accept the findings. For example, in evaluating the Illinois Gifted Program, we spent about two years convincing the program personnel that the demonstration centers, in which they had placed so many hopes and aspirations, were not nearly as effective as they had believed. During this time, we presented many types of information, piece by piece, and slowly, the program personnel came to believe what we were saying. This took patience, persuasion and persistence—traits not usually associated with evaluators. The demonstration centers were reorganized, but at no time did the program personnel make an overt switch and say "Yes, I see what you are meaning." The conversion was very gradual until eventually they accepted and then even championed the new ideas.

This type of relationship is to be found in what Rippey calls transactional evaluation. It involves an exchange, a two-way relationship between the client and the evaluator, with a common reference system in which both have an interest and understanding. One extreme of the transactional approach is perhaps best represented by the French anthropologist Jaulin (Morin and Mousseau 1971), who believes that unless one is entirely immersed in the culture one studies, one will inevitably destroy that culture. Transactional evaluation is most satisfying for the client and is the most effective way of implementing findings since the client internalizes the findings. It is evaluation's analogue to psychoanalysis.

Transactional evaluation does, however, demand a trade off. The establishment of such a relationship takes a great deal of time. Our evaluation of the Illinois Gifted Program took four years. Although most of that time was not spent in developing a transactional relationship, the length of time encouraged close ties. Most evaluators are not inclined to establish such a relationship. Generally those who dress themselves in the garb of a psychometrician are not given to such relationships, and nor do they see any need to. As they see it, the problem will be solved when the data are produced. Since most evaluators are moonlighters, whose real careers lie in university departments, their evaluations hold no rewards for their careers.

Because an evaluation is specific and not usually generally applicable, the results prohibit publication. A long-term evaluation offers even less reward.

Assuming the evaluator has both capacity and desire to engage in a complex relationship, we may find that the next danger is that he becomes so identified with the program that he turns into an apologist. Znaniecki (1940) describes the "sage" as a man whose function "consists in rationalizing and justifying intellectually the collective tendencies of his party." Such seems to be the fate of the evaluator who totally identifies himself with the program under study. He becomes immersed in its values and personal relationships until gradually he changes from an evaluator to an advocate of the program. This process is speedier if the evaluator's livelihood depends on the program. He simply cannot bring himself to challenge the tenets on which the program is based; eventually he is not able to see them at all. Rare is the sage who is able to overcome his socially determined role. As Znaniecki notes, some do and then manage to establish more comprehensive standards and norms, and create a new image for the program, and thus shape its future.

Perhaps the severest constraint on the consultant role has not been mentioned—that it is effective only with primary groups. The transactions of the group that negotiates face-to-face are not likely to be convincing to those who are not participating. If the group with which the evaluator works makes policy for the whole organization, any change in its image may have widespread effects. If it is not a policy making body, only the work group will be affected. In a large bureaucratic organization, the effects of a transactional evaluation are likely to be severely circumscribed, because, regardless of the effects of an evaluation within the program being evaluated, the evaluation itself will be subject to the organizational environment in which the program exists. Since bureaucratic organizations consist of constantly shifting coalitions of groups that are concerned about the internal distribution of power and status, a program director is likely to use evaluation data only to help him defend or expand his program *vis-à-vis* the rest of the organization. If the results are negative, the report is likely to be buried: forces within the bureaucracy prohibit a more objective stance. Change may be brought about by making the evaluation public—which means essentially giving ammunition to opposing political factions. (The political nature of evaluation I have discussed elsewhere [House 1972].)

Such was the case with the Pentagon Papers. The report was buried until Daniel Ellsberg took it upon himself to make it public.

Forces opposing the Vietnam war seized upon it immediately as a powerful buttress for their position. Even so, the report itself probably had little effect internally on the government—except to stop such internal evaluations for a while. As Ellsberg has said, people learn, bureaucracies do not. The report's powerful effect has been on the public's image of the government and, over the long run, it may contribute to some change within the bureaucracy. Few evaluators are willing to go as far as Ellsberg in releasing data to a program's enemies. A somewhat different method of making the evaluation results public is to agree in advance on the evidence of success and agree on how they will be made public. For example, there has been some discussion of "educational indicators" that might show the effectiveness of programs (U.S. Dept. of Health, Education and Welfare 1969; Rivlin 1971). National assessment results might serve as one indicator on a national level to which various people could respond. There is no reason why the evaluation of a local program could not establish modest indices of success and keep a running record of them over time. Of course, one of the many problems of such an approach is to get program directors to agree to public disclosure.

One evaluator's role worth exploring is that of the evaluator who dissents from doctrine. To induce change one must break through the image of the individual, the paradigms of the discipline, and the ideology of the organization. What if the evaluator limits himself to supplying information? Rokeach suggests that changes in beliefs may be evoked by *inducing* inconsistency between behavior and attitudes, by introducing new information, or by exposing the client to information about inconsistencies already within the belief value system. Evaluation can introduce conflict into the belief system of the individual or organization. The evaluator can ferret out inherent contradictions and unquestioned assumptions on which the program is based and question them. (For an interesting example of this type of evaluation, see Stake and Gjerde 1971.) The more basic the assumption, the greater the possible effects. Many of the challenges are likely to be rejected, but the client is not likely to perceive his program in exactly the same way as he once did. For example, the Office of Education and most state departments are notoriously reluctant to evaluate their own programs. While such organizations might routinely ignore the complaints from their clients, the opinions of legislators that the agency is incompetent, whether justified or not, are likely to produce consternation and possibly some change. In other words, the evaluator might feed to the client the opinions of influential groups. By carefully selecting data relevant to the client's value system, the evaluator can expect maximum change. For both individuals and organizations, such data are likely to be those that will influence future careers. The evaluator has a modest but important social function in bringing divergent and conflicting ideas to the attention of the client. The client, whether an organization or individual, will respond to evaluation data to the extent and in the direction that they affect his self-interest. The client is not usually aware of this; the evaluator should be.

REFERENCES

Boulding, K. E. *The Image*. Ann Arbor: University of Michigan Press, 1956.

Carter, R. K. "Clients' Resistance to Negative Findings and the Latent Conservative Function of Evaluation Studies." *The American Sociologist* 6, no. 2 (May 1971).

House, E. R. "The Conscience of Educational Evaluation." *Teachers' College Record* 73, no. 3 (February 1972): 404-414.

Kuhn, T. S. *The Structure of Scientific Revolutions*. Chicago and London: University of Chicago Press, 1962.

Morin, F., and Mousseau, J. "La Paix Blanche, A Conversation with Robert Jaulin." *Psychology Today* 5, no. 4 (September 1971): 62.

Rivlin, A. *Systematic Thinking for Social Action*. Washington, D.C.: Brookings Institute, 1971.

Rokeach, M. *Beliefs, Attitudes, and Values*. San Francisco: Jossey-Bass, 1969.

Stake, R. E., and Gjerde, C. "The Evaluation of T CITY, The Twin City Institute for Talented Youth." Mimeographed. Urbana, Ill.: Center for Instructional Research and Curriculum Evaluation, University of Illinois, Urbana, 1971.

U.S. Department of Health, Education, and Welfare. *Toward a Social Report*. Washington, D.C.: U.S. Government Printing Office, 1969.

Znaniecki, F. *The Social Role of the Man of Knowledge*. New York and Evanston, Ill.: Harper & Row, 1940.

15

PROGRAM EVALUATION IN SCHOOLS

DOUGLAS SJOGREN

The response to the demands for program evaluation by the U.S. Office of Education in the past decade has stimulated much model building but little evaluation work. Nearly every federally funded program has some kind of evaluation activity, but most of it is in the nature of tokenism rather than any commitment to evaluation in the classic sense of the word. The situation is almost a comedy. An "evaluator" is hired to play the role while both he and the project director know that the evaluation activity will make little real difference to anybody. While the evaluation role is being played, the real evaluations that do make a difference are being made by the project staff and the project constituents. The evaluator is often not even aware of their judgments. Program evaluation in unfunded programs differs from that in funded programs primarily in the absence of a formal evaluator. Not only does evaluation not occur in all programs, but also the typical formal evaluation efforts, when they are made, have little impact.

We who work in educational evaluation feel that systematic evaluation should be a part of every program because it will benefit the program and the educational community. My pessimistic observation, however, is that most of us have little impact either on the programs or the community. The question that must be squarely faced is, "Why do we have no impact?" Many answers might be offered, and it is likely that each will have some validity. Evaluators talk about inadequate funding, fear of evaluation, antipathy toward research, poor cooperation, and so forth. Such explanations may account for some of the problem, but I would suggest that there are more basic reasons.

THE SHORTCOMINGS

We have had little impact because what we have done should have little impact. Generally, the evaluation procedures are such that the information obtained is too little and too late for the program. The summative reports are written in the rigid style of research reporting, in an attempt to satisfy a clientele that will not read the report anyway, rather than in a descriptive style that will inform an interested audience. Consequently the report is virtually ignored by everybody. The program director pays us little attention because we give him little that deserves attention. The educational community does not heed our reports because they are not written for the right audience. Stake (1969) has stressed the importance of knowing the audience, but we have not taken his point.

These, however, are only symptoms, not causes. In my opinion we are "hung-up" on a research model that is not appropriate for evaluation. Our strategies are based on considerations of research design rather than of program needs. Several recently developed models for evaluation, those, for example, of Stufflebeam (1969), Stake (1967), and Alkin (1967), provide broad bases for designing evaluation activities according to program needs. At present, however, there are few examples of well-defined strategies for implementing the models. While several of the recently developed models, such as those cited, do not emphasize the classic research models, many evaluation methodologists stress the importance of designing evaluations as comparative experiments (Glass 1969; Scriven 1967). Scriven, for example, has emphasized that judgments of worth are comparative and that the proper evaluation of an educational program requires that a comparison basis be included in the evaluation study.

I agree that most judgments are of relative worth, but I disagree with the position that the comparison should be built into every evaluation effort. Comparisons can be made among programs without the comparison being built into the design. Anthropologists have been comparing cultures for years, not with control groups, but by obtaining comprehensive descriptions of them, descriptions comprehensive enough to permit comparison. Such comprehensive monitoring is needed in educational evaluation. With the descriptions that will be possible from such monitoring we can make the comparisons among programs. The models cited above, if implemented, do seem to be designed to obtain this kind of comprehensive description. Implementation of such models is difficult.

Misconceptions

I have identified two assumptions that make it difficult to establish the approach to evaluation that I feel is needed. First, there is the assumption that a control group is needed. Generally, the people who employ evaluators have had a course or two in research design and in measurements; they have learned that an experimental design is needed to establish cause and effect, and they want to *prove* that their program is better than any other at causing some effect. Consequently, they believe that the evaluation design should be an experiment or at least a quasi experiment. They also expect to be able to identify some instrument, which is universally reliable and valid, that will provide the necessary measure to establish their proof. In my own evaluations, when I suggest that a control group is not needed and that the perfect instrument is not around, the reaction, I feel, is that I am either "soft" or a charlatan.

The second assumption is not independent of the first, but it is somewhat different. This is the assumption that objectivity is characterized by the expression: "we need an outside evaluator who will be completely objective and tell it as it is." The evaluator is viewed as an external auditor who will not be prostituted by vested interests in the program. In fact the term "education auditor" has been used. The analogy is appealing, but it breaks down. Auditors do audit financial records, and this type of audit is appropriate in educational evaluation. But auditors do not look at processes and products. They determine whether the money was spent as intended but they do not determine whether the money was spent for the right alternative, or whether a certain product was the outcome. There are some important things that the outside evaluator-auditor can do well, but there are many things he cannot do well. The "objectivity" of the outside evaluator is a myth. He is usually retained on the basis of his being competent in the area, which means that he is probably a member of the establishment and has a viewpoint sympathetic to the intents of the program. His decisions about instruments and procedures are subjective. His data base is so limited, consisting as it does, mainly of test scores and brief observation protocols, that the analysis and interpretation are necessarily heavily loaded with judgments.

The relationship between the external evaluator and the project contains another problem. The typical reaction to the terms "evaluation" and "evaluator" is defensive: somehow we associate these terms with negative judgments. This reaction, found among teachers, administrators, and students, seriously limits the work of the evaluator. The defensiveness is manifested in obvious ways, such as situations that have been structured to appear favorable, or teaching that is geared to the test. I would suggest that there are also some subconscious reactions, such as forgetting to collect data or forgetting instructions, and so forth. Even with the best design and instruments, the external evaluator has only minimal control so that the data are likely to be contaminated by conscious or subconscious actions that sabotage the study.

A serious misconception is reflected in the two assumptions, a misconception about standards of proof. The notion seems to be that, if the hypothesis is supported in a well-controlled study, that is conducted objectively, the hypothesis is proved. Actually, one study does not an hypothesis prove; it is only when the result is replicated many times that the hypothesis can be accepted with confidence. Scientific literature in any field abounds with examples of occasions when (objective?) scientists have interpreted the same finding very differently. Some of the best examples may be found among the findings on learning behavior. Finally, despite all its elegant designs, the effectiveness of the external evaluation approach is very dependent on a rapport that is not likely to exist.

Thus far, the message has been that evaluation strategy based on experimental research and independent, objective models for judgment are neither realistic nor useful. The expectations held for such strategies are not reached and, in fact, the results are so far from the expectation that they are virtually useless for the program and the educational community. Despite these limitations, the expectations of evaluation strategies held by most administrators are just those described above. In advocating a different strategy, one of your first tasks will be to change attitudes.

THE ALTERNATIVE

An alternative strategy for the evaluation of educational programs is based on the premise that the primary responsibility of an evaluation is that of improving the program being evaluated. The production of information that can be applied generally is but a secondary goal or a by-product of the effort. The strategy will be called a transactional strategy, as is appropriate to the theme of this book.

The Evaluator's Role

The essential feature of the transactional strategy is that the evaluator is a fully participating member of the program staff, an evaluator full- or part-time, or a staff member with duties other than those of evaluation. The primary function of the evaluator is systematically to gather and interpret data and information for the program. He will assume that the program staff are competent and sincerely want the best possible program. Thus he expects the staff to be open to suggestion, criticism, and different approaches. At the same time, he recognizes that the data and information can be interpreted in different ways, and that conflicts among interpretations will need to be resolved in staff deliberation. The implications of the preceding sentence are important. The evaluator is actually a participating staff member whose primary task is to obtain data and information for the staff. He will interpret these data from his point of view, but he must recognize that staff members may arrive at a different interpretation. They may make decisions with which he will disagree. The evaluator should recognize and acknowledge his fallibility and should not accept a role of the ultimate authority. If he provides a reliable data base for judgments he has done his job well.

It is somewhat difficult to assume the role I have described. This kind of role is not the one typically envisaged by educators. I feel there are two areas to which the evaluator needs to devote immediate attention in order to legitimize such a role. His behavior should make it clear to the project administration that he is not preempting the administrator's role. Having worked with a transactional approach in several schools and projects, we have found that we were constantly tempted to become overly directive as we gathered and interpreted the data. Administrators become defensive as we become directive, and rightly so. Our effectiveness diminishes as the administrator becomes defensive and stymies our efforts. We have also worked with administrators who seem to be very willing to transfer authority to us. They ask for direction and seem to expect us to tell them what to do. In the short run, our direction might be useful, but we feel that, in the long run, it will be detrimental in that responsibility must remain with the program staff. We can offer suggestions and interpretations, but not caveats.

The second matter for immediate attention is the legitimization of our role with the staff. At first the staff tend to resent the outside expert. They feel that we are coming in to snoop, that we will discover only the negative things, or that we are "out to get somebody." We try to demonstrate early that our ego, too, is involved with the program, and that we, too, are committed to its success. An effective technique for gaining the staff's acceptance of our role is to deliver something early and to discuss it with the staff. We usually deliver a report on some aspect of the program that can be studied early. By presenting the report as our perception and focusing the discussion on the accuracy of that perception, we manage to convey to the staff that they can evaluate our work and provide input to the evaluation efforts. Our attendance at and participation in staff meetings, and our submission of evaluation plans and instruments to the staff for discussion and revision have been effective techniques for gaining acceptance of our role, and also for conducting an evaluation that was useful to the program.

Acceptance

Generally, we have tried, in our early work in a project, to support, rather than criticize, in order to facilitate our acceptance. Once the transactional relationship is attained, such sensitivity is no longer necessary. We have played the "devil's advocate" at times in order to expose the many facets of a decision, but such a procedure is not effective until an open relationship is established.

The evaluation role that I am advocating might be interpreted as the role of the "nice guy," the role in which the evaluator is a pleasant person who reinforces the staff and does not worry too much about gathering data. This is not the interpretation I intend. The evaluator will design a systematic evaluation plan; he will measure those things that are measurable; he will observe in a systematic fashion; in other words, he will bring a special expertise to the project in gathering, analyzing, and interpreting the relevant data and information. As decisions are faced by the staff, he will assist them in defining and then gathering the information they will be needing. He may review literature, conduct opinion surveys, or conduct a small research project. For example, in an evaluation of a Computer Assisted Instruction (CAI) project, one of the decisions to be made was on the number of video tape units needed to service the courses adequately. We designed an experiment to determine the effect that a delay in video tape presentations would have on learning, and to determine the students' attitudes to "dead time"—time wasted because the video tape units required by the program were not available when they were needed.

If the evaluator and the staff feel that outside evaluators are needed, there is no reason why they should not be brought in to provide a new perspective on a problem, to legitimize certain results, to examine specific components, as an auditor would the financial records, or for other reasons. Thus, the evaluator may employ any or all of the accepted evaluation procedures as they are appropriate to the project. His technique will be determined by the needs of the project and not simply be imposed on the project. The evaluation role we advocate will reduce the conflict between the evaluator and evaluated, and reduce the likelihood that the data are incomplete, masked, or in other ways made invalid and unreliable.

Criticisms

The main criticism of this evaluational role is that the evaluation it produces will not be objective. The critics, legitimately, say that the evaluator will identify himself too closely with the project and ignore, or gloss over, negative results. I submit, however, that negative results are easily masked to the outside evaluator and are thus ignored or glossed over, but in a different way. Science, as a process, is based on an important assumption about the honesty of the investigator. We assume that he is honest in designing the study, conducting the study, and reporting the results. Is it unrealistic to expect an evaluator to be honest? I think not. At the same time, however, we recognize that the scientist is biased. He reports the results honestly from his perception, but does not recognize the influence of his own biases. The mechanism of correction is acceptance by and criticism from one's peers, and replication. Likewise the evaluation report will be biased, but I submit that we cannot expect to control the bias by having an "objective" evaluator. There is no such person. The bias will be corrected in the same way: by acceptance by and criticism from peers, and by replication.

While the primary purpose of evaluation is to improve the program, I recognize, at the same time, that evaluation reports should be issued and that the evaluation plan should provide for the reports. The evaluation role that I have advocated can provide for such summative reports very well. In fact it should be possible for the evaluator to issue a summative report at any time: he will be obtaining data continuously, and at any time the available data could be synthesized into a summative report of the project up to that point.

I have read few evaluation reports that seem to be products of a transactional evaluation strategy, probably because the strategy has rarely been applied. However, Stake and Gjerde (1971), Brauner (1969), and Smith and Brock (1970) have published reports that do seem to be products of transactional-type evaluations.

REFERENCES

Alkin, M. C. *Towards an Evaluation Model: A Systems Approach*. Los Angeles: Center for the Study of Evaluation, University of California at Los Angeles, 1967.

Brauner, C. J. "The First Probe." *The Architectural Review* 146, no. 84 (December 1969): 451-456.

Glass, G. V. "The Growth of Evaluation Methodology." Research Paper No. 27, Laboratory of Educational Research. Boulder, Colo.: University of Colorado, 1969.

Scriven, M. "The Methodology of Evaluation." In *Perspectives of Curriculum Evaluation*, edited by R. Tyler, R. Gagne, and M. Scriven, pp. 39-83. AERA Monograph Series on Curriculum Evaluation, No. 1. Chicago: Rand McNally, 1967.

Smith, L. M., and Brock, J. A. M. "Go, Bug, Go: Methodological Issues in Classroom Observational Research." Occasional Paper Series No. 5, Central Midwest Regional Educational Laboratory (CEMREL), 1970.

Stake, R. E. "Evaluation Design, Instrumentation, Data Collection, and Analysis of Data." In *Educational Evaluation*, edited by M. W. Essex. Columbus, Ohio: State Superintendent of Public Instruction, 1969.

Stake, R. E. "The Countenance of Educational Evaluation." *Teachers' College Record* 68, no. 7 (1967): 523-540.

Stake, R. E., and Gjerde, C. "An Evaluation of T CITY, the Twin City Institute for Talented Youth." (Mimeographed.) Urbana, Ill.: Center for Instructional Research and Curriculum Evaluation, University of Illinois, Urbana, 1971.

Stufflebeam, D. L. "Evaluation as Enlightenment for Decision Making." In *Improving Educational Assessment and An Inventory of Affective Behavior*, edited by W. H. Beatty, pp. 41-73. Washington, D.C.: Association of Supervision and Curriculum Development, National Education Association, 1969.

16

DEFICIENCIES OF STATISTICS IN EDUCATIONAL EVALUATION: THE PROBLEM AND A SOLUTION

JOHN M. THRONE

In criticizing conclusions (such as those reached by Coleman et al. 1966) that academic achievement is *not* a function of scholastic variables, including teaching, it is common for the schools' defenders (for example, Guba and Clark 1967) to focus on the unfeasibility or impracticality of meeting the statistical, design, and treatment assumptions of inferential statistics that, more often than not, were employed in the studies on which such conclusions are based. Guba and Clark include: as requisite statistical assumptions, normality of distribution, randomness of sampling, and effective equality of treatments (additivity); as requisite design assumptions, comparability of experimental and control groups (to insure internal validity), and random selection of subjects, their random assignment to experimental and control groups, and their insulation from reactive or interactive effects extraneous to the independent variables under study (to insure external validity); as requisite treatment assumptions, *a priori* treatment explication, noncontamination (non-confounding) of treatment by extraneous independent variables, treatment invarance throughout the experiment, identicality of treatment application by all experimenters, and elimination of competing treatments.

Because these assumptions, at least in the aggregate, are difficult if not impossible to meet in academic settings, the schools' defenders consider that the use of inferential statistics to evaluate the effectiveness of teaching is inappropriate. But they do not go far enough. The assumptions of inferential statistics are *ipso facto* incompatible with teaching; therefore, they are inappropriate in evaluating the effectiveness of teaching under any circumstances. That is, inferential statistics are *not* inappropriate in evaluating the effectiveness of teaching because their assumptions are difficult or impossible to meet, which implies they would be appropriate if the case were otherwise; they are inappropriate in evaluating the effectiveness of teaching precisely to the extent that their assumptions *are* met. Yet, *unless* they are met, inferential statistics cannot be used validly to evaluate the effectiveness of teaching, or of any other independent variable, at all.

TEACHING AND EVALUATION

The assumptions of inferential statistics must be met in order to permit the effectiveness of independent-variable stimuli, uncontaminated by other, extraneous variables, to be revealed validly through inferential statistical analysis; an effectiveness that the data of inferential statistical analysis theoretically, but only theoretically, represent. To reveal the uncontaminated effectiveness of independent-variable stimuli through inferential statistics validly requires that, once the stimuli are played, no tampering with the dependent-variable responses that, presumably, result from such stimulation, may be permitted. But the operations implied by tampering are not only indispensable to, they are indistinguishable from, teaching: moment-to-moment manipulation of students' responses is the quintessential *modus operandi* of teaching. It is therefore necessary (unless teaching be subverted) that data on the effectiveness of teaching be yielded through the teaching operations that produce the responses that the data are presumed to represent. The criterion dependent-variable responses toward which teaching is aimed are, of course, the academic and related performances of students.

Teaching demands an epistemological framework within whose

bounds may be found a single set of operations for determining its impact in both of the senses, production and measurement, that the term, determination, implies (Throne 1970). In education, the reciprocal relationship between production and measurement is often missed: one can determine the dependent-variable *effects* of teaching by producing them—for example, by teaching spelling; or one can determine the independent-variable *effectiveness* of teaching by measuring its effects—for example, by counting words spelled correctly after spelling has been taught. Usually, operations to produce and to measure effectiveness are kept deliberately distinct. But they need not be. If education can be undertaken actively, by *manipulating* results to meet criteria, rather than passively, by *comparing* results against a theoretical expectancy (for example, null hypothesis testing), all operational distinctions between teaching and evaluation can be dissolved. Most educators believe (correctly enough) that the semantic signs (numbers) that evaluative operations *on* teaching yield ought to reflect only the operations *of* teaching (the teachers' performances), not those confounded with the operations of evaluation (the evaluators' performances). However, they also believe that, if the assumptions of inferential statistics are met insofar as is possible, only the operations of teaching will be represented by the semantic signs in terms of which the results of inferential statistical analysis are displayed. *Quite the reverse is true.*

Teaching versus Evaluative Operations

Ironically, it is precisely the operations of evaluation *in interaction with* those of teaching, and not those of teaching alone, that evaluators apply in measuring the effectiveness of teaching through inferential statistics whose assumptions, insofar as is possible, have been met. It is contradictory to say that only the independent-variable stimuli that are intrinsic to the operations of teaching are reflected by the semantic signs that constitute the data of inferential statistical analysis. Instead of being functions solely of the operations of teaching, these signs are partly functions of the operations of evaluation, with the operations of teaching (to the extent that the requisite assumptions have indeed been met) actually having been sacrificed to the operations of evaluation. (Evaluators using inferential statistical analysis may be teachers also, but they act in an evaluating, as opposed to a teaching, capacity; they function within a set of operational parameters kept deliberately distinct from teaching.) That, before evaluation, the students' responses to teaching have provided the flesh and bones over which the garment of inferential statistical analysis eventually is draped is not the issue. By the time the garment is completed, the shape of the body underneath is indiscernible and, to all intents and purposes, irrelevant. It is this traditional emphasis on the operations of evaluation at the expense of those of teaching—entailing the sacrifice of the latter to the former—that renders an evaluation of teaching that is based on inferential statistical analysis inappropriate. The difficulty or impossibility of meeting the assumptions of inferential statistics is thus beside the point.

Confirming Functionality of Teaching Operations

After the dependent-variable responses of students (that is, academic performances) have been manipulated by the independent variables of teaching, theoretical interpretations may be superimposed on the responses that result. These interpretations, perhaps defensible in theory, are quite gratuitous from the standpoint of the manipulations that were responsible for the responses in fact. At best, these interpretations may provide a basis for introducing theories about intervening variables contributing to the responses, intervening variables whose contribution to the responses was contingent on the interdiction of causal independent variables. (But the contingent intervening variables themselves did not cause the responses.) Acceptance or rejection of such theories depends on additional operations that still remain to be performed. At worst, these interpretations may be invoked to account for the responses on the basis of the responses themselves (tautological reasoning), or on the basis of a contingent relationship between the responses and the subjects through whom they were emitted (illogical reasoning). (For a fuller discussion of these points see Throne 1972; and Throne unpublished manuscript.)

However, aside from whatever value that interpretations of results (in this case, dependent-variable student responses produced through teaching) may have, it is only by effectively manipulating the independent-variable stimuli involved, that their functionality, in terms of criterion dependent-variable response effects, can be confirmed empirically. Functionally speaking, theorizing about the contribution of intervening variables to dependent-variable responses is needless if the causal effectiveness of independent-variable stimuli has been confirmed empirically. Functional relationships between independent-variable stimuli and dependent-variable responses can also be confirmed theoretically through the use of inferential statistics whose assumptions have been met. But a theoretical confirmation of a functional relationship cannot be substituted for its empirical confirmation. Theoretical confirmation of empirically confirmed functional relationships is unnecessary, while theoretical without empirical confirmation is insufficient.

Descriptive statistics, often recommended as an alternative to inferential statistics (for example, by Coats 1970), while appropriate insofar as no assumptions that are incompatible with teaching need be met, are insufficient for evaluating the effectiveness of teaching (Throne 1971a, b). Exactly as in the case of inferential statistics, the operations of descriptive statistics are kept deliberately distinct from those of teaching. Consequently, theoretical interpretations derived from descriptive, no less than from inferential, statistical analysis must be based on a presumptive functionality between the stimuli and the responses that the semantic signs (statistical data) theoretically represent. Results derived from descriptive, as well as from inferential, statistical analysis can lead only to theories of intervening variables contributing to relationships between stimuli and responses (between teaching and achievement) that still must be confirmed empirically. Thus we get the inevitable disclaimer: "Further research is needed."

There is no escaping the conclusion that teaching must be evaluated in circumstances entirely free of the restrictions on the moment-to-moment manipulations of teaching that the assumptions of inferential statistics impose. The effectiveness of teaching must not be measured according to a semantic-sign system that expressly precludes those very operations of teaching that produce the response effects in students that are presumed to reflect those operations.

OPERANT CONDITIONING

Fortunately, an approach to the evaluation of teaching that not only permits, but also requires, the moment-to-moment manipulation of dependent-variable response effects in students is available in operant conditioning, the empirical model of behavior originated by B. F. Skinner in the 1930s. (See, for example, Skinner, 1938, 1953, 1968.) Fundamentally, operant conditioning entails the controlled application of the consequential stimuli that responses encounter, contingent on responses to criteria being obtained. The basic principle of operant conditioning has been articulated by Skinner (1938): "Behavior is a function of its consequences." It has been referred to as *the principle of consequential determinism* (Throne 1970). Contingent application of consequential stimuli means that the responses that consequential stimuli follow must occur according to specifications, that is, on the basis of rules, in order for the consequential stimuli to be applied. Response criteria are always arbitrary: *the principle of criterial arbitrariness* (Throne 1970). They are selected, not capriciously, but on the basis of the functions to be served by teaching, by the objectives that teaching is to fulfill: *the principle of functional primacy* (Throne 1970). Usually, successive approximations of criterion responses are *differentially reinforced;* that is, they and they alone, are reinforced. Toward this end circumstances are scientifically arranged. Specifically, discriminative stimuli sufficient to produce successive approximations of criterion responses are introduced until the criterion responses themselves are achieved. Stimuli become discriminative when responses occurring in their presence are followed reliably by a reinforcing consequence. The strategy of differentially reinforcing successive approximations of criterion responses is called *shaping.*

Consequences can be extinguishing or punishing as well as reinforcing. Reinforcing consequences are functionally defined by subsequent *increases* in the frequency, percentage, or rate of responses emitted before the presentation (positive reinforcement), or withdrawal (negative reinforcement), of the consequential stimuli. If, and only if, the response class index (frequency, percentage, or rate) increases, the consequential stimuli are designated as reinforcing (positive or negative). Both extinguishing and punishing consequences are defined by subsequent *decreases* in prior response class indices. Withholding a reinforcing stimulus is an extinguishing consequence. Presenting an aversive stimulus (that is, a stimulus that the subject takes steps to avoid or escape) is a punishing consequence. Subsequent decreases in prior response class indices may also occur following withdrawal of a reinforcing stimulus—also a punishing consequence. Depending on which kind of consequential stimuli (reinforcing, extinguishing, punishing) are employed under which conditions, and depending on the experience of the subjects with related consequential stimuli, the amplitude, longevity, and generalizability of obtained responses (as well as any side effects) will be significantly diverse. (Consequential stimuli that subsequently neither increase nor decrease prior responses are designated as neutral.)

With the strategies and tactics of operant conditioning we can determine which independent-variable consequential stimuli cause which dependent-variable responses through contingent manipulation of the latter by the former. That is, the presentation, withholding, or withdrawal of whichever consequences demonstrably cause criterion responses, or successive approximations of them, to occur can be made contingent on the occurrence of these responses according to our specifications, on the basis of rules that we select. The principle of consequential determinism is therefore the key to the epistemological problem posed by the requirements of teaching for an evaluation system that is compatible with teaching. Through its application all operational distinctions between teaching and evaluation can be dissolved. If the dependent-variable response effects of teaching can be determined (produced) when the independent-variable stimulus consequences of teaching are contingently presented, withheld, or withdrawn, the effectiveness of teaching can be determined (measured) simultaneously by the same response effects. Evaluation can determine stimulus effectiveness empirically, in terms of manipulated response effects (students' performances); instead of theoretically, in terms of manipulated semantic signs (statisticians' numbers).

To summarize: Using operant conditioning, we can show empirically that teaching produces dependent variable response effects in students. At the same time, we can measure the effectiveness of teaching by the dependent-variable response effects it produces in students. Unlike the case in which inferential and descriptive statistics are used, evaluation can be undertaken in the process of, not separate from (or after) teaching. Stimuli responsible for students' responses can be empirically determined (measured) as a function of the very operations of teaching that determine (produce) these responses. If teaching is successful, an evaluation of the effective stimulus variables is determined by the dependent-variable response effects obtained. If teaching is not successful, an evaluation is also determined by the obtained effects (strictly speaking, the obtained *non*effects). In any event, neither the success of teaching nor its failure can be determined empirically independently of teaching. Positive results prove the presence of stimuli sufficient for success; negative results prove only that such stimuli were absent. The belief that the results of one set of operations, called teaching, can be determined empirically by another set of operations, called evaluation, is a fallacy.

The question of which of several components of effective independent-variable consequential stimuli are necessary to cause dependent-variable response effects, is separate from the question of whether the independent-variable consequential stimuli, which of course are constituted of these components, are as a whole effective or not. To the extent, and in the form, that it is desirable that the first question be answered, the strategy to be followed is one of differential reinforcement of responses to criteria by each of the consequential stimulus components involved, one by one. (That is, all components but one are alternately held constant or removed.) The question of the *necessity* of a consequential stimulus component is thus transformed into the question of its *sufficiency*. Indeed, the *principle of consequential infinitude* (Throne 1970), which postulates that determining consequential stimulus possibilities are unlimited, demands it.

OPERANT CONDITIONING AND TRANSACTIONAL EVALUATION

This brief addendum is a response to questions about operant conditioning that might conceivably be asked by an advocate of transactional evaluation as defined by the editor in chapter one of this book. The positions listed immediately below refer directly to specific issues he raises; all italicized words and phrases refer to positive statements that he makes about transactional evaluation. Obviously the chapter must be read before this addendum.

It would be misleading to imply that operant conditioning and transactional evaluation are obviously compatible but, as far as evaluation is concerned, they have several features in common.

Operant conditioning can be viewed as a variant of transactional evaluation if it is recognized that independent-variable stimuli within the educational system, including performances of teachers, are the *evaluative focus* of operant conditioning. The dependent variables within the system, including performances of students, are its *teaching focus*. The output of students validates the input of schools.

In operant conditioning, the *social, psychological, and communications* aspects of the educational system of primary concern to transactional evaluation (the independent variables of teaching), not the system's *manifest objectives* (the dependent variables of student performances), are its evaluative focus. From the standpoint of operant evaluation to improve the latter is but a means to improve the former.

In operant conditioning, as in transactional evaluation, *information is fed back* continuously into the educational system to improve it. Without this feedback, there would be no need to use the dynamic evaluation procedures of operant conditioning. The static procedures of inferential and descriptive statistics would suffice to yield the kinds of data required by institutions that are changing not continuously but continually (if at all).

In operant evaluation the teacher is no more *intrinsic,* the evaluator no more *extrinsic,* to the educational system than in transactional evaluation. On the contrary, the teaching evaluator (or evaluating teacher) who uses operant conditioning always functions within the system of which, in his reciprocal role, he is an integral part. Since his *is* a reciprocal role, he must evaluate teaching within the system without cost to teaching.

Operant conditioning, like transactional evaluation, places little or no stress on *conventional* considerations of reliability, validity, and objectivity, since *unconventionally* the responses produced by operant conditioning speak unequivocally for themselves; they need no transformation into the semantic signs of inferential or descriptive statistics in order to be explained. However, precisely those intervening variables that bear upon the attainment of the dependent-variable manifest objectives of educational systems (that is, student performances) through the independent variables of teaching, and that are of concern to the transactional evaluator, such as *timeliness, relevance, and feedback of evaluative information into the system,* concern the operant evaluator too. They constitute variables that contingently contribute to the effectiveness of the independent variables of teaching on student performances. By experimentally controlling these variables, the operant evaluator can prove their contingent contribution empirically, the statistical evaluator can prove it only theoretically, and the transactional evaluator, in his capacity as transactional evaluator (as defined in the Introduction), apparently not at all.

Thus, although the *primary aims of transactional evaluation are not the production of new knowledge, nor the attribution of causality, but, rather, the constructive channeling of the conflict energy that is associated with change through a clarification of the roles of those in the educational system who are involved in change programs,* operant conditioning offers a mechanism by which the transactional evaluator's aims may be fulfilled at the same time that the manifest objectives of the educational system are achieved. Operant conditioning can help the transactional evaluator look at any transaction within the system on his own terms without sacrificing the manifest objectives of the system itself.

Finally, nothing inherent in operant conditioning precludes

opponents of program design aspects of educational systems from participating in the development and implementation of evaluation plans. On the contrary, operant evaluation demands programmatic inputs from all sources to insure results. For both the operant conditioner and transactional evaluator there is everything to gain and nothing to lose from listening seriously to every suggestion, *substantive and/or apprehensive,* that can increase the probability of fulfilling programmatic aims of educational systems.

FOOTNOTES

This chapter is a revision of a paper, presented to the meeting of the American Educational Research Association, New York City, February 1971, and originally titled "Inappropriateness of Inferential and Insufficiency of Descriptive Statistics in Educational Evaluation: The Problem and a Solution."

Dr. Throne's contribution is the expression of rather an extreme stance—that of radical behaviorism. It is not necessary for one to accept all of the assumptions of radical behaviorism in order to accept the concept of transactional evaluation. However, we find it interesting to note radical behaviorism's support for the concept of evaluator and researcher involvement and intervention - *Editor.*

REFERENCES

Coats, W. "A Case Against the Normal Use of Inferential Statistical Models in Educational Research." *Educational Researcher* 21 (1970): 6-7.

Coleman, J. S., Campbell, E. Q., Hobson, C. J., McPartland, J., Mood, A. M., Weinfeld, F. D., and York, R. L. *Equality of Educational Opportunity.* Washington, D.C.: U.S. Government Printing Office, 1966.

Guba, E. G., and Clark, D. L. *A Proposal for the National Institute for the Study of Educational Change.* Bloomington, Ind.: National Institute for the Study of Educational Change, Indiana University, 1967.

Skinner, B. F. *Behavior of Organisms.* New York: Appleton-Century-Crofts, 1938.

Skinner, B. F. *Science and Human Behavior.* New York: Macmillan, 1953.

Skinner, B. F. *The Technology of Teaching.* New York: Appleton-Century-Crofts, 1968.

Throne, J. M. "A Radical Behaviorist Approach to Diagnosis in Mental Retardation." *Mental Retardation* 8, no. 3 (1970): 2-5.

(The published version of this paper contains several typographical errors. A corrected copy may be obtained from J. M. Throne, Center for Mental Retardation and Human Development, University of Kansas, Lawrence, Kansas 66044.)

Throne, J. M. "Statistical Analysis in the Evaluation of Teaching: Is it Necessary?" *Educational Researcher* (March 1971): 4-6. (a)

Throne, J. M. "Does Operant Conditioning Make Functional Distinctions Between Teaching and Evaluation Obsolete?" American Psychological Association *Proceedings* (1971): 557-558. (b)

Throne, J. M. "Confusion of Contingency and Cause in Cognitive Research in Mental Retardation: Zigler, Zeaman and House, Ellis (and Bijou)." *Mental Retardation* 1972, in press.

Throne, J. M. "Tautological and Illogical Reasoning in Linguistic and Cognitive Research and Practice: Chomsky, Piaget and Freud." Unpublished.

17

TRANSACTIONAL EVALUATION OF CLASSROOM PRACTICE

MAURICE J. EASH

The central assumption of this chapter is that classroom practice would be improved if research findings were better implemented. Having observed many classrooms in the past eight years and found corroboration for my observations in discussions with colleagues who are broadly acquainted with classroom practice, I feel it safe to assert that classroom instruction is basically untouched by research findings. Even where the research findings are most unequivocal and their implementation would require only limited modification of teacher behavior, systematic observation finds them absent in the repertoire of most teachers' classroom performance. One example of a research finding that is consistently neglected, though it is supported by substantial evidence, and has been documented at length, is that of the pretest in teaching spelling. Other obvious examples are as easily come by.

What is crucial to the dissemination of research findings is the *translation* of research findings and procedures into a framework of current practice, so that they become an integral part of the class-room behavior of teachers and students. The process of translation may be synthesized into three models, which draw data from litera-ture and the author's experience, and, in name, directly reflect the basic postulate guiding the process of relating research findings to classroom practices (Kaplan 1964).

DISPLACEMENT MODEL

Perhaps the most widely used, in that it reaches the most class-rooms, and valued, because it is thought to arouse less antagonism among teachers, is the displacement model. In this model the desired change in instructional practice, be it a research finding or an innovation, is fitted into the activity of the classroom by displacing a similar activity and forcing the teacher and students to use the replacement. One of the most common examples of the use of this model is in the adoption of new textbooks, containing new material, and a simultaneous prohibition against the old books; other examples would include the use of programmed materials instead of textbooks, or the requirement that a teacher use filmstrips, films, or educational television. Some of the work in computer-assisted instruction seems to be implemented by displacement: the classroom teacher is by-passed and his interaction with pupils replaced with a device and a program.

Where the teacher's cooperation and his knowledge of materials is critical, one hardly need dwell on the problems that arise. Schools have had disconcerting experiences when older instruction materials in mathematics and science were displaced by new programs and the teacher was unwilling or unable to cope with the new material. One leading proponent of the new mathematics, after viewing the misuse of his carefully developed materials, communicated his anguish in a paper delivered at a professional meeting that was reported by the mass media (Beberman 1964). His criticism was interpreted as a call for a halt to hasty adaptation of new curricular materials by the schools:

> New curricula have been introduced without proper attention to essential pedagogical principles or the need for relating mathematics to the real world, as well as relating it to the logical principles now receiv-ing great emphasis. Until pedagogical principles are

better established, it is criminal to push new programs
in this field.

Thus the model is criticized because it lacks the power of consistent application. Not infrequently, as in the case of Beberman's mathematics program, the new program is taught in the same way as the old; learning by rote is disastrous whether the material be symbol manipulation or mathematical law. (For a trenchant criticism of the new mathematics curriculum and its implementation, see Kline [1966].)

The displacement model for implementation is also criticized for its effect on the behavior of the teacher, who is a crucial agent. The displacement procedure on a wide scale requires money. It has been suggested that any heavy economic commitment may reduce the teachers' tolerance for feedback and stifle criticism.

It would be a comfort to harassed school administrators if the displacement model effortlessly implemented change in classroom practice, minimized conflict, and guaranteed the preservation of the innovation. Basically, however, the model is a mechanistic view of the instructional process, conceptualizing it as an assembly line, a conceptualization that overrides the human exponents and leaves unresolved the basic problem of making use of research findings while maintaining their authenticity.

AUTHORITY MODEL

The authority model has been widely used by those who believe that research findings are valuable and that, if teachers are aware of research, they will use the findings. This model emphasizes published findings, on the premise that they will be read and acted upon. The written word may carry authority in some circles, but the evidence is less than reassuring that research finds its way into the classroom through print—I am thinking of the teacher who independently seeks out and implements research. In a study by the National Education Association (1967) of reading habits of teachers, none of the six journals mentioned as most helpful (the magazines that were mentioned by between 1.3 percent and 15.8 percent of the respondents), specializes in educational research. An analogous study of other scientific journals does not make one optimistic for implementation by this route. Wilkinson observed, on the readership of articles in scientific journals (1964), that the average scientific contribution is read by 1.3 persons, and he concludes that, "since some contributions are read by several hundred, the import of this figure is that most papers are not read at all." The bald facts are that, if findings are not brought into the practitioner's awareness, there is no hope for their implementation.

Another approach of the authority model, to have researchers act authoritatively to bring the findings to practitioners, also poses special problems for implementation. Researchers in a university drew up an inventory of major research findings that pertained directly to classroom practices in a specific subject. From this inventory they drew up lists of teaching practices, those that were supported by research and those that were questionable in the light of research findings. Armed with these two lists, they administered inventory instruments on teaching practices, and elicited expressions of classroom teaching behavior. After tabulating the findings and sharing them with the group, the researchers proceeded to expatiate on the research findings on each of the practices mentioned. There were, almost needless to say, major discrepancies between the practices acknowledged by the teachers and the practices supported by research. Although the implementation of research findings is of great interest to the researchers and publication contributes to knowledge of the present state of teaching this particular subject, I would predict that the authority model will produce improved practices buttressed by research. The postulates on which the authority model proceeds are inadequate to secure implementation because:

1. The research findings are generally introduced without attention being given to their translation into the teacher's frame of reference, which includes a multitude of variables probably unaccounted for in the original findings. Hence the instructional patterns and procedures used by the teacher may prevent his seeing the relationship between the findings and his practice.

2. The interaction of the researcher and practitioner in the model, as in the example given, does evaluate present practice early in the relationship and requires an admission of inadequacy, which heightens tension and produces friction between the researcher and the teacher. (For an excellent discussion of the tension and friction that rise between practitioner and researcher as they operate in the same environment, and the conflict of their allegiances to different goals, see Rodman and Kolodny [1965].)

3. Correspondingly, where findings are introduced in a group meeting without follow-up there is little or no incentive for teachers to adopt new findings that require a modification of practice, and more incentive to avoid interrupting present classroom instruction.

4. The effecting of change through authority has a rather long

history in formal organization and considerable evidence has been accumulated on the ability of informal structures within the organization to resist implementation efforts.

COACTION MODEL

The third model, the coaction model, is based on the postulate that the implementation of research findings must be a two-way process engaging both the researcher and the practitioner.[1] This model is devised in an attempt to correct the inadequacies in the other two models by recognizing a fundamental condition of human interaction which was defined in a theoretical essay by the German sociologist, Georg Simmel. Simmel (1964) stated that the basis for a positive working relationship was lodged in an interaction in which the parties had a possible parity in the exchange: "All contacts among men rest on the schema of giving and returning the equivalence." He argued that one party is diminished where the relationship is not reciprocal, and the unequal party becomes dissatisfied in the relationship. Gouldner has labeled this inequity in relationships "reciprocity imbalance." The coaction model is intended to build a relationship between researcher and practitioner that will meet Simmel's condition for equivalence.

The following two case studies are drawn from my work, with teachers, in which selected findings were brought to bear directly on their problems and working hypotheses were derived and tested. In both cases I was working with one teacher, but I have worked with groups of teachers, and the critical variable in both instances is the researcher's generating a feeling of reciprocity between the two parties.

Conflict Resolution

In the first case study the teacher of an elementary class and the researcher were confronted with a problem that is endemic to selected elementary schools: the pupils resolved all their differences by physical aggression. The teacher was finding that the continual fighting was greatly interfering with her teaching. While direct physical altercations could be controlled in the classroom, they broke out on the playground, in the lunchroom, on the way home, and the students' hostility permeated the classroom. One child described his emotional state in the afternoon after a fight at noon, "It makes you so you can't think."

As a first step the teacher began to collect systematic accounts of their hostilities by talking to the children. These accounts were discussed with the researcher, analyzed, and some of the findings from conflict resolution were used to generate some rough hypotheses to test (Boulding 1962). From these raw data it appeared that, in any conflict of interests, these particular children would gravitate to a zero-sum game. (A zero-sum game is a situation in which whatever one party gains the other loses.) In most of the incidents the loss was status in the eyes of fellow students.

The researcher and teacher tried to move the conflicts from physical aggression to negotiation by setting up alternative routes to the resolution of differences. The procedure would also try to help students become more sophisticated in understanding the causes of their conflicts. The raw data harbored clues of social pressures that were producing many of the altercations and the participants were, in a number of incidents, unwilling victims of these pressures. We established a procedure whereby students would bring their conflicts before a nonjudgmental mediator (in this case, the teacher) whose prime role was to obtain data on the circumstances surrounding the conflict from the parties involved and other observers. Each party received an uninterrupted opportunity to state his views before the other participant and observers. Once the data were gathered, the parties to the conflict were asked to analyze the conflict, look for other alternative responses, and, if the conflict merited it, discuss the consequences of their actions and determine the punishment, usually a restriction of privileges. In some incidents the parties had to negotiate differences and arrive at a commonly acceptable decision.

A record was kept of the children's behavior after the negotiation procedures were inaugurated, used for two months, and compared with the original observations. There was a marked reduction in physical aggression, and the students had begun to use a variety of techniques to dampen down conflict before it escalated into physical aggression. Considerably fewer students were coercing or being coerced into confrontations in which the only recourse was to overt conflict to avoid a loss of status. In comparing the class before and after the new procedures were instituted, the teacher recorded that the greatest gain was in the class's sense of community—improved cooperation and reduction of hostility and conflict—that created a completely different climate for learning. The researcher and teacher had both learned from the endeavor that the findings from conflict resolution studies can be translated into the classroom and effectively used.

Classroom Organization

The second case study of the use of the coaction model demonstrates that effective coaction does not have to be founded on a compelling problem. In a passing conversation a teacher observed to the researcher that her fourth grade students enjoyed coming in every morning, and reading and discussing the lesson plans for the day. She eventually left her plans on her desk so the students could peruse them before class. The teacher and researcher began speculating on the students' interest and, subsequently, had conversations about human behavior and its response to an organization. (For a quick review of the research on organizations, see Berleson and Steiner [1966, pp. 374-379].) We then explored ways to increase effectiveness (the accomplishment of the common purpose) and efficiency (the satisfaction of the motives of individual contributors) in this fourth grade classroom. (These, and other conceptualizations for this project, were drawn from the literature on organization theory and research, a very useful summary of which is contained in Scott [1964, pp. 485-529].)

As one way of translating some of the research findings on organizations and human behavior to a classroom setting, a committee, with the rather elegant title, "Committee on Instruction," was organized. Composed of four students chosen by their classmates, the committee met every Friday for forty minutes and then discussed their work with the class for twenty minutes. Committee membership rotated every two weeks. A tape recording of the meetings was made, and the researcher and teacher analyzed the topics the committee discussed, the suggestions that were made, the class reaction. Data were collected through a postevaluation of the students' reactions and the teacher's observations. The students were enthusiastic about the committee's work and their greater sense of goal direction became evident. Some sample responses drawn from the children's data gathered in the postevaluation suggest that the committee's activities promoted effectiveness and efficiency in the classroom, which is an organization that meets formal goals and human needs.

In response to the stimulus question, would you like every teacher to have a committee on instruction? one girl replied: "Yes. Sometimes the children in the class do not understand the way the teacher puts things, and other children are able to put it the way they can understand it." Some other sample responses suggest that a significant awareness may have come out of the experience. One boy commented: "I have learned that I can help other people with their problems." Another child stated: "I've learned that other people can have better ideas that work." In looking at these fourth graders' responses, I was struck with the development of insight and awareness that they showed. To their advantage, I compared these children's sense of the committee experience with that of many a college committee on which I have sat.

Other behavioral consequences were noted by the teacher: less supervision of children's work periods was needed, the number of incomplete assignments decreased, the group was more cohesive and interested in school work, attendance was better. The researcher noted that the teacher was more enthusiastic about her work.

A classroom organization, like other formal organizations, has a similar predilection for entropy that, in a classroom, is often a product of the isolation in which the teacher frequently feels engulfed.

Who can fill the role of the outside agent in the coaction model? From these case studies some of the agent's qualifications are readily evident: a broad knowledge of research findings, an understanding of classroom functioning, the ability to translate research findings from other contexts into the classroom, and skill in interpersonal relationships—skills that Rubin (1966) has discussed in more detail. The coaction model also requires that the participants devote a considerable amount of time to the implementation of research findings, which in complex problems, is complicated by the form of the problem as well as by the state of the research findings.

That there has been a "reciprocity imbalance" in the relationship between educational researchers and classroom practitioners cannot be denied. That teachers are restive about their status and are demanding a new realignment of relationships may be observed in some scattered data. The president of a group of state school teachers said:

> In too many instances, teachers have played a very minor role in planning programs . . . Proposals are formulated by university professors, school administrators, supervisors, and research specialists with only a nod in the direction of the classroom teacher. (Foley 1966).

This sentiment, echoed against some of the recent statements of "spokesmen" for educational research, sounds like the dilemma sketched by C. P. Snow (1963), who, in the 1959 Rede Lectures at Cambridge University, expounded the thesis that a crisis condition existed in the two predominant academic cultures. He was talking about the hiatus between the sciences and the humanities:

> Between the two [lies] a gulf of mutual incomprehension—sometimes (particularly among the young) hostility and dislike, but most of all lack of understanding. They have a curious distorted image of each other. Their attitudes are so different that, even on the level of emotion, they can't find much common ground.

Lest this seem an incorrect parallel Cronbach (1966), past president of the American Educational Research Association, clearly recommends the creation of a state of affairs in educational research that would polarize educational researchers and classroom practitioners. Cronbach considered the isolation of the researcher and a minimal interaction between researcher and teacher as necessary conditions for basic educational research.

On this point Snow can be instructive. In 1964 he reexamined his 1959 thesis and the storm of criticism it invoked. He optimistically saw a basis for the emergence of a third culture, which could bridge the tragic polarization of the two cultures. If my thesis, on how little research findings are used in the classroom, is correct we should be thinking of building a third culture that encompasses both teacher and researcher, rather than advancing two polarized cultures. The coaction model, by placing transactional evaluation in the classroom, promises to influence the educational process directly. Very few acts or products of educational researchers can make this claim.

FOOTNOTE

1. I am indebted to Edward Haskell and Harold G. Cassidy for the concept of coaction that they enunciated in an unpublished paper "General Systems Theory and Education: On the Unification of Science."

REFERENCES

Beberman, M. In "Peril to Doing Sums Seen in 'New Math.'" *New York Times*, 31 December, 1964, p. 22.

Berleson, B., and Steiner, G. A. *Human Behavior: An Inventory of Scientific Findings*. New York: Harcourt, Brace and World, 1966.

Boulding, K. *Conflict and Defense: A General Theory*. New York: Harper and Row, 1962.

Cronbach, L. J. "The Role of the University in Improving Educational Research." *Phi Delta Kappa* 47 (1966): 539-545.

Foley, A. A. "The Teacher: Central Change-Agent of Society." *New York State Education* 54 (November 1966): 19-22.

Kaplan, A. *The Conduct of Inquiry*. San Francisco: Chandler, 1964.

National Education Association. *Reading and Recreational Interests of Classroom Teachers*. Research Report—R2. Washington, D.C.: National Education Association, 1967.

Rodman, H., and Kolodny, R. "Organization Strains in the Researcher-Practitioner Relationship." In *Applied Sociology: Opportunities and Problems*, edited by A. W. Gouldner, and S. M. Miller. New York: The Free Press, 1965.

Rubin, L. "The Professional Growth of the Educator." Occasional Paper. Santa Barbara: Center for Coordinated Education, University of California at Santa Barbara, 1966.

Scott, W. R. "Theory of Organization." In *Handbook of Modern Sociology*, edited by R. E. L. Faris. Chicago: Rand McNally, 1964.

Simmel, G. *The Sociology of Georg Simmel*. Translated by K. H. Wolff. New York: The Free Press, 1964.

Snow, C. P. *The Two Cultures and a Second Look*. New York: Mentor Books, 1963.

Wilkinson, J. "The Quantitative Society, or What are You to Do with Noodle?" Occasional Paper. Santa Barbara, Calif.: The Center for the Study of Democratic Institutions, 1964.

18

ISSUES IN THE EVALUATION OF SOCIAL PROGRAMS

FRANCIS G. CARO

Efforts in the past decade to reduce the incidence of major social problems have stimulated a new interest in program evaluation. Numerous writings have appeared on the use of the concepts and methods of behavioral research in evaluating these interventions. This chapter is a review of that literature. It surveys evaluation programs designed to produce some identifiable change in individual or social groups.

BASIC CONSIDERATIONS

Attempts to define evaluation reflect concern with both the results and the desirability or value of programs. Greenberg (1968), Brooks (1965), and Suchman (1967a) emphasized the information-seeking aspect of evaluation. Greenberg (1968, p.260) defined it as "the procedure by which programs are studied to ascertain their effectiveness in the fulfillment of goals." Brooks (1965, p.34) listed as evaluation objectives the determination of: the extent to which the program achieves its goal, the relative impact of key program variables, and the role of the program as contrasted to external variables. Suchman (1967a, pp.31-32) defined evaluation as "the determination of the results attained by some activity designed to accomplish some valued goal or objective." He also identified (1966, p.68) four evaluation categories: effort (the amount of action), effect (results of effort), process (how an effect was achieved), and efficiency (effects in relation to cost).

The judgmental dimension was emphasized by Scriven (1967, pp. 40-41) who defined evaluation as a "methodological activity which combines performance data with a goal scale." Glass (1971) similarly stressed that evaluation is an attempt to assess the worth or social utility of a thing. He argued that, since the desirability of announced program goals might be questioned, evaluation should include procedures for the evaluation of those goals.

Methodology

Several distinctly different approaches to evaluation methodology can be identified. Legislators, administrators, practitioners, recipients of services, and journalists are among those who typically rely on impressionistic or informal evaluation. Stake (1967) described informal evaluation as dependent on casual observation, implicit goals, intuitive norms, and subjective judgment; he characterized it as of variable quality—sometimes penetrating and insightful, sometimes superficial and distorted. Similarly, Mann (1969) noted that observations by participants may provide suggestive leads for interpreting the effects of programs but, because the extent of their bias is unknown, it is impossible to judge the accuracy of their conclusions.

Among formal approaches to evaluation, a distinction can be made between those emphasizing inputs and those emphasizing outputs. Educational accrediting agencies, municipal building inspectors, and fire insurance underwriters base their evaluative judgments on inputs, using explicit checklists and formulas. Educational programs are evaluated on the basis of such factors as teacher qualifications and the ratio of library books to students; adequacy of housing is judged on the basis of plumbing facilities and sleeping arrangements; fire insurance raters consider the nature of building materials and fire fighting equipment. Data are typically obtained through site inspections. Glass (1971) pointed out that, since it is based on subjective judgments, this approach is weak in the areas of objectivity and validity.

The program accounting approach to evaluation also emphasizes input of efforts. It focuses on the maintenance and quantitative analysis of project activity records. The extent of actual practitioner-client contact and the number of clients exposed to programs are typical concerns. Outputs or effects tend to receive little attention; program accounting is tied to routine agency records, and agencies can rarely undertake the extensive follow-up activities necessary for complete information on the outcome of services. However, since it can provide information on the ability to establish contacts with clients and the cost of program-client contacts, program accounting is useful as a procedure for determining the administrative viability of programs.

An emphasis on outputs or effects and a concern with the use of the scientific method characterizes evaluative research, the approach of primary concern here. Suchman (1969, p.15) distinguished between evaluation, a "general social process of making judgments of worth regardless of the basis for such judgments," and evaluative research, the "use of the scientific method for collecting data concerning the degree to which some specified activity achieves some desired effect." Similarly, Hyman and Wright (1967, p.742) called for evaluation based on "methods that yield evidence that is objective, systematic, and comprehensive." The emphasis of evaluative research on outputs need not imply a lack of concern for input variables. Scriven (1967), for example, suggested "mediated" evaluation as a way of combining input and output variables to permit study of the process through which goals are pursued.

Program Development and Administration

Evaluation may be viewed as a phase in systematic program development. Ideally, action programming is preceded by a planning process that includes: identification of problems, specification of objectives, analysis of the causes of problems and the shortcomings of existing programs, and an examination of possible action alternatives. Evaluation follows program implementation and provides a basis for further planning and program refinement. (Although evaluation may follow implementation, it is, of course, desirable that evaluation activities begin prior to implementation.) The planning-action-evaluation cycle may be repeated indefinitely until objectives are realized or problems and objectives are redefined. Results of evaluation may be used to modify programs already in progress to increase the likelihood of realization of long-term goals. When evaluation is viewed as part of a process of planned change, the utilization of evaluation findings in decision making becomes a key concern.

Evaluative research is concerned with stable and well established programs as well as with new programs for which viable administrative patterns are being sought. Scriven (1967, p. 43) introduced the terms "formative" and "summative" to distinguish between these two evaluation concerns. Formative evaluation is designed to improve a program while it is still fluid; summative evaluation is designed to appraise a product after it is well established.

A predisposition toward gradual and moderate change is thought to produce an interest in evaluative research. Where change is thought to be undesirable or impossible, little interest in evaluation can be expected from the guardians of societal institutions. Groups demanding rapid and radical change are also unlikely consumers of evaluative research; their inclinations are likely to be ideological rather than empirical, and evaluative researchers are not likely to respond to their information needs rapidly enough.

Emphasis on evaluative research is most appropriate when program effects cannot be expected to be directly and immediately evident (Coleman 1969). Such is often the case in contemporary large-scale education, welfare, and social service programs whose effects are often subtle and diffuse. Large-scale programs also tend to increase the physical and social distance between policy makers and recipients of services. When they are in close contact with clients, policy makers may have reason to be confident of their own informal evaluations of programs. As their contacts with the client population decrease, however, policy makers may recognize the need for more formal evaluation procedures (Trow 1967).

In principle, evaluation activities may generate judgments regarding effectiveness of performance on such varied levels as programming approaches (for example, remedial reading or income-maintenance programs), administrative units (for example, schools, departments, or agencies), individual practitioners (for example, physicians or teachers), and recipients of services (for example, patients, clients, or students) (Cronbach 1963). In practice, for reasons discussed below, evaluators whose primary concern is with program effectiveness usually deliberately avoid making judgmental statements regarding particular administrative units, practitioners, or recipients of services.

Evaluation may be considered a programming input, subject to evaluation in the same manner as other inputs. In cost-benefit terms, the cost of evaluation should be related to the benefits that evaluation data and judgments contribute to programming efficiency or effectiveness. A heavy investment in formal evaluation is most likely to be justified when a program is expensive, its impact is potentially great but uncertain, and the potential for diffusion of programming concepts is great. Glass (1971) contended that decisions to conduct evaluative research should reflect estimates of the cost of evaluation, the extent to which there is uncertainty regarding program effectiveness, and the cost of implementing alternate programs.

Theoretically, evaluative research may be undertaken without any formal sponsorship, may be based on a wide range of value perspectives, and its findings may be reported to a variety of audiences. In practice, however, because of problems of cost and access to information, formal evaluation is usually a sponsored activity. External funding agencies (for example, private foundations or the federal government) and top administrators of action organizations are the most common sponsors. Whether the evaluation is conducted by an internal unit of an organization or by outside consultants, the researchers usually are directly linked to persons high in the administrative structure of the action organization. Those who actually carry out the programs to be evaluated are, then, subordinate to those to whom evaluators report. The issues addressed by evaluation and the manner in which results are reported are strongly related to sponsorship. Consequently, the interests of the general public, practitioners, and recipients of services are often not fully served by evaluators.

Science, Research, and Evaluation

From a behavioral science point of view, evaluative research represents an application of the scientific method, which is quite different from that of basic research. Some insist on a sharp distinction between research and evaluation, while others classify evaluation as a form of research. Wrightstone (1969, p.5) suggested that

> Research is more concerned with the basic theory and design of a program over an appropriate period of time, with flexible deadlines, and with sophisticated treatment of data that have been carefully obtained. [Evaluation on the other hand] may be concerned with basic theory and design, but its primary function is to appraise comprehensively a practical activity to meet a deadline.

Suchman (1969) argued that the distinction between basic research and evaluative research is one of purpose rather than method. Evaluative research applies the scientific method to problems that have administrative consequences, while basic research is concerned with problems of theoretical significance. Cherns (1969) distinguished between pure basic research, which is stimulated by the perceived needs of an academic discipline, and action (evaluative) research, which is concerned with an ongoing problem in an organizational framework and involves the introduction and observation of planned change. Cherns also pointed to differences in diffusion and generality between the types of research. In the case of basic research, the potential for generality is great but the potential for immediate utilization is limited. Evaluative research has a limited potential for generality but the potential for immediate utilization is great.

Evaluative research represents only one form of applied or action research; research may contribute to social action without assessing the effects of specific interventions. Research on the causes of problem behavior, on the incidence and concentration of patterns of social problems, and on public knowledge of and attitudes toward existing services may all have important policy implications without being specifically evaluative.

For social scientists interested in contributing to programs of direct change evaluative research is only one possible role. Alternately, social scientists may contribute to training programs and engage in consulting activities. Brooks (1965) suggested that social scientists provide ideas for experimentation and encourage the greatest possible rationality in the planning process. They can aid in the identification of objectives and action alternatives and the prediction of consequences of possible courses of action. (See Bennis 1965; Likert and Lippitt 1953.)

THE ORGANIZATIONAL CONTEXT

Although the rationale for a central role for formal behavioral evaluation is often strong, effective participation by evaluative researchers in social programming is much less common. When evaluation is examined from an organizational and occupational perspective, some of the practical problems in establishing and maintaining the evaluation role become apparent.

Of fundamental importance is the fact that, traditionally, decision makers have not accorded evaluative research a major role in policy formation and change in social programming (Rossi 1969). Policy has been formed without considering the kinds of evaluation data needed to sustain the worth of a program. Objective evidence of the effects of programs has not been demanded as a basis for modifying programs. Satisfied with informal evaluation, administrators have often included evaluative research only when it was required by a funding agent. Recent emphasis on evaluation in education, for example, stems largely from a provision of the Elementary and Secondary Education Act of 1965.

Some administrators may consider evaluative research expensive and of little practical value. They may also have important covert reasons for resisting formal evaluation. For example, the presence of an evaluation component invites administrators to consider the possibility that their policies do not lead to the effective realization of announced objectives. Because administrative claims for programs are usually extremely optimistic, evaluative research results almost inevitably are disappointing (Rossi 1967). Campbell (1969) observed that ambiguous results help to protect administrators where there is a possibility of failure. Freely available facts might reduce the privacy and security of some administrators, making them vulnerable to inquiries about their honesty and efficiency. In addition, administrators may resent evaluators who raise questions about basic organizational premises or suggest evaluative criteria which may be embarrassing to the organization.

Horowitz (1969) identified several other reasons why administrators may consider social scientists who belong to an internal research unit troublesome members of an action organization. Social scientists often demand preferential treatment, which is resented by other employees. Presuming superior wisdom on their own part, social scientists may seek direct access to top decision makers, thereby threatening bureaucrats who are bypassed. Further, the extracurricular involvement of social scientists in writing, teaching, and the like are often resented.

At the same time, administrators interested in evaluative research have often found it difficult to recruit and hold qualified behavioral scientists. Like other scientists, behavioral scientists often prefer to be oriented toward the general scientific community rather than the needs and goals of the organization that employs them (McKelvey 1969). Scientists typically wish to do research that contributes to a scientific body of knowledge. Administrators, however, typically expect scientists whom they employ to do research that contributes directly to the goals of their organizations. Social scientists who may wish to publicize their work also resent the norm of secrecy prevailing in some organizations (Horowitz 1969). In contrast to administrators who want social scientists to work within the framework of established policy, social scientists may want to challenge an agency's ideological premises (Horowitz 1969). In addition, some social scientists have been concerned that agreement to undertake the evaluation of a program may be interpreted as implicit commitment to the philosophy or goals of that program; they may give a program a legitimacy they do not believe it deserves (Ferman 1969). Other deterrents have been the low prestige accorded to applied research in academic settings, exasperation with the methodological and administrative problems of conducting research in an action setting, and disagreements regarding the use of research results.

Administering Evaluative Research

Successful administration of evaluative research depends on cooperation from agency administrators and practitioners charged with implementing action programs. Even though they often advocate extensive collaboration and communication with administrators, evaluative researchers typically insist that ultimate responsibility for research design and execution is theirs. Administrative interference with what social scientists consider critical issues in the design and execution of research is seriously resented (Smith, Sim, and Bealer 1960).

Whether or not researchers are agency employees, they are readily drawn into staff-management conflicts. A number of observers noted that acceptance of evaluative research at upper management levels was often accompanied by suspicion of research at lower levels (Rodman and Kolodny 1964; Lippitt, Watson, and Westley 1958; Argyris 1958; Whyte and Hamilton 1964; Likert and Lippitt 1953). Because evaluation is linked to top administration and involves examination of the activities of staff subordinates, evaluators are sometimes accused of being management spies. Staff practitioners interested in avoiding criticism of their work are likely to attempt to conceal real or imagined shortcomings. Such steps, of course, would add greatly to the evaluator's difficulties in obtaining valid data.

Research neutrality is also likely to pose a problem with practitioners who consider a strong value commitment to their programs important. Scriven (1967), for example, reported that some practitioners feel that the skepticism of evaluative researchers may dampen the creativity of a productive group. Argyris (1958) argued that research neutrality leads to subject alienation which then produces anxieties in the researcher, resulting in invalid observations.

The purely mechanical demands of data collection may also create a burden. Practitioners, perhaps correctly, consider themselves over-burdened with record keeping. Typically, even when record keeping is emphasized, records are not sufficiently accurate or complete to satisfy research criteria. Conflict between research and service goals may also interfere with the collection of research data. When a research design calls for action inconsistent with immediate service goals, practitioners may disregard research needs in favor of providing services. Compounding the problem, practitioners may neglect to inform evaluators that clients were shifted from a control or comparison group to an experimental group.

Different conceptions of efficient use of time may lead to mutual annoyance. A professional evaluator, for example, is not accustomed to turning in daily time sheets, but his failure to do so may be interpreted as a sign of indolence by an administrator with time and cost concerns. Bynder (1966, p.67), reflecting on his research in a social work unit of a general hospital, observed that "thinking is not a tangible use of time, and therefore, could not be accepted in an agency which measured work in terms of clients interviewed, physicians contacted, meetings attended, and pages written." An insecure social scientist may respond by engaging in activities that make him appear busy but that are detrimental to long-term evaluation objectives.

Status ambiguities may further strain relationships, especially if an evaluator has had more formal education but less clinical experience than administrator and practitioner counterparts. The social scientist may bring to the situation an academic disrespect for practical problems; administrators and practitioners, in turn, may be defensive about their educational inferiority and highly sensitive to what they interpret as the snobbism of evaluative researchers. Deteriorating relationships have led threatened practitioners to claim that evaluators are incompetent because they do not understand the practical problems of an action agency. The evaluators, perceiving themselves as exposed and defenseless members of a minority group in the action organization, sometimes react at this point by looking for ways to return to an academic setting.

Two basic problems were discussed in the literature concerning the publication of evaluative research results (see, for example, Rodman and Kolodny 1964). Agencies often impose controls on the publication of "sensitive" data because a negative report may threaten not only the agency's public image but also its access to funds. If it is agreed that project results should be reported, there may be disagreements about publication credits. The evaluation researcher, who contributed the research design, data analysis, and write-up, may regard the report as a scientific publication for which he is solely responsible. The administrator, emphasizing the content of the project, may believe he deserves major recognition for conceiving and implementing the program.

A final important issue is the availability of the funds needed for evaluative research. Action organizations nearly always operate on tight budgets. Administrators must attempt to use funds to provide as much service as possible. The cost of the elaborate data collection and analysis essential to evaluation research may represent a substantial proportion of the total project budget. Given the often intangible and uncertain contribution of evaluative research, requests for evaluation funds may be among the first to suffer in times of budget curtailment.

Using the Results of Evaluation

Since the ultimate purpose of evaluation is a contribution to the effectiveness of action programs, implementation of research results is a critical phase in the evaluation process. Yet numerous writers have warned that even the most carefully designed and executed evaluative research does not automatically lead to meaningful action. (For some examples of cases in which findings of evaluative research were ignored or rejected by program administrators, see Rossi [1967] and Hall [1966].) Disregard for results of evaluation appears to stem from a variety of sources.

Some of the nonuse of evaluation results is attributable to limitations of the research itself. In discussing demonstration projects, Rein and Miller (1967) noted that evaluative research often cannot produce results early enough to be a major factor in short-term policy decisions. Mann (1969, p.13) similarly reflected on the dilemmas of rigor, timing, and utility of evaluation:

> The better the study, the longer it takes, and consequently the less usefulness it may have. Conversely, the sloppier the procedure, the more likely it is to provide information on questions of interest even though this data will be of doubtful validity.

Weiss (1966) indicated that the influence potential of evaluation may be limited because results are indefinite, show only small changes, and fail to indicate the relative effectiveness of various components or the reasons for a program's success or failure.

Of basic importance in cases where pertinent evaluation results are ignored is the evaluator's lack of authority. Since the evaluator's capacity is that of an advisor, policy makers are under no obligation to accept his recommendations. Nonuse of evaluation findings is sometimes explained by the fact that evaluation was included for the "wrong reasons." Downs (1965) pointed out that professional advice is sometimes sought to justify decisions already made or to postpone action. Several commentators suggested that an evaluation component is sometimes supported because it lends an aura of prestige to an action enterprise (Rodman and Kolodny 1964; Bynder 1966; Rosenthal and Weiss 1966; Schulberg and Baker 1968). An administrator may support an evaluator in the hope that the evaluator will provide other services—for example, the organization of information to justify grant requests (Miller 1965a; Luchterhand 1967). As previously indicated, evaluation sometimes is included in action programs only because it is required by law or the administrative regulations of a funding agent. In these cases evaluation results may be ignored because administrators do not adequately understand or appreciate their relevance or, perhaps, because they resent evaluation as an imposition. Discrepancies between the findings of evaluative research and informal evaluations, the personal convictions and professional ideologies of decision makers, and judgments of the competence of evaluators also contribute to the nonuse of evaluative research findings (Sadofsky 1966).

Disagreements regarding evaluative criteria sometimes contribute to nonuse of findings. Rossi (1969) observed that administrators sometimes discount evaluation findings by claiming that the "real" goals of the project were not measured. Schulberg and Baker (1968) questioned the wisdom of the usual practice of building evaluation on the public goals of an organization because administrators may have no intention of achieving those goals. An evaluative researcher, then, may be ineffective because he misread the administrator's real intent.

Tension Between Researchers and Administrators

It has been shown that strained relations between evaluative researchers and administrators often occur in the introduction, execution, and utilization of evaluative research. Many of the specific obstacles to effective collaboration can be summarized by consideration of several basic orientations in which administrators and evaluative researchers are likely to differ markedly: service versus research, specificity versus generality, methods status quo versus change, academic versus practical experience, and explanations for failures.

Service versus Research. In contrast to the practitioner who is concerned with the immediate and specific application of knowledge, the evaluative researcher is responsible for the acquisition of knowledge. The service-research tension is most evident in field settings where research and service perspectives call for opposite courses of action. An evaluative research design may call for the assignment of a client to a control group when, from a service perspective, it appears preferable that he receive the experimental treatment (Argyris 1960; Freeman 1963; Perry and Wynne 1959). In addition, evaluative researchers, reflecting their academic backgrounds, are likely to have a greater appreciation than practitioners for the acquisition of knowledge for its own sake.

Specificity versus Generality. In contrast to administrators who emphasize the solution of immediate problems, researchers are often more interested in long-range problem solving. Similarly, administrators emphasize the uniqueness of their agency and program while researchers prefer to generalize in both time and space. What is of theoretical significance to the scientist may be trivial from a practical viewpoint (see Shepard 1956; Warren 1963; Merton 1957; Rodman and Kolodny 1964; Cherns 1969).

Methods. Although administrators and researchers usually agree on the use of rational methods in program development, they often do not mean the same thing by "rational." Evaluative research requires explicit statements of objectives and strategies to which administrators find it difficult or undesirable to commit themselves (Schulberg and Baker 1968). Administrators may be displeased with evaluative research that, in emphasizing organizational outputs, often tends to neglect administrative activities that are needed to maintain the organization as a viable system (Etzioni 1960). At another level, the researcher's commitment to scientific decision-making procedures may run counter to the administrator's confidence in intuition. Evaluative researchers have a professional interest in being able to show that the scientific method is superior to conventional wisdom as a basis for decision making (Ferman 1969).

Status Quo versus Change. Implicit in the evaluation role are attempts to discover inefficiency and to encourage change. Administrators, however, usually prefer to conceal inefficiency and tend to resist disruptive change. A claim to superior knowledge of human affairs predisposes social scientists to dramatize inadequacies in the conventional wisdom on which programs are often based. Administrators, however, look for evidence of success in past and current programs to assert their competence. Evaluative researchers are, thus, predisposed to see a need for fundamental change while administrators are inclined to defend the programs with which they have been identified (see Argyris 1958; Ferman 1969). (When they are new to their positions, however, administrators may be receptive to suggestions from evaluators for basic changes since major weaknesses in programs can be attributed to a previous administration.)

Explanations of Failure.   Evaluators and administrators frequently emphasize different explanations for the persistence of social problems. Again, apparently because of a desire to assert their competence, administrators tend to accept the validity of the theoretical premises on which their programs are based. Attributing failure to the inadequate resources available for the application of his approach, the administrator is likely to call for an expansion of present efforts. Evaluators who are free to question program premises often attribute failure to an inadequate understanding of the basic problem. They are likely to suggest that a radically different programming approach is needed in order to address the problem effectively. (In arguing that what is needed is "more of the same," the practitioner may also serve his professional interest in expanding the demand for his services. Evaluative researchers similarly have a vested professional interest when they argue that more effective programming requires an expanded emphasis on evaluation.)

When administrators and evaluators both acknowledge difficulties in implementing programs, administrators are likely to look for explanations that are individual (for example, incompetence or emotional instability) and moral (for example, dishonesty or laziness), in contrast to social scientists who emphasize amoral and structural factors. Part of what is at issue here is the social scientist's sensitivity to the impact of organizational structure on the person who occupies a particular position. Insiders, on the other hand, tend to explain organizational behavior in terms of the personal characteristics of the individuals who hold positions. Also involved is the evaluative researcher's more secular explanation of human behavior which leads him to emphasize factors outside the realm of free choice.

Academic versus Practical Experience.   Because the evaluative researcher typically approaches social action from the perspective of an academic discipline, his knowledge of practical affairs is usually highly incomplete. Unless he has had administrative experience in an action setting, the evaluative researcher is not likely to comprehend fully the administrator's position. Political constraints, budgetary problems, and limitations of personnel and facilities are among the realities that an evaluative researcher, preoccupied with the substance of programs, may underestimate. Similarly, it is difficult for administrators with limited research training to understand the evaluative researcher's emphasis on methodology.

Client Activism

Much of the innovative social programming in recent years has been directed at a reduction of the incidence of poverty. At the same time, group self-consciousness has been growing among the minorities who represent a substantial portion of the poor. Stimulated by the civil rights movement and by professional community developers, minority activists have taken a significant interest in local community affairs—including the social programs directed at the poor. As clients or spokesmen for clients of anti-poverty programs, activists have pressed for extensive participation in, if not full control of, these programs by clients, at the levels of both policy and implementation. Anti-poverty programs consequently have often been surrounded by substantial and continuous conflict over such matters as representation on and authority of boards, employment policies and practices, and the substance and administration of programs. Beyond the direct programming implications of minority activism, the movement has added to the challenges with which the evaluative researcher is confronted.

Even though evaluative researchers may firmly believe that their efforts contribute ultimately to the cause of the poor, minority activists may confront them with great hostility. Part of what is involved is that the basic issues that strain evaluator-administrator relations even more thoroughly set evaluative researchers apart from low-income program clients. Preoccupied with the immediate, tangible, dramatic, and personal, the minority activist is likely to be impatient with the evaluator's concern with the future, abstract concepts, orderly procedures, and impersonal forces. In contrast to the activist, who often seeks to generate open conflict, the evaluative researcher typically emphasizes cooperative approaches to problem solving. The evaluator may also find himself in an awkward position in the power struggle between client spokesmen and professional administrators. If he entered the program at the invitation of a funding agency or a professional administrator, the evaluative researcher is likely to be mistrusted immediately by minority activists who see him as a potential spy. Indeed, if evaluative criteria are limited to those acceptable to administrators, and if evaluation findings are subject to administrative review prior to being publicized, client spokesmen have good reason to challenge the evaluator's contribution.

Some of the minority activist's hostility toward the evaluator is attributable to a general antipathy toward social research. A widespread complaint of minority spokesmen is that they have been "surveyed to death." Perhaps social research has come to symbolize for some the powerlessness of the poor. Resentment is obvious in the poverty spokesman's view that social research on poverty has nearly always been initiated by outsiders and addressed to issues defined by outsiders. The cooperation of the poor has been solicited with rhetoric that links research to desired social goals; yet, it is difficult for the poor to see tangible benefits stemming from social research. In fact, many activists cynically view research as a substitute for needed action. General antagonism toward social research is also linked to the activist's political ambitions. The independent social scientist who does poverty research is a potential competitor for the activist who would like to control the flow of information from poverty areas. The indigenous, would-be spokesman for the poor has reason to be anxious if his claims are challenged by respected social scientists.

Client representatives are additionally justified in challenging evaluative researchers if they have reason to question the latter's assurances of confidentiality in the use of information about persons. Walsh (1969) reported an incident that developed in the evaluation of an Office of Economic Opportunity project concerned with delinquent gangs. After confidentiality had been pledged and significant information on individuals had been collected, the study group complied (however reluctantly) with a Senate committee's subpoena of raw data.

Establishing and Maintaining the Evaluation Role

A number of experienced evaluators have suggested strategies for dealing with the problems that can be expected in establishing and maintaining the evaluation role.

A basic administrative issue is the comparative advantages and disadvantages of "inside" and "outside" evaluators. The "inside" evaluator is a staff member of the organization whose programs are evaluated; the "outside" evaluator is a consultant from outside the organization. The following are some of the arguments which have been presented in favor of outsiders: they tend to be better able to maintain their objectivity, they are more likely to be able to include evaluative criteria that question basic organizational premises, they may be able to mediate more effectively if there is extensive internal conflict, they usually are better protected from problems of marginality and status incongruity, and they are better able to avoid unwelcome nonresearch tasks. It has been suggested that insiders have the following advantages: they are usually able to develop a more detailed knowledge of the organization and its programs, and they are in a better position to do continuing research. Likert and Lippitt (1953), Weinberger (1969), Weiss (1966), McEwan (1956), and Rodman and Kolodny (1964) are among those who have addressed themselves to these arguments. Luchterhand (1967), however, pointed out that outsiders cannot always be counted on to be more objective than insiders. When they are concerned with maintaining good relations with clients, outsiders may slant their interpretations to accommodate their clients' interests; alienated inside evaluators may be inclined to report on their agencies' programs with stark objectivity. Yet, funding agencies, spokesmen for clients, and the general public usually consider the reports of external evaluators more credible. As Lortie (1967) pointed out, persons and organizations cannot be trusted to act as judges in their own cases. Their self-appraisals cannot be accepted without question. When evaluation is conducted for the purpose of accounting to an outside body, utilization of external evaluators appears preferable. If, on the other hand, evaluation is conducted to assist an organization in its program development efforts, an internal evaluation unit may be able to contribute more effectively.

If the evaluative researcher hopes to contribute to internal program development, it has been suggested that he take early steps to establish effective ties with those who make key programming decisions. Sensitivity to the locus of decision making is important. Relations with administrators are always important, but in more decentralized and democratic organizations, evaluative researchers may find it appropriate to work more closely with the professional practitioners (for example, physicians, social workers, teachers) who are more concerned with the substance of programs.

Some authors emphasized the importance of the evaluator's organizational position (see Argyris 1958; Bennis 1965; Rosenthal and Weiss 1966; Suchman 1967a; Whyte and Hamilton 1964). The evaluator's prestige and power are considered to be positively related to the likelihood that his findings will be implemented. If the evaluator is an insider, it is important that he have a prestigious position within the organization. Similarly, if he is an outsider, it is helpful if he has strong professional and organizational credentials. It is also important for an outside evaluator to be associated with someone of high status in the action organization—a relationship that Sussman (1966) called the "Merlin role." However, when he makes status claims, the evaluator must concern himself with the possible resentment of staff subordinates. If they believe he receives more status prerogatives than he deserves, staff subordinates may withhold their cooperation from the evaluation effort.

As he begins working with agency representatives, it is important for the evaluator to create what Likert and Lippitt (1953) called an "image of potential." The evaluator must, for example, provide administrators and practitioners with assurance of his technical competence, his understanding of the action setting, and his personal integrity and decency (Warren 1963).

A mutual clarification of expectations at an early stage in the relationship would be useful. Administrators, for example, should be informed of some of the limitations of the contribution of evaluative research. Evaluators might need to explain that their work cannot resolve fundamental value issues nor can it, by itself, resolve deep-seated conflicts between administrators and their staff or between the agency and its clients. If evaluation is to be used for program development purposes, evaluators should attempt to gauge the extent to which policy makers tolerate challenges to their basic premises. An early agreement regarding the manner in which evaluation results will be publicized should also be sought. If the purpose of the evaluation is summative and it is externally sponsored, advance agreement is desirable on the extent to which persons and organization units will be identified in published reports. The evaluative researcher's interest in pursuing professional research interests should also be discussed. For his work to be relevant in the action setting, the evaluative researcher may have to postpone the pursuit of some of his personal intellectual interests. It may be desirable for him to reach an early and explicit agreement with the funding agency and program administrators on the extent to which he is free to use his time and project data for professional research purposes. The evaluative researcher should inform himself not only about available action alternatives, but about the timing of decision making. If results are to be used, evaluation must be addressed to pertinent issues and results must be available when needed.

Evaluators may be able to make a greater contribution if they can modify the policy maker's approach to programming. Sadofsky (1966) suggested that the program operator's fear of failure might be diminished if action projects were considered as experiments. Failure, then could be seen as a learning opportunity. Weiss (1966) recommended that instead of judging programs in simple success or failure terms, the administrator should be encouraged to ask questions about the relative effectiveness of alternative programs.

It is generally suggested that evaluators work closely with administrators in establishing evaluative criteria so that evaluators may become more fully aware of administrative concerns and so that administrators may become more committed to the evaluation process (Freeman and Sherwood 1965). Collaboration in the identification of criteria or goals may help evaluators base their work on variables more explicit, realistic, and perhaps more comprehensive than the objectives shown in official program documents. Stake (1967), however, introduced a note of caution. He argued that administrators or practitioners should not be expected to work at the high level of abstraction required for the writing of behavioral goals. Rather, evaluators should draft statements of objectives that attempt to reflect and clarify the intent of administrators. Coleman (1969) similarly pointed out that, because administrators are often not fully aware of their decision-making criteria, evaluative researchers themselves may have to discover these criteria.

A number of writers pointed to a need for evaluative researchers to consider a wide variety of potential program effects, including those that are unintended and undesired. Scriven (1969) emphasized the evaluator's responsibility to focus his efforts on appropriate evaluative criteria. Campbell (1969), concerned with undesired side effects, recommended that several outcome measures be utilized including those proposed by "loyal opponents." However, because of limited evaluation budgets and the relatively narrow range of alternatives that the administrator sees as open, the evaluator often finds it prudent to narrow the range of his inquiry. Aware of his lack of power, but hopeful of being able to influence policy makers within a limited but significant range of decision alternatives, the evaluator might find it desirable to ignore some potential evaluative criteria.

It is important for the evaluator to take some steps to obtain cooperation, not only from administrators, but also from staff members who carry out programs. Staff support is critical if programs are to be carried out as designed and if program records, essential for evaluation purposes, are to be maintained. Staff cooperation, however, cannot be taken for granted. A basic problem here is that the evaluator's relationship with top administrators puts him in the same organizational position as an inspector or policeman. If he hopes to obtain staff cooperation, the evaluator must insist that program evaluation is quite different from the evaluation of individuals or organizational units. Thus, Likert and Lippitt (1953, p.161) emphasized that staff members must be assured

> that the objective of research is to discover the relative effectiveness of different methods and principles and that the study is in no way an attempt to perform a policing function. The emphasis must be on discovering what principles work best and why, and not on finding and reporting which individuals are doing their jobs well or poorly.

Staff subordinates must, then, be given emphatic assurance of confidentiality and anonymity. It is also desirable to obtain a commitment from administrators to share evaluation findings openly with subordinates. If evaluation will add to the record-keeping duties of practitioners, evaluators may be wise to provide practitioners with added compensation or staff support.

Because of pressure to produce results quickly, timing may be a critical concern in the organization of evaluation efforts. Time pressures, must, of course, be given strong consideration in the selection of a methodological strategy. Grobman (1968) suggested that evaluators use a formal planning procedure such as Program Evaluation and Review Technique (PERT) to assure that evaluation work is completed within a tight time schedule. In some cases evaluators may wish to report interim findings, either to aid in an immediate decision problem or to keep administrators interested in the evaluation process. Early feedback, however, is a problem for evaluators if it causes administrators to change substantially programs before enough cases have been observed to satisfy the requirements of an experimental design.

Utilization of evaluation findings may depend on the manner in which results are reported. Some authors pointed to the need for clear, concise, and even dramatic presentation of findings. Sadofsky (1966) warned that to deliver results to an administrator publicly, without warning, may produce a defensive reaction to findings. It may be desirable to supplement written reports with personal meetings with administrators. Mann and Likert (1952) recommended a series of small group meetings, both at top administrative levels and through the ranks of subordinates, to facilitate communication of results and to stimulate interest in following through on the action implications of results. They argued that the pressures generated in small groups increase commitment to implementation of recommended changes. Argyris (1958) proposed asking administrators and practitioners for their own diagnoses first to reduce the likelihood that they reject research findings as too obvious.

Cooperation from Client Spokesmen

Where clients' cooperation with evaluators may be a problem, support of client spokesmen should be sought at an early stage. Funding agencies or administrators should initially explain the rationale for evaluation and the allocation of evaluation funds. Participation of client spokesmen in the selection of an evaluator may also be advisable. Since employment opportunity is a central concern among minority activists, it is desirable for evaluators to employ some members of the population served by programs. (Such a commitment may make it necessary for the evaluator to place more emphasis on staff training and supervision than he would otherwise.) Even more than staff subordinates, client spokesmen need assurance that confidential personal information will be used only for overall evaluation purposes. They also need to be convinced that, unlike basic research, evaluative research is designed to have immediate action implications. Client spokesmen need assurance that evaluation results will be available to them and that they will have full opportunity to participate in their interpretation. An evaluator may be able to satisfy some of the personal concerns of poverty groups by spending enough time with minority spokesmen so that they know and trust him as an individual.

In some situations the level of conflict between client spokesmen and established agencies may be so great that cooperation in program evaluation is not a realistic possibility. In these cases it may be preferable for each group to sponsor its own evaluation enterprise. Funding agencies may find it advisable in these cases to provide organized client spokesmen with the funds needed for their independent evaluation of programs.

METHODOLOGICAL CONSIDERATIONS

The methodological principles that apply to the evaluation of social programs are not different from those of general behavioral science inquiry. There is some regularity, however, in the problems of measurement and design that arise in evaluative research.

Texts and manuals on the methodology of evaluative research include those written by Hayes (1959), Herzog (1959), Fairweather (1967), Suchman (1967a), and Grobman (1968). Writings on field experiments by such persons as French (1953), Campbell (1957, 1967, 1969), Campbell and Stanley (1963), and Barnes (1967) are also highly relevant to evaluative research. Among those who have written extensively about methodological problems in evaluation work are Hyman, Wright, and Hopkins (1962), Cronbach (1963), Whyte and Hamilton (1964), Mann (1965), Greenberg (1968), Lerman (1968), Scriven (1967), Stake (1967), and Glass (1971).

Measurement

A basic step in evaluation is the identification of objectives and their measurement. Suchman (1966) suggested that formulated objectives have five aspects: the content of the objective (that is, the social conditions or behavior patterns to be changed by the program), the target of the program (that is, the population to which the program is addressed), the time within which the change is to take place, the number of objectives (if they are multiple), and the extent of expected effect. Freeman (1965), Suchman (1967a), Greenberg (1968), and Weiss (1966) urged a distinction among immediate, intermediate, and ultimate objectives. Measurements focused on immediate and intermediate objectives are particularly important when evaluation results are needed before ultimate objectives can be realized. If immediate and intermediate objectives are used as substitutes for ultimate objectives, however, the burden is on the evaluator to argue the validity of the hypothesized links to ultimate objectives. When programs fail to realize ultimate objectives, utilization of a hierarchy of objectives may also be useful in accounting for their limited success.

Because the realities of program operations are often inconsistent with public project descriptions, measurement of program inputs has also been recommended. Greenberg (1968) termed observation of administrative patterns and analysis of service statistics as "quasi evaluation." Coleman (1969) urged a distinction between resources allocated by organizations and services actually received by clients. Analysis of these administrative data may be useful for preliminary program screening purposes. To the extent that organizations are unable to deliver services to clients, expectations of program effectiveness are, of course, diminished.

As discussed previously, it is also desirable for the evaluator to anticipate and measure possible unintended effects of programs including those that are undesirable. Scriven (1967) recommended that evaluators consider secondary effects of programs, such as impact on the individuals and organizations who conduct programs, and impact on those who regularly interact with program beneficiaries.

Identification of variables is only a first step in the measurement process. Evaluators are often confronted with serious obstacles in seeking the valid, reliable, and sensitive measures they need. Lerman (1968) and Campbell (1969) pointed to the shortcomings of the agency records on which evaluators are often dependent. When he uses agency records, the evaluator must take into account the fact that these data may reflect the organizational, professional, and individual interests of those who maintain the records as much as they reflect the behavior that they are supposed to measure.

Because of his refined information requirements and the poor quality of agency records, the evaluator frequently must collect original data. When he gathers his own data, the evaluator is faced with additional problems. Data collection may add enormously to the cost of evaluation. Administrators and practitioners may object that it interferes with their programming efforts either because it takes away from the time available for programming or because it may jeopardize client or community acceptance of the program. Evaluators may be concerned that through their data collection activities they may enhance client awareness of the program, thereby adding artificially to its apparent or actual effectiveness. The evaluator may cope with these data collection problems by using unobtrusive measures (Webb et al. 1966) or by disguising the relationship between his data collection and the program (Seashore 1964). He may also address these problems through his selection of a research design. Campbell (1957) suggested use of the Solomon four-group design or a design requiring only posttest measurements. Also see Suchman (1967a) and Wuebben (1968). Although Hyman, Wright, and Hopkins (1962) reviewed evidence indicating that the sensitizing or practice effects of pretesting are often negligible, the evaluator is clearly advised to take steps to guard against this potential source of measurement error.

Freeman (1963) urged that evaluators use behavioral rather than attitudinal measures of program objectives because policy makers are more likely to be impressed with behavioral data. Deutscher (1969) similarly argued in favor of direct behavioral measures because they pose fewer validity problems than do procedures designed to provide estimates of hypothetical behavior.

Beyond the sensitizing effects of measurement, widespread

awareness of evaluative criteria and measurement procedures can have important undesired effects on the ways in which programs are administered and interpreted by clients. The danger is that administrative units, practitioners, or clients may artificially redirect their behavior to affect the outcome of evaluation. The problem is particularly acute when incomplete sets of evaluative criteria and imperfect measures are used to judge the performance of participants. Considerable attention has been given to this problem in higher education, where it has been argued that faculty are often excessively concerned with numbers of publications and students are overly preoccupied with grades. By emphasizing their concern with program concepts rather than specific participants, evaluative researchers may be able to deal with this problem with some effectiveness.

Timing of measurement is another serious issue in evaluative research (Freeman and Sherwood 1965; Hyman and Wright 1967; Harris 1963). It is often not clear how soon program effects can be expected. The stability and durability of changes brought about by programs may also be in doubt. Ideally, the problem is addressed through continuous or at least repeated measurement of output variables. Many evaluative researchers, however, find themselves in situations where they have an opportunity only for a single posttreatment measurement. The timing of such a measurement may have most important implications for the outcome of evaluative research.

Design

To assure that changes in measured behavior can be attributed exclusively to the program at hand, evaluative researchers prefer to employ some form of an experimental design. From an evaluation perspective, it is desirable that clients be assigned randomly to treatment and control groups. Adequate control, however, is difficult to achieve in an action setting. Suchman (1967b) cited two obstacles to the effective use of control groups: service orientation—administrators, practitioners, and client representatives are reluctant to allow services to be withheld from those who might benefit from them; self-selection—it is difficult either to refuse service to those who seek it or provide service to those who resist it. Mann (1965) further observed that in an organizational setting, innovative approaches may "spread like a disease" to control groups. In discussing the evaluation of communitywide programs, Greenberg (1968) pointed out the added problem of finding truly equivalent communities. Where control groups are not possible, experimental control may be approximated through some design adjustments. One approach is to match participants with nonparticipants and compare them through the use of analysis of covariance. The time-series design (Hyman, Wright, and Hopkins 1962; Campbell and Stanley 1963; Campbell 1969; Gottman, McFall, and Barnett 1969) is an alternative by which the treatment group is used as its own control through repeated measurements of outcome variables beginning well before program implementation. For treatment of further design possibilities, see Campbell and Stanley (1963) and Campbell (1969).

Lerman (1968) argued that evaluators should resist the common administrative assumption that evaluation is based on those who complete treatments. Rather, evaluation should be based on the population in need of services. Lerman pointed out that the issue is particularly critical among private agencies that can be selective in whom they accept as clients.

It may be possible to use comparison groups in action settings where control groups are unacceptable. Unlike the control group, which receives no treatment, the comparison group receives an alternate treatment. Where policy makers are committed to the principle of providing additional services, a comparison group design may actually provide more useful information than a design using only a strict control.

Social programs usually are not expected to produce a dramatic impact. If evaluation is to document subtle but important changes, large samples or highly sensitive designs are necessary (Freeman 1963). The conservatism regarding rejection of null hypotheses that often prevails in academic research may also be inappropriate in the formulation of decision criteria for evaluative research. Rather, evaluators may wish to be cautious in drawing negative conclusions regarding innovative programs (Miller 1965b).

A persistent problem in the design of evaluative research is the separation of effects of program content from effects of practitioners' characteristics. Staff enthusiasm and confidence may be critical variables in innovative programs. Design adjustments are particularly difficult when the number of practitioners is small. Greenberg (1968) suggested that program personnel be rotated between treatment and control conditions. Some of Rosenthal's (1966) suggestions for controlling experimenter expectancy effects in social psychological research appear to be applicable. Special training and supervision of practitioners may be introduced to reduce variability in practitioner behavior. Alternately, it may be possible to conduct some programs with minimal practitioner-client contact.

Program recipients sometimes contribute to the effectiveness of a program through their feelings of self-importance as persons selected for special attention (Hawthorne effect) or through their faith in the program (placebo effect). The impact of the Hawthorne or placebo effects is likely to be particularly great when the program is new and experimental and the participants are volunteers. Scriven (1967) suggested the use of multiple experimental groups to separate these effects from those of programs. He urged that enthusiasm be held constant while treatments are varied. Trow (1967), however, pointed out that some administrators may try to capitalize on Hawthorne effects by attempting to build an experimental climate into their normal programming. Sommer (1968, p.594) similarly argued that the Hawthorne effect is not an extraneous disruptive influence; rather it is an important and ever present factor in any field situation:

> Environmental changes do not act directly upon human organisms. They are interpreted according to the individual's needs, set, and state of awareness.

The implication seems to be that, if the effects of social programs are to be fully understood, it is important that the client population's predisposition toward and interpretation of programs be an integral part of comprehensive evaluative research.

New programs often pose difficulties for evaluators that are not present in the case of well-established programs. On the one hand, the evaluative researcher must be prepared to deal with the positive effects of novelty, special attention, and enthusiasm. On the other hand, he must look for some of the strictly administrative problems common in the implementation of a new program that can account for the failure of an otherwise soundly conceived program (Hyman and Wright 1967). In the case of innovative programs, it is particularly important that administrators be free to modify their procedures on the basis of their early experiences in implementing the program (Marris and Rein 1967). These modifications pose an enormous problem for evaluation if research designs call for a lengthy commitment to a highly specific set of procedures. If, as Glass (1971) recommended, evaluators focus on program concepts rather than specific procedures, their experimental designs may be able to accommodate procedural adjustments as long as basic concepts of the program remain intact.

Program outcomes may also be affected by many other variables that cannot be controlled in a single evaluative study. Among these variables are the physical characteristics of the program site, and the duration and intensity of the program.

Because action programs are often ineffective and because experimental evaluation is often very expensive, Rossi (1967) recommended a two-phased approach to evaluation. First, correlational designs would be used to identify promising programs. Then, controlled experiments would be conducted to evaluate the relative effectiveness of those programs that passed the initial screening.

Rigid evaluation designs are most easily implemented in the programs conducted by highly centralized organizations having extensive control over their clients. Prisons, hospitals, and residential schools are among the organizations most likely to have these characteristics. When programs involve a number of autonomous organizations, are conducted by practitioners with considerable personal and professional autonomy, and are directed at client populations whose willingness to cooperate is highly uncertain, evaluators often must be satisfied to use limited methodological tools. Effective programming is, of course, also very difficult under these circumstances.

Contemporary communitywide anti-poverty programs are among those in which it is most difficult for evaluators to use highly controlled experimental designs. The relative contribution of various components of these large-scale programs may be difficult to determine because of clients' uncontrolled exposure to several programs. It may also be difficult to determine the extent to which new programs are supplements to rather than substitutes for earlier programs. Weiss and Rein (1969) further noted that, in the case of highly diffuse and unstable programs, it is particularly difficult to select and operationalize evaluative criteria that are sufficiently broad in scope to reflect a program's full range of consequences—especially consequences that are unintended.

In these settings the evaluator must look for research strategies that are realistic and, at the same time, yield a maximum of useful information. Particularly in the case of completely innovative programs for which evaluation results are needed at an early stage, informal approaches usually associated with exploratory research may be most appropriate. Observational techniques and informal interviewing can often provide more useful and rapid feedback than can formal experimentation (Weiss and Rein 1969). Lazarsfeld, Sewell, and Wilensky (1967) observed that, because the decision process in these programs is continuous, evaluation must take place at many points. They recommended concurrent evaluation, a procedure by which records are kept of all decisions, including information on rejected alternatives and expected outcomes. Perhaps, as Benedict et al. (1967) suggested, what is needed is evaluation that combines rigorous experimental data with a "natural history" account of events and actors before, during, and after program implementation.

Decision makers are usually concerned with efficiency as much as they are with effects of programs. Evaluators, therefore, should be prepared to deal with the relationship between cost and effectiveness. In some cases cost analysis is straightforward; in others, it adds another complex dimension to evaluation.

CONCLUDING THOUGHTS

Clearly, evaluative research is an activity surrounded by serious obstacles. Satisfied with informal and impressionistic approaches to evaluation, policy makers are often reluctant to make the investment needed to obtain verifiable data on the effects of their programs. Evaluative researchers are typically confronted with problems of measurement and design that greatly restrict their ability to reach unambiguous conclusions. Abrasive relations with practitioners and clients can add to the evaluator's difficulties in obtaining information. Evaluative research is often addressed to a distressingly narrow range of issues; results are not as fully or widely disclosed as they might be; highly pertinent findings are often ignored by policy makers. It is little wonder that many social scientists regard evaluative research as a dubious enterprise.

Yet, the argument for emphasizing evaluative research in social programming is strong. Expenditures in this country for social service programs are enormous. Yet there is reason to be dissatisfied with the effectiveness of many of these programs. Increases in program costs tend to be much more conspicuous than improvements in the quality of services. If it is agreed that social programs should be strengthened and that improvement is most likely to come about through the use of rational methods, it is clear that the evaluation role is important and should be emphasized. The often subtle results of social programs require the methods of empirical research to obtain precise information on program effectiveness.

Evaluative researchers can take a number of steps to improve their contributions to program development. They can become more skillful in applying their methodological tools to specific evaluation problems. They can become more knowledgeable about the decision problems of action organizations, and thus recommend more appropriate evaluation strategies. Greater personal familiarity with action settings may make evaluators more effective in working with practitioners and clients. The climate for evaluation might be improved if evaluators were to place more emphasis on educating administrators, practitioners, and client representatives regarding the role of evaluation in program development. Evaluators might develop more effective ways of communicating the action implications of their findings. Behavioral scientists who assume administrative roles in programs can also help by showing how programs can be structured to accommodate evaluation requirements.

If, however, evaluative research is to make its full contribution, substantial changes must be made in society's overall approach to social programming. Legislators and other public officials, reflecting widespread public concern, must significantly raise their demands for the effectiveness and efficiency of programs. In addition, they must learn to focus more on program goals so that they can assume a more experimental attitude toward specific programming strategies (Campbell 1969). Such fundamental changes in orientation toward social programming would lead to greatly expanded interest in evaluative research. If there were a more serious emphasis on performance standards and on the search for more effective program approaches, evaluative researchers would be more often able to obtain the political and administrative support needed to employ experimental designs. Behavioral scientists who hope to contribute to the effectiveness of social programs through evaluative research need to concern themselves not only with immediate methodological and organizational problems but also with the larger issues concerning the social context in which social programs are conducted.

REFERENCES

Argyris, C. "Creating Effective Relationships in Organizations." *Human Organization* 17, no. 1 (1958):34-40. Republished: In *Human Organization Research*, edited by R. Adams and J. Preiss. Homewood, Ill.: Dorsey, 1960.

Barnes, L. "Organizational Change and Field Experiment Methods." In *Methods of Organizational Research*, edited by V. Vroom. Pittsburgh: University of Pittsburgh Press, 1967.

Benedict, B. A., Calder, P. H., Callahan, D. M., Hornstein, H. A., and Miles, M. B. "The Clinical-Experimental Approach to Assessing Organizational Change Efforts." *Journal of Applied Behavioral Science* 3 (1967):347-380.

Bennis, W. "Theory and Method in Applying Behavioral Science to Planned Organizational Change." *Journal of Applied Behavioral Science* 1 (1965):337-360.

Brooks, M. "The Community Action Program as a Setting for Applied Research." *Journal of Social Issues* 21 (1965):29-40.

Bynder, H. "Sociology in a Hospital: A Case Study in Frustration." In *Sociology in Action,* edited by A. Shostak. Homewood, Ill.: Dorsey, 1966.

Campbell, D. T. "Validity of Experiments in Social Settings." *Psychological Bulletin* 54 (1957):297-312.

Campbell, D. T. "Administrative Experimentation, Institutional Records, and Nonreactive Measures." In *Improving Experimental Design and Statistical Analysis,* edited by J. Stanley. Chicago: Rand McNally, 1967.

Campbell, D. T. "Reforms as Experiments." *American Psychologist* 24 (1969):409-429.

Campbell, D. T., and Stanley, J. C. Experimental and Quasi-Experimental Designs for Research on Teaching." In *Handbook of Research on Teaching,* edited by N. L. Gage. Chicago: Rand McNally, 1963. Republished: *Experimental and Quasi-Experimental Design.* Chicago: Rand McNally, 1966.

Cherns, A. "Social Research and Its Diffusion." *Human Relations* 29 (1969):209-218.

Coleman, J. S. "Evaluating Educational Programs: A Symposium." *The Urban Review* 3, no. 4 (1969):6-8.

Cronbach, L. J. "Course Improvement Through Evaluation." *Teachers' College Record* 64 (1963):672-683.

Deutscher, I. "Looking Backward: Case Studies in the Progress of Methodology in Sociological Research." *American Sociologist* 4 (1969):35-41.

Downs, A. "Some Thoughts on Giving People Economic Advice." *American Behavioral Scientist* 9, no. 1 (1965):30-32.

Etzioni, A. "Two Approaches to Organizational Analysis: A Critique and a Suggestion." *Administrative Science Quarterly* 5 (1960):257-278.

Fairweather, G. *Methods of Experimental Social Innovation.* New York: Wiley, 1967.

Ferman, L. A. "Some Perspectives on Evaluating Social Welfare Programs." *Annals of the American Academy of Political and Social Science* 385 (1969):143-156.

Freeman, H. E. "Strategy of Social Policy Research." In *Social Welfare Forum,* edited by H. E. Freeman. New York: Columbia University Press, 1963.

Freeman, H. E., and Sherwood, C. "Research in Large-Scale Intervention Programs." *Journal of Social Issues* 21 (1965):11-28.

French, J. "Experiments in Field Settings." In *Research Methods in the Behavioral Sciences,* edited by L. Festinger and D. Katz. New York: Holt, Rinehart and Winston, 1953.

Glass, G. V. "The Growth of Evaluation Methodology." In *Perspectives of Curriculum Evaluation.* American Educational Research Association Monograph Series, no. 7. Chicago: Rand McNally, 1971.

Gottman, J. M., McFall, R. M., and Barnett, J. T. "Design and Analysis of Research Using Time Series." *Psychological Bulletin* 72 (1969):299-306.

Greenberg, B. G. "Evaluation of Social Programs." *Review of the International Statistical Institute* 36 (1968):260-277.

Grobman, H. *Evaluation Activities of Curriculum Projects: A Starting Point.* Chicago: Rand McNally, 1968.

Hall, R. "The Applied Sociologist and Organizational Sociology." In *Sociology in Action,* edited by A. Shostak. Homewood, Ill.: Dorsey, 1966.

Harris, C. W. *Problems in Measuring Change.* Madison: University of Wisconsin Press, 1963.

Hayes, S. P. *Measuring the Results of Development Projects.* New York: UNESCO, 1959.

Herzog, E. *Some Guidelines for Evaluation Research.* Washington: U.S. Government Printing Office, 1959.

Horowitz, I. "The Academy and the Polity: Interaction Between Social Scientists and Federal Administrators." *Journal of Applied Behavioral Science* 5 (1969):309-335.

Hyman, H., and Wright, C. "Evaluating Social Action Programs." In *The Uses of Sociology,* edited by P. Larzarsfeld, W. Sewell, and H. Wilensky. New York: Basic Books, 1967.

Lazarsfeld, P., Sewell, W., and Wilensky, H., eds. *The Uses of Sociology.* New York: Basic Books, 1967.

Lerman, P. "Evaluative Studies of Institutions for Delinquents: Implications for Research and Social Policy." *Social Work* 13, no. 3 (1968):55-64.

Likert, R., and Lippit, R. "Utilization of Social Science." In *Research Methods in the Behavioral Sciences,* edited by L. Festinger and D. Katz. New York: Holt, Rinehart and Winston, 1953.

Lippit, R., Watson, J., and Westley, B. *The Dynamics of Planned Change.* New York: Harcourt Brace, 1958.

Lortie, D. C. "The Cracked Cake of Educational Custom and Emerging Issues in Evaluation." Paper read at the Symposium on Problems in the Evaluation of Instruction, December, 1967 at the University of California, Los Angeles. Mimeographed.

Luchterhand, E. "Research and the Dilemmas in Developing Social Programs." In *The Uses of Sociology,* edited by P. Lazarsfeld, W. Sewell, and H. Wilensky. New York: Basic Books, 1967.

Mann, F., and Likert, R. "The Need for Research on the Communication of Research Results." *Human Organization* 11, no. 4 (1952):15-19.

Mann, J. *Changing Human Behavior.* New York: Scribner's, 1965.

Mann, J. "Evaluating Educational Programs: A Symposium." *The Urban Review* 3, no. 4 (1969):12-13.

Marris, P., and Rein, M. *Dilemmas of Social Reform.* New York: Atherton Press, 1967.

McEwen, W. J. "Position Conflict and Professional Orientation in a Research Organization." *Administration Science Quarterly* 1 (1956):208-224.

McKelvey, W. "Expectational Non-Complementarity and Style of Interaction Between Professional and Organization." *Administrative Science Quarterly* 14, no. 1 (1969):21-32.

Merton, R. "Role of the Intellectual in Public Bureaucracy." In *Social Theory and Social Structure,* edited by R. Merton. New York: The Free Press, 1957.

Miller, S. M. "Evaluating Social Action Programs." *Trans-action* 2, no. 3 (1965):38-39. (a)

Miller, S. M. "Prospects: The Applied Sociology of the Center-City." In *Applied Sociology*, edited by A. Gouldner and S. M. Miller. New York: The Free Press, 1967. (b)

Perry, S. E., and Wynne, L. "Role Conflict, Role Redefinition and Social Changes in a Clinical Research Organization." *Social Forces* 38 (1959):62-65.

Rein, M., and Miller, S. M. "The Demonstration Project as a Strategy of Change." In *Organizing for Community Welfare*, edited by M. N. Zald. Chicago: Quadrangle Books, 1967.

Rodman, H., and Kolodny, R. "Organizational Strains in the Researcher-Practitioner Relationship." *Human Organization* 23 (1964): 171-182. Republished: In *Applied Sociology*, edited by A. Gouldner and S. M. Miller. New York: The Free Press, 1965.

Rosenthal, R. *Experimenter Effects in Behavioral Research.* New York: Appleton-Century-Crofts, 1966.

Rosenthal, R., and Weiss, R. "Problems of Organizational Feedback." In *Social Indicators*, edited by R. Bauer. Cambridge, Mass.: MIT Press, 1966.

Rossi, P. "Evaluating Social Action Programs." *Trans-action* 4 (1967):51-53.

Rossi, P. "Evaluating Educational Programs: A Symposium." *The Urban Review* 3, no. 4 (1969):17-18.

Sadofsky, S. "Utilization of Evaluation Results: Feedback into the Action Program." In *Learning in Action*, edited by J. Shmelzer. Washington: U.S. Government Printing Office, 1966.

Schulberg, H., and Baker, F. "Program Evaluation Models and the Implementation of Research Findings." *American Journal of Public Health* 58 (1968):1248-1255.

Scriven, M. "The Methodology of Evaluation." In *Perspectives of Curriculum Evaluation*. American Research Association Curriculum Evaluation Monograph Series, no. 3. Chicago: Rand McNally, 1967.

Scriven, M. "Evaluating Educational Programs: A Symposium." *The Urban Review* 3, no. 4 (1969):20-22.

Seashore, S. "Field Experiments with Formal Organizations." *Human Organization* 23 (1964):164-170.

Shepard, H. A. "Nine Dilemmas in Industrial Research." *Administrative Science Quarterly* 1 (1956):295-309.

Smith, J., Sim, F., and Bealer, R. "Client Structure and the Research Process." In *Human Organization Research*, edited by R. Adams and J. Preiss. Homewood, Ill.: Dorsey, 1960.

Sommer, R. "Hawthorne Dogma." *Psychological Bulletin* 70 (1968):592-595.

Stake, R. "The Countenance of Educational Evaluation." *Teachers' College Record* 68 (1967):523-540.

Suchman, E. "A Model for Research and Evaluation on Rehabilitation." In *Sociology and Rehabilitation*, edited by M. Sussman. Washington: American Sociological Association, 1966.

Suchman, E. *Evaluative Research.* New York: Russell Sage Foundation, 1967. (a)

Suchman, E. "Principles and Practice of Evaluative Research." In *An Introduction to Sociological Research,* edited by J. Doby, 2nd ed. New York: Appleton-Century-Crofts, 1967. (b)

Suchman, E. "Evaluating Educational Programs: A Symposium." *The Urban Review* 3, no. 4 (1969):15-17.

Sussman, M. "The Sociologist as a Tool of Social Action." In *Sociology in Action,* edited by A. Shostak. Homewood, Ill.: Dorsey, 1966.

Trow, M. "Methodological Problems in the Evaluation of Innovation." Paper read at The Symposium on Problems in the Evaluation of Instruction, December 1967 at the University of California at Los Angeles. Mimeographed.

Walsh, J. "Anti-Poverty R & D: Chicago Debacle Suggests Pitfalls Facing OEO." *Science* 165 (1969):1243-1245.

Warren, R. *Social Research Consultation.* New York: Russell Sage Foundation, 1963.

Webb, E. J., Campbell, D. T., Schwartz, R. D., and Sechrest, L. *Unobtrusive Measures: Nonreactive Research in the Social Sciences.* Chicago: Rand McNally, 1966.

Weinberger, M. "Evaluative Action Programs: Observations by a Market Researcher." *The Urban Review* 3, no. 4 (1969):23-26.

Weiss, C. H. "Planning an Action Project Evaluation." In *Learning in Action,* edited by J. Schmelzer. Washington: U.S. Government Printing Office, 1966.

Weiss, C. H. "Utilization of Evaluation: Toward Comparative Study." Paper read to the American Sociological Association, September 1966 at Miami Beach. In *The Use of Social Research in Federal Domestic Programs.* Part III "The Relation of Private Social Scientists to Federal Programs on National Social Programs." Washington: U.S. Government Printing Office, 1967.

Weiss, R., and Rein, M. "The Evaluation of Broad-Aim Programs: A Cautionary Case and a Moral." *Annals of the American Academy of Political and Social Science* 385 (1969):133-142.

Whyte, W. F., and Hamilton, E. *Action Research for Management.* Homewood, Ill.: Dorsey, 1964.

Wrightstone, J. W. "Evaluating Educational Programs: A Symposium." *The Urban Review* 3, no. 4 (1969):5-6.

Wuebben, P. "Experimental Design, Measurement, and Human Subjects: A Neglected Problem of Control." *Sociometry* 31 (1968):89-101.

Wynne, E. "Evaluating Educational Programs: A Symposium." *The Urban Review* 3, no. 4 (1969):19-20.